Koala edu. enterprise & services. inc.
ALL RIGHTS RESERVED.
COPYRIGHT @2016-2036
BY SOO IL YOU

NO part of this book may be reproduced in any form, by phtosat, Microfilm, PDF or any other means, or incorporated into any information retrieval system, electronic or mechanical, without the written permission of the copyright owner

All inquiries should be addressed to: Koala edu. enterprise & services inc.
satvancouver@gmail.com

Also Available:

SSAT Middle Level, SSAT Upper Level.

ISEE Lower level, ISEE Middle Level. ISEE Upper Level.

SAT Practice tests.

Learn from the author of this book!
For private and group tutoring via Zoom,
contact at satvancouver@gmail.com

READ ME

Correct Answers Can Be Found FREQUENTLY Without Reading the Passages

For almost all students preparing for the SSAT, one of the biggest concerns must be the uncertainty of the Reading and the verbal scores. This book presents several practical techniques rather than relying on conventional approach.

The purpose of this book, if summarized into a short phrase, is to shift your focus from the reading passage to the question patterns In fact, many correct answers can be found without even reading the passages.

To make it more objective and verifiable, we are going to use the official test. Go to the SSAT Website ssat.org, the one that you've registered or will register for the test. Sign up and click on the SSAT practice test. Then choose the upper level. Go to the first reading passage. Please do not read the passage yet.

Jimin: Okay! Hold it! I've got it. The title is "Channel Islands National Park," right?

Great! Have you ever been to a national park, Jimin?

Jimin: Yellowstone!

What did you see there?

Jimin: Lots of trees, rabbits. flowers, and some guys collecting money at the gate.

Can you imagine the Yellowstone without trees or flowers but only with animals?

Jimin: Nonsense!

How did you get there? By car? or by bus?

Jimin: My dad drove all the way.

Okay! Let's get back to the title: "Channel Islands National Park." Can you think of the unique feature about the park in the title?

Jimin: It's in Islands.

Correct! Can you drive there?

Jimin: No. By boat, maybe?

If you have a friend living in the islands, can you visit him or her very often with lots of your mutual friends?

Jimin: I don't think so.

When you look at the title, tell me Jimin, do you think the passage is a fiction?

Jimin: I think it is either history or science genre.

READ ME  A LOT OF

How to Find Correct Answers Without Reading the Passages

 That's right! It is either science or history, which tends to use informative neutral tone. So, don't choose too positive or too negative tone from the choices. Do it now! Jimin: (3minutes later) Amazing! I've got all five of them right!

Did you read the passage? Jimin: Not a single word! I don't understand how this could happen.

Here's what happened. You've applied logical thinking.

Much in the questions and five choices depends on logic rather than on information in the Reading passages. Even to those with very low English scores, questions 1, 2, 4 must have been a piece-of-cake.

Jimin: Can I use this logic with any type of questions, any type of reading passages?

Yes, of course! But don't get me wrong. What I am trying to show you here is not to dissuade you from reading the passages, far from it. To really improve, reading skills are integral.

By applying logic, we can almost always eliminate a couple of incorrect answers from each question, without or less relying only on information from the reading passage.

Jimin: I still believe that reading the passages is the first thing to do because it is the most Important thing. Otherwise, it'll be all guessing. I don't like taking a chance on my important test.

The problem is, by focusing too much on reading, we've been de-emphasizing the importance of analyzing the questions and incorrect-answers. Test creators care only for the questions they create and the logic beneath them. For them passages are nothing more than justifications for the correct answers.

Jimin: Does it work in my school homework too?

It works with your school homework, SSAT, ISEE, SAT, ACT, TOEFL, GRE, GMAT. In fact, the higher the level of test becomes, the more important is understanding the questions and logic.

This book does not pivot on the correct answers Usually the answers are found right there in the passage. No need to think. It is better to pay more attention to the questions, incorrect answers. and logic behind them. If you cannot find the official SSAT test materials from the SSAT.org, request through email at: satvancouver@gmail.com. I will send you the link.

READ ME

How the Top 0.1 Percent Students Solve the Reading Section

Imagine you're one of the top 0.1 percent students. In order to experience in this experiment more realistically and more objectively, we should choose extremely difficult reading passages and very, very hard questions.

Google the "GRE BIG BOOK PDF." That's the test material for graduate students. Randomly pick two long reading passages. We will solve each of them by applying two different methods.

First Reading: Follow Your Present Reading Pattern
Start reading the first passage that you picked from the GRE Big Book. You'd never know what's going to come in the questions. So you must focus on every detail in every single line to thoroughly understand the entire passage. Now, start solving questions one by one by repeatedly going back to the passage. Completed, you may feel totally exhausted, very frustrated with your dismal performance despite of enormous time and energy consumed, unless you had given up already.

Second Reading: Follow Your Future Reading Pattern
This time, pick and read a couple of questions including all the choices. Try to understand the tone and the key concept, and remove intuitively incorrect choices, anticipate the type of passage before reading. Now, read the passage, but, this time, intentionally avoid irrelevant information. Focus on the lines that are directly related to the questions. Go back to the questions. Make sure there are logic and traps everywhere. How? By dividing each choice into several pieces of word-groups. Hit or miss, it's all practice. Your eye vision would be clearer on each question because you've intentionally increased your attention and time to the questions instead of the passage.

What Made the Differences?
With the first passage, you had only one goal: complete understanding and remembering the entire passage, which is nearly impossible, worse yet unnecessary. Proportionately, the time allotted to understanding questions had shrunken.

Meantime in the second passage, you had no other way but being forced to focus on questions; being forced to find the keywords, tones, and tried to eliminate incorrect answers based on feeling. As you read the passage, the trace of you memory follows and become more analytical although you may not have noticed.

It may take indefinite time to Improve scores through passage reading. By shifting the attention to questions, you may develop analytical skills, read the passage more strategically. It all comes naturally.

**A reminder to the elementary & Lower level students: The purpose of this page and the following exercise is not to let you solve the overwhelming questions.
It is to encourage you to grasp the concept underlying the questions.**

·

READ ME

How to Eliminate Incorrect Answers Without Reading the Passages

A reminder to the elementary & Lower level students: This page and the following exercise are not to let you solve this overwhelming question. It is to encourage you to grasp the concept underlying the questions

Incorrect answers may or may not require information from the passage.
In many cases, we can actually take a very good guess whether choices are correct or incorrect. This guessing technique can be improved through practice.
The following question is randomly taken from the GRE Big Book page 1053, question 21.

Analysis 1. Identify the type of question. This is the main idea question. That is to say, the correct answer must be using a broad-term. In other words, choices with very specific terms are highly likely to be incorrect. For they must be representing some specific issue, albeit very important in some paragraph.

Analysis 2. Identify the genre and tone. This must be a science genre. Thus, the correct answer tends to maintain a neutral tone. Contrary, Incorrect answers use negative or emotionally positive words.

21. The **primary purpose** of the passage is to
A) **discuss the techniques** of analyzing lead isotope composition
B) **propose a way to determine** the origin of the copper in certain artifacts
C) **resolve a dispute** concerning the analysis of copper ore
D) **describe the deficiencies** of a currently used method of chemical analysis of certain metals
E) **offer an interpretation** of the archaeological record of the Bronze Age.

Choice A could be the correct answer. For it uses a broad term, maintains a neutral tone. Rely not too much on the phrase "lead isotope compositions." It may or may not be the primary words. The deciding factor must be the phrase "discuss the technique"

Choice B could be the correct answer. For it uses a broad term, maintains a neutral tone. As said, the Key point is not to rely too much on the phrase "copper in certain artifacts" It may or may not be the primary words. The deciding factor must be the phrase "propose a way to determine"

Choice C could be incorrect. For it uses a negative term, "resolve a dispute" The passage may or may not show this issue. Regardless, it is highly unlikely to be the primary purpose.

Choice D could be incorrect. For it uses a negative term, "deficiencies" The passage may or may not show this issue. However, it is highly unlikely to be the primary purpose.

Choice E could be incorrect answer. For it uses generalization. Generalization is a typical incorrect answer technique, widely applied throughout the reading questions. Generalization refers to a phrase that sounds generally true, by using an impressive words taken from the passage. However, it usually fails to inform the primary purpose (See Chapter 1)

READ ME

Exercise:
How to Eliminate Incorrect Answers Without Reading the Passages

Now, let's try SSAT level questions. Mechanisms are the same as GRE, but much simpler and easier to understand.

Try to find the possible incorrect answers and possible correct answers for the following three questions without reading the passages.

1 SSAT Elementary Level

"Thirteen-year-old...people's minds (line 1)chiefly suggests
A) a girl's naivety
B) Chrissy's humble nature
C) importance of reading
D) all young girls' dreams
E) superpower the girl possesses

1 SSAT Middle Level

The primary purpose of the passage is to
A) criticize the King, George III
B) describe the relation between the English Parliament and the King
C) discuss the origin of modern stamps
D) celebrate the Stamp Act
E) introduce the brief history behind the development of Stamp Act

1 SSAT Upper Level

According to paragraph 2 (lines 6-12), the old Dashwood invited Mr. Henry Dashwood because
A) he felt contempt for Mr. Henry
B) Mr. Henry had some financial issue
C) he had more than one reason
D) he needed to repent his wrongdoings
E) Mr. Henry was still single

READ ME

Explanations:
How to Eliminate Incorrect Answers Without Reading the Passages

1. Elementary Level SSAT

"Thirteen-year-old...people's minds (line 1)chiefly suggests
A) a girl's **naivety**
B) Chrissy's **humble** nature
C) **importance of reading**
D) **all young girls'** dreams
E) **superpower** the girl possesses

Analysis 1. Identify the type of question. This is the local type question, requiring specific information.
Analysis 2. Identify the genre. This is the literary genre.
Analysis 3. identify the key word in the question. "Thirteen-year-old" is the keywords. The correct answer, then, must be about this character, nothing else.

Choice A could be the answer. The word "naivety" contains negative connotation.
Choice B could be the answer. The word "humble" contains positive connotation. Thus, it is important to identify the correct tone in line 1. if line 1 is positive about the character, the answer is choice B; negative, choice A.
Choice C, D could be incorrect. For they use generalization. Generalization refers to a phrase that sounds generally true in any circumstance, in any type of passage, by using an impressive words taken from the passage. However, it usually fails to inform the primary purpose of passage. (See Chapter 1)
Choice E is highly likely to be incorrect. It can be eliminated with commonsense. It is illogical to say a child possesses superpower.

1. Middle Level SSAT

The **primary purpose** of the passage is to
A) **criticize the King,** George III
B) describe the **relation** between the English **Parliament and the King**
C) discuss the origin of **modern stamps**
D) **celebrate the Stamp Act**
E) introduce the **brief history** behind the development of **Stamp Act**

Analysis 1. Identify the type of question. This is the main idea question. The correct answer must be using a broad-term. In other words, choices with very specific terms are highly likely to be incorrect.
Analysis 2. Identify the genre and tone. This must be a history genre. Thus, the correct answer, especially in SSAT, tends to maintain a neutral tone. Contrary, Incorrect answers use negative or emotionally positive words.

HOW TO USE THIS BOOK

READ ME

Explanations:
How to Eliminate Incorrect Answers Without Reading the Passages

Choice A is highly likely to be incorrect. Whether true or not, criticizing the king could be at best a localized issue in one paragraph but would not represent the entire passage.

Choice B is highly likely to be incorrect because the phrase focuses on the parliament and the king. Whether stated or not, the relation between them may not be the primary purpose of the entire passage.

Choice C is highly likely to be incorrect. It can be eliminated with commonsense. It is illogicl to discuss modern.

Choice D, E could be the correct answer. Unlike choice A, B, C, they approach a broad concept, the Stamp Act. If the author spoke in negative tone with the Stamp Act, however, then choice D will be incorrect answer.

---

1 Upper Level SSAT

According to paragraph 2 (lines 6-12), the **old Dashwood invited** Mr. Henry Dashwood because
A) **he felt contempt** for Mr. Henry
B) **Mr. Henry** had some financial issue
C) he had more **than one reason**
D) he needed to **repent his wrongdoings**
E) **Mr. Henry** was still single

Analysis 1. Identify the type of question. This is the local type question, requiring specific information.
Analysis 2. Identify the genre. This is the literary genre.
Analysis 3. identify the key word in the question.
 We have two characters in this question: the old Dashwood and Mr. Henry Dashwood. The old Dash wood is the keyword. For it's the subject. The correct answer, then, must be about him, not Mr. Henry.

Choice A is highly likely to be incorrect. It can be eliminated with common sense. For it is illogical to invite someone contemptuously.

Choice B, E are highly likely to be incorrect because the two phrases focus on Mr. Henry, not the main subject of the question.

Choice C, D could be the correct answer. Unlike choice B, E, they focuses on the subject of the question.

Because this is literary genre, it must carry the tone of each character. If the old Dashwood is a negative character, the answer could be D. If not, however, the answer could be C.

SSAT ABSOLUTE PATTERNS

READ ME

Top 0.1 Percent?
How about the Bottom 1 % Who Keeps on Going South?

Jimin: Is this method applicable only to top 0.1 percent and up?
For me, my real problem arises from more fundamental level. I lose my mind when I try to read the passages, especially difficult passages. Barely knowing the passages, I just can't focus when I start reading the questions. Simultaneously, all kinds of things pop out in my head. I recently took this I.Q. test and got less than three digits. Easy to remember.

Observing the interaction between predator and prey probably help you understand and solve your situation. You know these animals have no considerable form of intelligence. They act based on experiences (practice) and instinct (consciousness).
Starting from freely floating awareness, they both suddenly become extremely awaken when a subtle feeling arouse their conscious.

They are now super-focused, hold consistent breath. Once in that state, everything stops. Within them they both find each other's presence, nothing else. Such an arousal stimulates them to experience a type of prediction (finding incorrect answers without reading the passage). Although stimulated not by intellectual analysis, but by instinctive aggression and fear, their acute sense of alertness undoubtedly allows them to be in amazing level of consciousness, superior to human intelligence.

So, before you read the passage, do this simple practice. Put earplugs into your ears. Close your eyes and breathe in and breathe out five times. It will be your normal breath, but with the earplugs in, you could actually hear your breath.

Try to find stillness in your mind. Open your eyes. When you start reading the passage, do the same thing till the last sentence, breathe in and breathe out. and listen to your breath. If you are unconscious while reading the passage, you will be either unable to understand or forget immediately what you're reading.

Listening to your breath will constantly hold your attention. While listening to your breath, nothing will pop out from your head.

If you read so fast, yet your score does not reflect your speed reading skills, slow down by listening to your breath. Contrary, if you do not understand what you are reading, some people find this problem from the student's lack of vocabulary. That's a separate issue. Try to listen to your breath. Consciousness comes along. And with it, understanding the passage.

HOW TO USE THIS BOOK

READ ME

Why Is It So Hard to Improve Reading and Verbal Scores?

Do you feel stuck when it comes to your Reading and Verbal scores, Jimin? Do you know why you can't improve your scores?

Jimin: yeah. Because I'm a turkey. That's why they eat me alive.

It's because you use the same approach as everybody does. You buy a book, solve a bunch of questions, look at the answer keys, and when you don't see any improvement you feel disappointed in yourself.
Isn't it true that during the practice you don't pay attention to your errors?   You know why? Because you grow more and more frustrated looking at your faults and quickly move onto the next questions.
From the beginning to end, you rely on your own judgment and avoid looking at your mistakes!

Jimin: Any suggestions? Sure! This book can quickly and dramatically improve your scores.

You've been focusing too much on passage analysis. With all due respect, reading skills such as speed reading and analytical thinking progress only through years of sustained effort. They cannot immediately be improved overnight.

You should not start with the answer keys. Instead, like you always do during the real test, you should start out from incorrect answers with very little—sometimes with absolutely no—information from the passage. "The Relevancy Check" is the most critical step to start with.

 Jimin: What do you mean by that?

SSAT ABSOLUTE PATTERNS

READ ME

Because What You Actually Do is Guess!

 Sound paradoxical though, you should develop skills to find the incorrect answers, not the correct answer, by following systemic and logical patterns. For many students during the test, complete understanding of the passages is next to  impossible, let alone analyzing the passage. What students actually do is *guess!*

Through guess, rather than through complete understanding, students eliminate incorrect answers. It is natural for students to follow their intuition—due to their limited understanding of the passages. If then, the better way to improve your score is to improve your guessing skills that eliminate those incorrect answers in systematic ways. Let's call this "The Relevancy Check" or the incorrect-answer verification process.

Practicing incorrect answers through guess, indeed, is as pivotal as, if not more important than, practicing the correct answers through passage analysis.  Think this way. How can you guarantee that the correct answer is really correct without verifying all the incorrect answers, which are easier to verify than the correct answer? In theory, the correct answer cannot exist if incorrect answers do not exist because there would be no comparison. Only a true statement would exist. There are so many incorrect answers with true statements.

The passage analysis justifies the correct answer. You will never improve your score in a short time by following evidence from the passage. Why? Because test creators seriously focus on incorrect & correct answer mechanism, not on the passage.

Analysis	Test-Creators think	You think
Incorrect Answers	Most Important	Less Important
Correct Answer	Less Important	Most Important
Passage	Less Important	Most Important

Test creators in fact consume enormous amount of time creating incorrect answers based on logic and patterns. On the contrary, they spend little time creating the correct answer.  You do the exact opposite. While practicing, you spend least amount of time on incorrect answers, and consume most of the time finding the correct answer. To materialize, you read the passage repeatedly. Imagine you are taking the actual test during which the answer keys are absolutely unavailable. You very often do not comprehend, even worse, misjudge the passages and questions.

HOW TO USE THIS BOOK

READ ME

 **Fatal Mistakes Always Come From Misunderstanding the Questions Played by the Logic. It, Thus, Explains Why You Miss Certain Questions Repeatedly.**

As we have observed so far from a series of experiments, the questions and incorrect answers are made of highly sophisticated logic.

As the test you take becomes higher-level, the more difficult and sophisticated those incorrect answers become. It, thus, indirectly explains why you miss certain questions repeatedly.

When asked, 10 out of 8 average-score students insist they understood the passage clearly but made mistakes. Can the scores actually be improved through practice by reducing mistakes? The answer is No.

Why not? Because that's not mistakes. Believing that's pure mistakes will let you keep focusing on the passages, not on the logic behind the questions. Only when you see the answer keys after the test do you realize that you were being trapped in logic.

In each choice A, B, C, D, and E for each question, meaningful words from the passages are repurposed. Test creators follow common rules such as Direct Contradiction (DC); True Statement but inconsistent with the question (TS); Extreme Word Usage (EX); Generalization (GE); New Information (NI); Insufficient Information (IS); and Tonal Incongruity (TI).

SSAT Elementary level uses very straightforward incorrect-answer patterns. SSAT Middle and Upper level use more complex incorrect answer patterns. SAT or ACT uses sophisticated patterns, GRE uses highly sophisticated form of incorrect answers. But one thing is clear. They all use above five patterns.

What if you can predict incorrect answers even before reading the passages?

You can greatly improve your confidence by following 10 patterns for the Reading section, 5 common patterns for the incorrect answers, and 12 patterns for the Analogy section.

SSAT ABSOLUTE PATTERNS

READ ME

Therefore, the Secret is in Improving Your Guessing Skill, Stick to It, Love It, and Take Good Care of It!

Focus on Answer Explanations in each test. To try out, Test 1 doesn't start with the test, but starts with the answer explanations.

After studying chapter 1, you will be able to tell which type of question you're dealing with, which logic and pattern sustain each incorrect answer, and from which part in the passage the correct answers are originally created.

If you focus on questions and the choices that come along, you will experience drastic enhancement to your attention when you read the passages. How?
Because you know what you are reading. The quality of your reading skills improves. You'll see each key point very clearly. Eventually, you will learn by yourself how to improve scores drastically.

Once you completely understand chapter 1 and the answer explanation for test 1, move on to the next page. You'll see the same questions under the same name "TEST 1." Try to get them all in third of the time-limit. You'll see that your scores have improved at a head-spinning rate.

Jimin: Improving scores at a head-spinning rate?

I know! When you try something new, it feels sort of wearing a brand-new underwear, a bit uncomfortable inside. But soon will you find a comfort zone as if it's part of your skin.

How to Use This Book

The Relevancy Check = The Mechanics Inside Your Guess

The passage supports which of the following about China and Egypt in line 4?
A) They were as big as Europe--NI
B) They were less advanced than Western Europe--DC
C) They had no civilization--EX
D) They were as competitive nations as India--V

You may, as shown on the left, write initials on each question based on 10 Reading Patterns and 5 Incorrect Choice Patterns.
The Relevancy Check—finding and eliminating incorrect answers through guess—is the only way to drastically improve your score.

The remaining tests 2 to 7, however, start with the questions.
If you still feel uncomfortable, it's your book, read the answer explanations first until you feel confident about what you're doing.

Once you identify what kind of questions you are dealing with, you'll have a much clearer idea for what will be the important information in the passage.
Knowing what is being asked and what will be important in the passages makes a huge difference in finding the correct answers. Believe it or not, you'll be able to find many correct answers without even reading the passages.

How top 0.1 percent student solve questions?

Have you ever seen any brilliant friends who can find the answers so quickly and so naturally? But somehow he/she cannot seem to explain the reasons for the answers so that you can understand? Luck? Yes! Can this be developed by practice? Yes! All those above 0.1-top-scorers, although they may think they are just good readers, have highly developed guessing skills that find incorrect answers consciously but without definite terminologies they can explain.

To prove, this book starts with the official tests taken directly from SSAT that you can download from Google.

How to Use This Book

Do you know, Jimin, that every single reading and analogy question is created with the unique but repeating pattern? Jimin: I didn't. What are they like?

The Reading and Analogy Sections use the same repeating patterns.
The official SSAT creates questions based on these patterns. This book focuses on these patterns.
Each question is categorized based on 10 Reading Patterns, 5 Incorrect Choice Patterns, and 12 Analogy Patterns.
Instead of solving each individual question endlessly without knowing the patterns and logic behind it, practice with hidden patterns, memorize them and check whether you follow the patterns until they become natural to you

How to Understand the Answer Tables

Each box that represents each question focuses on the question pattern and the Relevancy Check for the incorrect answers.

Q31. Question Pattern: The primary function of the first paragraph is to describe the
AP 10: Understanding the Structure of the Passage: Find the structural pattern of the paragraph or the passage

- **Question Keyword/Key phrase:** "primary function"
- **Incorrect Answer Patterns:** A) man's specific concern—NI   **B) setting of the place**
   C) difference between the Palais Royal and the Palais Cardinal—DC   D) luxurious details inside the Palais Royal—IS   E) self-awareness of the man sitting in a splendid chamber—IS
- **What Does The Question Really Ask?** First of all, identify the key phrase in this question: "primary function." That is, this is the "function question," not a "content question." Thus, this question mainly asks the functional structure of the passage.
- **Reading Tip:** In literary genre, in SSAT level, exists only one function for the opening paragraph: "to describe the settings," such as the settings of place or the main characters.
- **Relevancy Check:** Choice A, C, D, E, whether truly stated or not in the passage, cannot be the "function" of the paragraph.

B is the best answer. In line 1, the narrator states the settings of the place "In a splendid chamber of the Palais Royal"

How SSAT Analogy Section is Created

Jimin: Does each analogy question ask one analogy at a time?

Each question, in its fundamental level, is made of one analogy-stem and five potential answers that usually use different analogies. That's for the elementary level though.

As level moves up to the Middle and Upper level, you'll see many questions apply several logic and analogies like multi-layer stems. For instance, the question-stem "Evil is to God" basically uses the Antonym Pattern. But it also has the Negative and Positive Pattern, the Intangible and Tangible, the Subjective and Objective, and the Mental Pattern.

Jimin: What? five patterns are squeezed into one question? How can I possibly find the correct answer if one question is buried with so many patterns?

Depending on the complexity of five choices, the level of difficulties will be determined in each question.

Understanding the analogy-stem in each question is critical. identifying the Analogy-stem is your first task!

Remember, the analogy-stem (the question) is quite often interpreted in more than one analogy.

Observe each question-stem from various perspectives. In fact, seeing one question from many different analogy patterns eventually become less complex than treating it as a simple analogy question. For you'll know immediately when you start reading each choice.

How to Use This Book

Can This Book Guarantee My Score?

Yes. Absolutely!

With the lower level tests (or easy questions for you), you may not need to understand the patterns. For they are easy anyway. However, the more complex and difficult the test becomes, the less will you be relying on passages. It is because while easy questions nearly copy and paste the answer from the passage with little logic, difficult questions, in spite of the same passage, provide only limited information from the passage.

The problem is penetrating the questions. They all are fortified by logic and tricks. Whether impenetrable or not depends on your consciousness and practice rather than intelligence and reading skills. Chapter 1 provides all the patterns and solutions. Be familiar with the patterns and the terms used in chapter 1.
Remember! There's no overnight solution. You should work very hard to memorize your vocabulary.

What is The Minimum Vocabulary and is it in This Book?

For students aiming for 99% in the Reading and Verbal section, it is recommended to memorize:

SSAT Upper Level: ……….1500 word vocabulary

SSAT Middle Level: ………1000 word vocabulary

SSAT Lower Level…..600 word vocabulary

Request your free ABSOLUTE vocabulary book at: satvancouver@gmail.com

CONTENTS

How to use this book 2-14

Chapter 1 .... 15– 89

SSAT official test analysis....17-34

10 Absolute Patterns for the Reading Section... 35-51

*Absolute Pattern 1: Main Idea (Focus Shifts) Question

*Absolute Pattern 2: Summary Question

*Absolute Pattern 3: Example Question

*Absolute Pattern 4: Word-In-Context Question

*Absolute Pattern 5: Understanding the True Purpose

*Absolute Pattern 6: Analogy Question

*Absolute Pattern 7: Inference Question

*Absolute Pattern 8: Understanding Attitude (Tone) Question

*Absolute Pattern 9: Relationships Question

*Absolute Pattern 10: Understanding the Structure of the Passage

5 Common Patterns for *In*correct Choices 52-59

1. Direct Contradiction—DC

2. Insufficient Information—IS

3. Irrelevant Words—IW

4. New Information—NI

5. Extreme Word Usage—TI

12 Absolute patterns for Analogies...................60-89

How SSAT Analogy Section is Created

*Absolute Pattern 1. The Category Pattern

*Absolute Pattern 2. The Synonym/Antonym

*Absolute Pattern 3. the Purpose (Tool) Pattern

*Absolute Pattern 4. The Characteristic Pattern

*Absolute Pattern 5. The Degree Pattern

*Absolute Pattern 6. Definition Pattern

*Absolute Pattern 7. Mental (Emotion) Pattern

*Absolute Pattern 8. The Production Pattern

*Absolute Pattern 9. Syntax Pattern

*Absolute Pattern 10. Positive vs. Negative Pattern

*Absolute Pattern 11. Subjective vs. Objective Pattern

*Absolute Pattern 12. Human-Nonhuman Pattern

Chapter 2..122-330

Complete Answer Explanations for Test 1.....90-108
Test 1....109-121

Test 2.....122-134
Complete Answer Explanations for Test 2 with Absolute Patterns 135-152

Test 3 153-166
Complete Answer Explanations for Test 3 with Absolute Patterns 167-182

Test 4 183-195
Complete Answer Explanations for Test 4 with Absolute Patterns 196-211

Test 5 212-223
Complete Answer Explanations for Test 5 with Absolute Patterns 224-240

Test 6 241-253
Complete Answer Explanations for Test 6 with Absolute Patterns 254-269

Test 7 270-282
Complete Answer Explanations for Test 7 with Absolute Patterns 283-298

Test 8 299-312
Complete Answer Explanations for Test 7 with Absolute Patterns 313-330

SSAT

Chapter 1

10 Patterns for the Reading Section
 5 Common Patterns for Incorrect Choices
 12 Patterns for Analogy Section

Koala SSAT

10 Patterns for the Reading Section

 Each question consists of three structures: the base-form, keyword or phrase, and the logic chain.

 The base-form in the question rarely changes. But it's the keyword or key phrase that changes always, which makes each question unique.
The logic-chain controls the level of difficulty, provides hints, or test your reasoning skills.

Q10. Question Pattern: <u>The author uses</u> **"*While* these...brain,"** (lines 6-7) <u>to make which of the following points?</u>
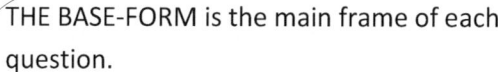

THE BASE-FORM is the main frame of each question.
The frame—just like the house frame—seldom changes. So limited is the number of these unchanging base forms, In fact, that there are only 10 of them.

 These same patterns of base-forms will appear on your test.
Confusion may arise to some questions in identifying the correct patterns. Quite a few questions may seem, for instance, an inference question and the main idea question simultaneously.

It is not because the question is intentionally misleading or defective, but because it is a multi-layered question.
Don't be too concerned though. For identifying the question base-form is to limit the reading scope thereby removing unnecessary information, so that only necessary information can be considered. The above question Q10, for instance, uses two phrases "The author uses" and "to make which of the following points?" as the question base-form. From which we can find that the question is asking the true purpose of using the word "while" and the keyword.

 THE QUESTION KEYWORDS OR KEY PHRASE refer to the most important words in each question.
Test creators, to create each question, look for keywords from the passage and then plug those keywords into the question base-form.
At this point, some students, when asked, find fancy words from the question such as "very," "extremely," or "so much," believing they are the keywords. They are not. They are meaningless adverbs only good enough to put them in the garbage can.

10 Patterns for the Reading Section

The keywords or key phrase must be very unique words that stands out in each question. "these....brain" in above question is the unique word that stands out more than any other words in the sentence.

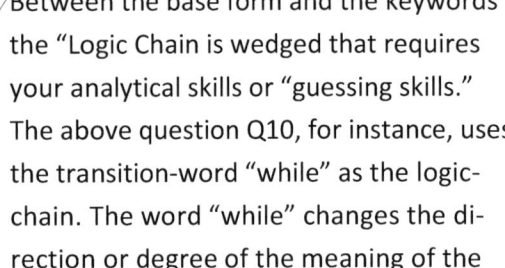

Between the base form and the keywords the "Logic Chain is wedged that requires your analytical skills or "guessing skills." The above question Q10, for instance, uses the transition-word "while" as the logic-chain. The word "while" changes the direction or degree of the meaning of the sentence.

Test creators can create over dozens of the correct answers or incorrect answers using this word "while," the logic-chain.

As seen above, the Base-Form, the Key-word or key Phrase, and the Logic-Chain are wired together into one question.

To sum up, every time you read the question
1. Identify the question Base-Form.
2. identify the Key Phrase.
3. Identify Logic.
4. Decide whether reading the passage is necessary for such a question. If then, ask yourself where to read? What information do I need to find?

Now, you are starting to focus more on the questions, less on the passages.

The more you practice, the more will you understand how to penetrate the questions and the mechanisms lay under them. Upon which you will value less on the passage.

10 Patterns for the Reading Section

CATEGORY A: THE CONTENT QUESTION -HAS FIVE PATTERNS

The entire questions in the reading section, for both literary and informational passages, can be categorized into two parts:
Category A: Content Question
Category B: Technique Question

CATEGORY A: THE CONTENT QUESTION

▶ **Pattern 1: The Main Idea (Focus Shifts) Question**

Find the main idea of the entire passage or the paragraph

▶ **Pattern 2: The Summary Question**

Summarize the sentence or the entire paragraph

▶ **Pattern 3: The Example Question**

Find the primary reason for using the example sentence

▶ **Pattern 4: The Word-In-Context Question**

Find the clue words and keywords from the sentence

▶ **Pattern 5: Understanding the True Purpose**

Find the explicitly stated true purpose of the sentence

10 Patterns for the Reading Section

CATEGORY A: THE CONTENT QUESTION - HAS FIVE PATTERNS

The Content Question contains mostly the Local Question. That is, the Content Question, either with the line reference number (i.e. line 5) or without it, normally asks localized, detailed information from one or two sentences in the passage.

Decide before reading the passage —using the key-word you have from the question—where to read. Remember, read only one or two sentences, not the entire passage.

Students who are unfamiliar with this concept find the answer, for example, from line 35 when the question indicates "line 5." The question-and-the-correct-answer relation doesn't work that way. For that's not the characteristic of the content question. Even the highest-level tests such as GRE, GMAT does not create questions that way.

On the contrary to the local question, the Main Idea Question requires holistic understanding of the passage. More often than not, the main idea question tends to appear sooner than other types of questions in each passage. In that case, it's best to leave it alone and come back later. Called the "universal type question" such as the "main idea question" or "understanding the structure question" would be so much more easier when other questions are handled properly. This advice is especially important to the students with average scores.

PATTERN 1: THE MAIN IDEA QUESTION

Find the main idea of the entire passage or the paragraph

The main idea question asks a big question. It also includes focus shift (climax) in the Passage.

When the question asks the main idea of the passage, the answer is most likely to be located in the topic or concluding paragraph where, in many cases, you may find the author's final message with a clear tonality.

10 Patterns for the Reading Section

PATTERN 1: THE MAIN IDEA QUESTION
Find the main idea of the entire passage or the paragraph

First, Be familiar with various terms used in each question pattern.

→ A good idea is to memorize the repeating terms and phrases used in this book. Otherwise, It could sometimes be confusing what the question really asks.

→ For instance, question number 1 on your actual test may start with the phrase "What happens to Ms. Sally?"

If you don't understand the phrase "what happens?" and don't treat it as the main idea question, the correct answer may not come to you by simply reading the first sentence.

 Second. Location, location, location!
Incorrect answers for the main idea question can be roughly discovered by identifying the location of the key words.
For example, if choice A was found in the middle of the second paragraph while choice B was in the concluding paragraph, then choice B would more likely be the answer because the author generally finalizes his/her central argument in the conclusion.

Count the keywords in the passage. For example, if choice A has the keyword that occurred in the passage once or twice while the keyword in choice B occurred ten times, then B is more likely to be the answer.

 This is the real story. A student knowingly picked the incorrect answer in her actual test. She picked choice A "war" that was mentioned only once in the passage, while dumping the correct answer D "peace" mentioned 12 times. The student commented "I don't know. Maybe the word "war" sounds more impressive?"

Minor Ideas
Distinguish the minor ideas from the main idea.
To milk the main idea the author writes the supporting details or example sentence. For example, the phrase starting with "For example"—as in this sentence—is the minor idea that helps you understand better the main idea. Thus, the choices describing the example sentence can never be the main idea.

10 Patterns for the Reading Section

Pattern 1: The Main Idea Question

Find the main idea of the entire passage or the paragraph

What should I do when I am stuck with two equally true answers?

1. Review the introduction, the conclusion, and then choose the answer that holds the most frequently used keywords.

2. Don't trust the answer clothed in very specific words such as a specific name, place, or thing. For they are highly likely to be the minor idea. The main idea is supposed to cover the entire passage without specific words

3. Choose the answer that reflects the same tonality with the passage. It may sound easy, but very tempting to pick the opposite tone.

Amplifier
Amplifier is the technique used in the main idea question.
The sentence describing the main idea of the passage may not reveal the correct answer. Yet, an amplifier creeps up on you when you least expected. The amplifier phrase normally starts with a pronoun, such as "It" or "This" located right after the main idea sentence or clause. However, many students often ignore such a pronoun, which, in fact, emphasizes—or de-emphasizes—the preceding main sentence.

Premises and Consequence
The premise-and-consequence attached with transition words such as "because," "but," "however" are one of the major logic chains used in the main idea. So, pay attention when you see those words in the passage.

Focus Shift
Focus shift may occur in the passage in several forms. The author, for instance, may change his mind and disagree with the critics whose opinion was initially valued by the author; the author may eventually agree or disagree or raise his own opinion in the concluding sentence; a character may eventually change his or her arguments. Therefore, it is important to read the Conclusion.

10 Patterns for the Reading Section

PATTERN 2: THE SUMMARY QUESTION

Summarize the sentence or the entire paragraph

SSAT uses this pattern more than any other patterns. The basic technique is almost the same as the Main Idea pattern. Unlike the Main Idea pattern that requires the holistic understanding of the passage, the reading scope in this pattern is limited to a few lines, or at most one paragraph. Therefore, it is not necessary to read the entire passage. Try to avoid reading the following paragraph. For it is extremely important not to mix one paragraph with another paragraph. For instance, if the question asks the summary of the second paragraph, never choose the one that contains information from the first paragraph. For that is the bait! Treat as if each paragraph in the passage is written by different authors.

Focus on tonality: the tonality of the entire passage, the tonality of the author, the tonality of each character. The tonality can usually be divided into the positive, negative, and neutral. For instance, if the author is critical to the quote "I have a dream" by Martin Luther King for its idealism and cliché, you should never pick the answer with the positive tonality—although students may take for granted that the correct answer must be, without doubt, a positive.

Treat Each Paragraph in the Passage is Written by Different authors. That is, focus only on one paragraph per question.

Focus on the tonality of the very first word in each choice. The first word, such as "blame," "criticize," "celebrate," "approve" or "disapprove" becomes the deciding factor to the correct answer.

The type of passage also decides the correct answer.
Between (A) playful and (B) celebratory, for example, the correct answer—although they both are positive words—is likely to be (B) if it were the informational passage.

A summary question, unlike the main idea question, is supposed to be specific and it focuses on one or two lines in the passage. If choice (A) contains a number, specific name, or things, whereas choice (B) contains a general statement, the correct answer is highly likely to be (A).

10 Patterns for the Reading Section

PATTERN 3: THE EXAMPLE QUESTION

Find the reason for using the example sentences

Jimin: I love reading example sentences.

Because it's easy! Example sentences are easy to understand because the authors use a scenario to illustrate and clarify their main argument.

Rarely does the example sentence contain the correct answer, however. For the example sentence merely supports, through the illustration, the main idea of the author, the narrator, or the character

The Example Question sometimes uses a historical figure's monologue, an authority's quote, an analogy, or Aunt Sally's note. Many students try to find the answer by scrutinizing the example sentence. For it is easier to understand than the main argument. The correct answer, however, is located directly above or below the example sentence, where the author presents his main idea

For instance, if the question asks lines 5-8, and if it is identified as the example question, the answer should be located either in line 4 or in line 9—directly above or below the example. Incorrect answers are, conversely, very visible, located in lines 5-8, where everyone can see easily.

Sometimes, the last sentence in the paragraph would be the example sentence.
Many students dig out the root of every single word within that paragraph, looking up hoping to find if there's something dangling similar to the answer. Yet, students overlook the topic sentence of the
following paragraph, where the author's main argument for that example sentence actually starts.
This is the only case when two paragraphs merge as one information.

10 Patterns for the Reading Section

PATTERN 4: THE WORD-IN-CONTEXT QUESTION

Find the clue words and keywords from the sentence

Jimin: Do I need to memorize lots of vocabulary for this pattern?

Yes. You should. The Word-in-Context Pattern presents two types of questions: first, the vocabulary test. It asks whether you know the precise meaning of the word—normally a high-level word; second, it asks the figurative meaning used to word in a sentence.

WARNING

Avoid using the technique so-called "the Plug-in method."
Students try to "plug" every word in each choice into the sentence until the correct answer is found. It wouldn't work that way, and worse yet, the "plug-in method" would create only confusion.
For the incorrect answers are created using the very plug-in method intended to create confusion.

SOLUTION: The Mirroring Technique

Word-in-Context questions almost always leave *a "clue word"* in the question sentence. You must find the clue word first.
Jimin: how do I know which one is the clue word?
The clue word is usually the most important word in the sentence that contains most critical information, therefore comparable to the question word.
Step 1: Find the clue word from the sentence-in-question.
Step 2: Eliminate the incorrect answers that cannot be replaced with the clue word.
Step 3: The correct answer should be the synonym to the clue word.

Thus, you must use the clue word as a mirror to reflect the answer.
It is a very risky practice to attempt to find the answer by plugging words, without having a clue word.

10 Patterns for the Reading Section

PATTERN 4: THE WORD-IN-CONTEXT QUESTION

Find the clue words and keywords from the sentence

The Literal-Meaning Question
If the Word-in-Context question asks a difficult word, it is most likely to be the question asking for the literal meaning of the word. In this case, consider only the very first definition from dictionary, not the second or third ones.

The Figurative-Meaning Question
If the Word-in-Context question seems to be so easy, don't choose the first answer that looks like the one. It is almost guaranteed that you would miss the question.
Why do you think such an easy word would appear in the first place? Because test creators are nice?
Read the passage and find a clue word to decipher the figurative meaning of the word in the sentence.

The Word-in-Context Question is not a piece-of-cake just because the question phrase is short.

Some questions use clue-word trick!
Last but not least, distinguish the "clue word" from the "correct answer".
The clue word is NOT the correct answer. It is the *reflection* of the correct answer.
Potential answers may use a flamboyant adjective or adverb, mainly for distraction.
Beneath it may you find the correct answer as simple as "it" (the singular pronoun).
Rarely does the impressive adjective or adverb become the correct answer.

For example, which one would you choose between these two potential answers?
(A) foreboding relationship (B) it
Sound more sophisticated though, choice A could be wrong if the passage shows the positive relations.

10 Patterns for the Reading Section

PATTERN 5: UNDERSTANDING THE TRUE PURPOSE

Find the explicitly stated true purpose of the sentence

The correct answer must be based on irreducible, fundamental concept.
It has to reach to the rock solid concept where logic, reasoning, or common sense is not violated. That is to say, find the self-sufficient word.

Here is a simplified version for this type of question.
Q: This pen is
A) yellow
B) cheap
C) pretty
D) plastic

The correct answer is D. For "plastic" represents the fundamental substance of the pen. Unlike choice D, all the other incorrect answers become secondary information at most, if not untrue. Take this way. They all contain subjective values. However, choice D, whether stated in the passage or not, cannot be disputed. No one can.

Jimin: But my pen is made of metal.

You're not listening, Jimin. Do you see the word "metal" in the choices?

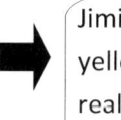

Jimin: My pen is also yellow, very cheap, and really pretty.

Gosh! Isn't it plastic?

Take this way: the concession phrase.
"*Although I was hungry*, I didn't eat."
Considered all the choices are true statements, the correct answer—unless stated otherwise, must describe the phrase "I didn't eat"—primary information.

In absolutely no way, concession phrase *alone* can convey the author's true purpose. Explaining "why I was hungry" or "how it feels to go hungry" does not answer the question. They are definitely not the true purpose nor should be the correct answer.

10 Patterns for the Reading Section

CATEGORY B: THE TECHNIQUE QUESTION-HAS FIVE PATTERNS:

If Category A: Content Question is about the interior of the building, Category B: Technique Question is about the foundation and skeleton that support the building.

Category B: Technique Question-has five patterns:

▶ Pattern 6: Analogy Question
Find the logically-supported similar situation

▶ Pattern 7: Inference Question
Find the indirect suggestion behind the sentence

▶ Pattern 8: Understanding Attitude (Tone) Question
Find the tonality: positive vs. negative, mental vs. physical, subjective vs. objective

▶ Pattern 9: Relationship Question
Find the relationship between cause and effect, between characters or ideas

▶ Pattern 10: Understanding the Structure of the Passage
Find the structural pattern of the paragraph or the entire passage

10 Patterns for the Reading Section

PATTERN 6: THE ANALOGY QUESTION
Find the logically-supported similar situation

Don't be overwhelmed when you see choices containing totally different information from what you've just read from the passage.
In the analogy question—unlike all the other types of questions—the choices use completely new Information.
It may suddenly ask, for example, (A) a school teacher (B) frogs (C) hardwood floor (D) Odyssey

The analogy questions in the Reading section ask the logical consistency between the correct answer and the passage. To find the situational similarities with the passage—that uses the logic chain—requires more than passage information.

The logical analogies typically contain
Positive *vs.* Negative;
Active *vs.* Passive;
Physical *vs.* Mental;
Quantity *vs.* Quality;
A single person *vs.* Multiple persons involvement;
Part *vs.* Whole

Take this example.
If the passage contained "a mother who lost her son during the war," the incorrect answers often contain such words as "mother," "son," "war."
The correct answer, however, must contain one or more of the following logic:
(1) two-person involvement
(2) negative tonality
(3) external impact
Remember. The correct answer has no keywords in the passage.

10 Patterns for the Reading Section

PATTERN 7: THE INFERENCE QUESTION

Find the indirect suggestion behind the sentence

Suppose you were a 2-year-old kid and very hungry. If you saw the McDonald's sign on the street and pointed that out to your mom, what would it mean?
(A) I want to have that McDonald's sign
(B) I want to have a hamburger.
That's the example of inference question.

Just as the kid wanting to have a hamburger, not the McDonald's sign, whatever directly copied from the reading passage should never be the answer. Alas!

You may expect the question phrases will send you a strong signal such as " what it refers to…" or "what it implies…" so that you would be ready to snatch the correct answer in no time.

In ideal situation, yes! It should stamp its indication on its forehead.
The problem is that the inference question very frequently won't send you any signal.

For example, the question phrase "what does it indicates?" does not sound at all the inference question. Yet it may use the Inference pattern for the correct answer.

Conversely, some questions send a strong signal, such as "what it implies" or "the author infers" that appears to be, without doubt, the inference question.
As it turns out to be nothing like the inference question.

SOLUTION
Treat all questions as Inference Questions. Take a guess—an educated guess—based on sound reasoning we have practiced and will practice in this book.

10 Patterns for the Reading Section

PATTERN 8: UNDERSTANDING ATTITUDE (TONE)

Find the Tone such as Positive-Negative, Active-Passive, Mental-Physical, Subjective-Objective

In this pattern, find the correct answer that maintains the same tonality as you have seen in the passage.

It may be easy to find the correct answer with a negative tonality for the negative character in the passage. On the contrary, it requires more skills to identify how the author would react to that negative character, or how the critics would view the negative character.

The author in informational passages may maintain a neutral tone to the ghastly Holocaust, for instance. Or the main character would praise World War II.
For it contributed to the advancement of science and technology. Identify from whose point of view—whether it is from the author, a character, or a quote from the previous paragraph— the answer must be determined.

Understanding tone plays a key role in all the other questions. For there exists a unique tonality in virtually all correct answers in the reading questions.

HOW TO USE THIS BOOK

10 Patterns for the Reading Section

PATTERN 9: THE RELATIONSHIP QUESTION
Find the relationship between cause and effect, between characters, and between ideas

This pattern asks many different types of relations found in the passage.

(1) The relationship between the cause-and-effect situation: focus on transition such as "because," "since," "for," "as," "but."

(2) The relationship within a compare-and-contrast situation flagged by "more," "better," "never," "often," "if," or "unless." Both the passage and the correct must contain a comparative.

(3) The relationship between historical events, between characters, between ideas, or between arguments.

Focus on the main character: The Reading passages with several characters are very confusing. Even more confusing are, for example, different types of fungus or different types of planktons in biology. If the passage contains more than one character, focus on, no matter what, the main character. Again, focus only on the main character—unless the question asks different character. Potential answers may change the character's name but still use the true statement. (e.g., (A) Chessy's mom was relieved   (B) Chessy was relieved

Common Mistakes!

If the question asks:

"compared to paragraph 1, paragraph 2...is?"

Use your pencil to cross out irrelevant information.
(e.g., "compared to paragraph 1, paragraph 2...is?")

The phrase "compare to paragraph 1" is merely a "complement."
Many students—as would in the "EXCEPT" questions—take the bait and pick the wrong answer—frequently choice (A)—that fits in paragraph 1. Use your pencil always.

For this pattern, the keywords in the passage are usually located at/near to the:
  √ contradictory conjunction "but (or synonyms)"
  √ paired comparisons such as "more ~ than"
  √ transition words/phrases, such as "on the other hand," "in fact," consequently"

SSAT ABSOLUTE PATTERNS

10 Patterns for the Reading Section

PATTERN 10: UNDERSTANDING THE STRUCTURE
Find the structural pattern of the entire passage or its organizational relationship

This question pattern has little to do with the content of the passage. It never means that you don't need to understand the content. One of the typical phrases in this type of question is "What is the primary function of the first paragraph?"

Consider the following sample question.
Q: Which choice best describes the function of the first paragraph?
  (A) It discusses the harmful impacts of protein
  (B) It introduces clinical results with examples

The answer is (B) because the major function of the first paragraph is to introduce things.
Choice A is incorrect because it would be nonsense to say "harmful impacts" is the function of the paragraph. On the contrary, choice A could be the correct answer had the question been the "Summary question."

Before choosing the answer, you need to identify the key phrase from the question so that you know what is being asked.
Without understanding this fact—no matter how well you understood the reading passage, you may pick the wrong choice.

5 Common Patterns for Incorrect Answers

At the beginning of this book, I presented, using the official SSAT test, how to find the correct answers without even reading the passage!"
Although it may sound overly simplistic with full of stretched exaggeration, many high scorers, indeed, consistently use this method.

Either consciously or unconsciously, many students pick the incorrect answers due to limited understanding, and worse yet, misunderstanding of the passage.

Take this way.
Obtaining no information at all by not reading the passage could have been better to find the correct answer without bias.

What if you are able to identify incorrect answers even before reading the passage—no matter how difficult the passage is?

Are there any patterns in all incorrect answers?

Yes! There are 5 Common Patterns for Incorrect Answers.

Consider "Generalization," for instance. Many incorrect answers apply generally acceptable but vague statements. Thus, "Generalization" sounds so plausible that will make you difficult to resist but to choose it as the correct answer.

The 5 common patterns for incorrect answers are:
1) Direct Contradiction
2) Insufficient Information
3) Irrelevant Word
4) New Information and Generalization
5) Extreme Word

5 Common Patterns for Incorrect Answers

DIRECT CONTRADICTION—

Direct Contradiction (DC) is a type of incorrect answer that contradicts the original statement.
This pattern appears most frequently.
So readily applicable is the use of antonym or opposing concept to the reading passage that almost all questions apply Direct Contradiction (DC) in one of their four incorrect answers. There are several ways to express direct contradiction.

Tonal Incongruity (TI)
Tonal incongruity switches positive to negative tone or vice versa.
The more you practice, the more will you observe questions using this simple but very powerful tool.
First, Identify the tonality of the question, then identify the tonality in choices A,B,C,D, and E. Second, think whether each choice's either positive or negative tonality corresponds to the reading passage's tonality.

Contradicting Situation, Characters, or Concept
Incorrect answers may use a contradicting situation or characters that go against the question or the passage. Characters in the passage have their own tonalities. A villain, for example, maintains the negative tone and so does a pungent onion that the villain uses in the passage. A butter that represents a positive character or situation becomes the positive concept because it is made of natural ingredients, while "margarine" becomes the negative concept because it uses artificial ingredients, so, too, negative is Aunt Nancy's artificial happiness to her husband. Direct contradiction may also use an abstract idea or concept. For instance, the passage may use one of our five senses "smell," "hearing," "touch," "sight," "taste"—e.g. sour (for taste); sickly (for smell); silky (for touch); squawking (for hearing); neat (for sight). Through the words that contain human emotion can we identify the physical and tonal contradiction.

Synonyms + Contradicting Adjectives or Adverbs
Majority of correct answers rely on the synonym pattern. That is, most correct answers do not use the exact wording from the passage, but instead, deploy synonyms.
Incorrect answers in this method can be created by simply placing contradictory adjectives or adverbs right next to the synonyms that otherwise could have been the correct answer.
Take this example. It is obvious that the term "acceptance" contains the positive tone.
Can you, however, distinguish "acceptance" and "mild acceptance" and "guarded acceptance?"
The term "acceptance" has an emphatic tone; "mild acceptance" shows a reduced positive tonality; "guarded acceptance" has a negative tone.

TO BE CONTINUED ⇨

5 Common Patterns for Incorrect Answers

 ## Direct Contradiction—

Depending on the word added to the keyword of each choice, test creators can adjust the difficulty level of the question. Easy questions, for example, may add a word that drastically changes the meaning of the answer; but in difficult questions, only a slightly contradicting word—that eventually changes the original meaning of the answer—will be added. Ex) A) known in U.S. B) once known in U.S. C) not known in U.S.

Concept Comparison
Concept comparison normally presents two opposing concepts, such as "Physical *vs.* Mental," "Negative *vs.* Positive," "Passive *vs.* Active," "Part *vs.* Whole," and "A single-individual *vs.* Two-individuals."   As seen from the analogy pattern, concept comparison focuses on logic chain within statement. Take this example, (A) COVID-19 was not known in 2018   (B) COVID-19 did not exist in 2018 Choice A uses the passive tone that leaves out some possibility, whereas choice B uses the active tone with no possibility. More often than not, choice A has high probability to be the correct answer.

Subjective *vs.* Objective Tonality
Subjective tonality is usually found in literature passages, and is represented by the first person or the narrator. Subjective tonality cut cross a clear positive and negative tonality. On the other hand, most informational passages such as history or science genre use objective tonality saturated with more tempered, analytical, and neutral tone. For example, between (A) "analyze…" and (B) "describe…," choice B "describe" is more likely to be the answer in literary genre. By contrast, choice A is more likely to be the answer in the information genre. In more complex version, if the question focuses on the narrator's view in the literary genre, choice A would be the answer because the narrator usually possesses the critic's view.
Now, which would you choose between (A) "playful…" and (B) "celebratory…" in informational genre?

Quantity and Quality Contradiction
The phrase "one-fourth," for instance, describes "quantity." Thus, the correct answer must indicate a certain amount.   Incorrect answers, however, frequently use such a subjective value as "good" or "bad."
A classic such as "The Great Gatsby" definitely implies a high quality writing. "comics," meanwhile, represent low quality. The correct answer therefore is decided by subjective view, such as "good" or "bad."

Finally, some students find themselves quandary in determining "direct contradiction" "semi-direct contradiction," and "little contradiction." It does not matter as long as they contradict the passage.

5 Common Patterns for Incorrect Answers

INSUFFICIENT INFORMATION—

Insufficient Information (IS) is a type of incorrect answer that uses true but only partially true statement, thereby giving not full, but insufficient information. Take this example.

Passage: Sally ate a pizza and a hamburger.
Question: What did Sally eat?
A) pizza B) nothing C) hamburger D) pizza and hamburger => D) is the best answer.

Choice (A) and (C) each contains one true keyword while choice (D) has two. Then choices A and C are incorrect because they are insufficient although true statement.

IRRELEVANT WORDS—IW

Irrelevant words or information (IW) is a type of incorrect answer that uses meaningful words from the passage but irrelevant to the question. While displaying meaningful words from the passage, incorrect answers do not answer the question. For instance, some incorrect answers may use the correct answer for the previous question that may instantly appeals to you.

Primary Idea *vs.* Minor Ideas
In the Main Idea Question minor ideas become irrelevant information. In Summary Question, on the contrary, the main idea loses its relevancy where requires specific information such as a specific name, place, thing, or history.

The Repetition of the Question
Fooling students is never easier when the answers paraphrase the question instead of answering it. Some questions may look extremely easy at first sight only because the potential answer paraphrases the question. For instance, that a question phrase ends with "because" should find the consequence as the correct answer, not the reason in the passage. This leads some students end up finding the phrase from the passage very similar to the question and believe they found the answer.

To be continued ⇨

5 Common Patterns for Incorrect Answers

 **IRRELEVANT WORDS—IW**

True but Inconsistent Statement (TS)

True but inconsistent with the question is a type of incorrect answer.

Suppose a question asks "the author's main concern in lines 15-22, paragraph 3."

-Choice A) is a true statement from lines 15, *but states what the critics say,* not what the author says

-Choice B) is a true statement from lines 1-5, paragraph 1, *not from paragraph 3*

-Choice C) is a true statement from paragraph 3, *but states an example sentence, not the main concern.*

-Choice D) is a true statement from line 20, paragraph 3 that states the author's main concern.

As seen above, you must Identify to "whom" in "which line" the question is being asked.

In short, you should decide exactly what information is need under what passage limitation.

Shifting the Argument

The author may change his/her argument later on. For example, in paragraph 1, the author introduces what the critics argue with one issue. But then, the author later in paragraph 2 opposes to the critics. In more complex passage, the author himself suddenly changes his opinion or corrects his previous misunderstanding.

It is important to verify clearly the author's final statement and his tonality, and they are normally located at the end, not in the middle of the passage, which will be considered irrelevant information.

Follow the Instruction Given in Each Question

Imagine one paragraph (a total of 15 lines) is composed of a single long complex compound sentence.

Such a long single sentence can be broken down into all four potential answers.

(A) lines 1-2 ("Although"-phrase...)   (B) lines 3-5,(the author's main argument)

(C) lines 6-15 (the author's minor argument)   (D) lines 35-45 (the author's main argument)

If the question asks about the author's main concern in the first paragraph (lines 1-15), the answer must be (B).

Strictly follow the line reference stated in the question. For it is part of the question. That is, you are assigned to read and find the answer only from the lines given to you.

5 Common Patterns for Incorrect Answers

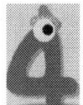
NEW INFORMATION—NI

New Information (NI) is a type of incorrect answer that shows completely unrelated information. However, it is tempting to pick such obviously incorrect answers when they use familiar common sense, well-known facts, or heroic figures. It may look good to add Martin Luther King Jr.'s name in the passage about Frederick Douglas. Or, the ancient Greek philosopher Plato could be a great answer to history genre. New information, however tempting, must not be the correct answer if it is not stated in the passage.

Generalization (GE)
Generalization uses elusive or too broad concept. For instance, choice (A) "to convey the reader's interest" choice (B) "to suggest the significant role of science," both of which can be practically applied to almost any questions in any scientific passage. Yet, it stops short of answering the specific issue in the question. To Identify generalization, use your common sense rather than reading the passages.

Unknown Prediction (UP)
Unknown Prediction (UP) not stated in the passage is considered incorrect, however persuasive it is. They include the verb in the future tense or the future adverbial phrases, such as 'likely to be,' "seem," "will," "perceive," or "anticipate."
Rarely does the correct answer predict the future not stated in the passage.
Just as there is no consequence without the premise, prediction cannot exist to the passage that describes only the present moment, present experiment, present condition, and present limitation.

5 Common Patterns for Incorrect Answers

 ## Extreme Word Usage—EX

Extreme Word (EX) is the type of incorrect answer that uses extreme words or phrases.
Some obviously extreme adverbs such as "always," "only," "never," etc. are relatively easy to eliminate as the incorrect answers. Some people take them as automatically incorrect answers. But there is no such a thing that is automatically wrong.
In the passage, for instance, that introduces an endangered species, terms such as choice (A) "only dwindling" or (B) "always compromised" are more likely to be the correct answers than choice (C) "extinct" or (D) "failed." For choice C and D are relatively more extreme than choice A and B.

Active *vs.* Passive Voice
Suppose that you have two competing answers A) sympathy   B) sadness
Can you tell the difference between them?
Imagine that you are watching a movie preview. in the scene, a female character is dying in bed.
Would you feel sad for her?   No, you would feel at most sympathy for her. Choice B) "sad," compared to choice A, becomes "extreme" expression.
Now imagine that your close friend died of cancer. Would you feel "sympathy" for her? No. The same word "sympathy" now becomes a weak implication.
As seen above, the keywords or key phrases in passage determines whether a term is "extreme" or not.
*Please note that this Active-Passive voice is not the same thing as the active-passive voice in grammar.

12 PATTERNS FOR THE ANALOGY SECTION

How SSAT Analogy Section is Created

Jimin: Analogy is really confusing! I sometimes experience a brain freeze when dealing with these guys.

To improve your score in Analogy, we must first understand how questions are actually created. Look at the chart below.

Elementary Level	Middle Level/Upper Level
1. Antonyms	1. Antonyms
2. Synonyms	2. Synonym
3. Degree	3. Degree
4. Part/Whole	4. Part/Whole
5. Characteristic	5. Whole/Part
6. Category	6. Type/Kind
7. Product to Producer	7. Association
8. Uses	8. Cause-Effect
9. Users	9. Function
10. Homonyms	10. Purpose
	11. Defining relationships
	12. Individual to Object
	13. Word
	14. Noun/Verb

The reason we're looking at all three levels is to consolidate the structure from its foundation. The foundation starts with the elementary level—from which the middle and the upper level branch out using slightly different terminology. As you can see from the table above the fundamental concept of all three levels are no different at all.

Analogy Starts From a Simple Comparison Between Two Things

Jimin: If all three levels use the same analogy patterns, why would they use different names?

Analogy starts from a simple comparison between two things. But as level moves up or questions get harder, the comparison becomes more complex such as involving human perception and logic beneath it. The higher the level is, the more complex the logic becomes, and so does the terminology.

Elementary Level	Middle / Upper Level
1. Antonyms	1. Antonyms
2. Synonyms	2. Synonym
3. Degree	3. Degree
4. Part/Whole	4. Part/Whole
5. Characteristic	5. Whole/Part
6. Category	6. Type/Kind
7. Product to Producer	7. Association
8. Uses	8. Cause-Effect
9. Users	9. Function
10. Homonyms	10. Purpose
	11. Defining relationships
	12. Individual to Object
	13. Word
	14. Noun/Verb

As you can see above, most analogy patterns are overlapping in all thee levels.

The Basic Concept of Analogy

Now, let's take a look how each analogy and its basic concept are working.

Elementary Level

Antonyms: Expensive is to cheap as cold is to hot
Explanation: Expensive is an antonym to cheap as cold is an antonym to hot

Synonyms: Man is to male as feeling is emotion
Explanation: Man is a synonym to male as feeling is a synonym to emotion

Characteristic: Beaver is to build as bee is to sting
Explanation: Beaver has a characteristic of building dam as bee has a characteristic of sting.

Homonyms: Sand is to sandwich as sunny is to sun.
Explanation: Sand sandwich make the same sound as sunny and sun make the same sound.

Degree: Dime is to cent as kilogram is to gram.
Explanation: Dime is greater than cent as kilogram is greater than gram.

Part/Whole Tire is to car as keypad is to cell phone
Explanation: Tire is part of car as keypad is part of cell phone

Category: Chicken is to bird as bear is to mammal
Explanation: Chicken belongs to bird category as bear belongs to mammal category.

Product to Producer: Pig is to bacon as chicken is to egg
Explanation: Pig produces bacon as chicken produces egg.

Uses: Knife is to cut as hammer is to pound
Explanation: We use knife to cut as we use hammer to pound.

Users: Professor is to projector as student is to paper
Explanation: Professor uses projector as student uses paper.

The Basic Concept of Analogy

Middle/Upper Level

Defining relationships: Chef is to meal as plumber is to water pipe.
Explanation: The job of chef is to make meal as the job of plumber is to fix water pipe.

Type/Kind: Poetry is to reading as whisky is to drink
Explanation: Poetry is a type of reading as whisky is a type of drink.

Whole/Part: Car is to tire as cell phone is to speaker.
Explanation: Car includes a tire as cell phone includes a speaker.

Word: Fly is to flew as go is to went
Explanation: Flew is the past tense of fly as went is the past tense of go

Noun/Verb: Dance is to dancer as sing is to singer
Explanation: Noun does verb: dancer dances as singer sings.

Individual to Object: Professor is to projector as student is to paper
Explanation: Professor uses a projector as student uses a paper

Function: Knife is to cut as hammer is to pound
Explanation: We use a knife to cut as we use hammer to pound.

Cause-Effect: Pig is to bacon as chicken is to egg
Explanation: We raise pig for bacon as we raise chicken for egg

Purpose: Bike is to ride as radio is to listen
Explanation: The purpose of bike is to ride as the purpose of radio is to listen

Association: Chameleon is to change as skunk is to odor
Explanation: Chameleon is known to change its skin colors for protection as skunk is known to use its odor for protection.

Question-Stem Usually Uses More Than One Analogy

Jimin: So, does each analogy question ask one analogy at a time?

Each question, in its fundamental level, is made of one analogy-stem and five potential answers (five analogies). As level moves up to the Middle and Upper level you would see a large portion of each question-stem consists of several analogies like multi-layer stems.

For instance, the question-stem "Evil is to God" basically uses the Antonym Pattern in elementary level. All you have to do is to find an antonym analogy from the choices, say Woman is to Men. But from the view of the middle and the upper level, it can also has the Negative vs. Positive Pattern, the Intangible vs. Tangible, the Subjective vs. Objective, and the human vs. nonhuman, to name a few.

Jimin: What? five patterns are squeezed into one question? How can I find the correct answer with so many variables? Should I apply every single pattern to each question? Impossible!

It depends on how complex five potential answers are presented in each question.

Just as understanding the question pattern is critical in the Reading section, so too is understanding the analogy-stem. That is, identifying the Analogy-stem is your first task! Remember, the analogy-stem (the question pattern) can be interpreted in more than one analogy.

For example, one question-stem would simultaneously indicate the degree pattern, the characteristic pattern, and positive and negative pattern.

It is important to identify the question-stem from various perspectives. In fact, seeing more than one analogy from the question-stem is always safer and easier to find the correct answer than not seeing anything at all.

Because this concept sustains the principle of so many analogy questions, we will discuss about this over and over.
Now, let's combine all the analogies from the Elementary level to the Middle and the Upper Level, and then further simplify all these analogies by grouping them into similar categories.

SSAT ABSOLUTE PATTERNS

Fundamental Analogy Concept

Fundamental Analogy Concept (Elementary/Middle/Upper Level Combined)

1. Synonyms/Antonyms
2. Part/Whole & Whole/Part
3. Characteristic/Type/Kind/ Category/Association
4. Degree
5. Product to Producer/ Individual to Object/Defining relationships
6. Purpose/Cause-Effect/ Function
7. Homonyms
8. Noun/Verb
9. Word

So far, we have identified the entire SSAT analogy concepts and then have grouped them into the nine fundamental categories.

Now, we will review all these categories along with four additional but equally indispensable categories from the fundamental level to more complex level. Once mastered, It is guaranteed that not a single analogy question can escape from your hands.

CAUTION: As noted, you may find that some question-stems contain several analogies. That is to say, each pattern in 12 absolute patterns for Analogy may contain more than one analogy. However, we must pin one single primary analogy and forget about other possibility or other analogies that may arise from our thinking.

For example, the sample question-stem in the Degree Pattern may look as the Production pattern from different angle. Forget about the Production pattern for awhile. Otherwise, it will be never-ending story that eventually gets you nowhere. Worse yet, many students give up SSAT test for this confusion arising each time when solving questions. We must prevent this confusion by adopting 12 absolute patterns.

12 Patterns for the Analogy Section

Pattern 1. The Category Pattern
Find the Part/Whole, the Same Type/Kind, Association

Q1. Smell is to pungent as
A) sight is to strong
B) hear is to Mozart
C) touch is to fire
D) taste is to sweet
E) sense is to anger

This question-stem uses the Category Pattern. You should find part from the whole, the same type or kind, or the associated category with the question-stem.

The correct answer is D

The question-stem focuses on our five sensory devices (touch, smell, hearing, sight, taste).
The pungent smell is a strong smell. It is a very strong smell like your fart after eating a lot of onions because they're cheap. "Pungent" is associated with "smell" as "sweet" is associated with "taste." You can also say "pungent" is a type of smell as "sweet" is a type of taste.
A) strong, B) Mozart, and C) fire and E) anger are all unrelated words to the question-stem.

Jimin: I didn't know what "pungent" was.

If the question contains a word that you didn't know, look from the five potential answers the most meaningful word that can be paired with the question-stem.

Jimin: For me, "Mozart" in Choice B sounds more meaningful than others.

"pungent" (even though you didn't know the meaning) is an adjective. You can tell that much, can't you? Then, it is more logical to find the same adjective than a noun because nouns and adjectives cannot mix regardless of their meanings. Choices B and C are incorrect because "Mozart" and "fire" are nouns. Choice A doesn't have an analogy. For "strong" does not belong to five senses.

Jimin: What is this pungent smell! Did you eat onions?

12 Patterns for the Analogy Section

Pattern 2. The Synonym/Antonym
Find the similar or opposite meaning between the words

Q2-1 Chronicle is to history as

A) epoch is to era
B) businessman is to entrepreneur
C) dancer is to choreography
D) ending is to beginning
E) inform is to reform

Q2-2. Antipathy is to sympathy as love is to

A) abhor
B) dislike
C) friendship
D) illusion
E) magic

(Q2-1) The correct answer is A

"Chronicle" is a synonym to "history" as "epoch" is a synonym to "era."

Jimin: Isn't the word "entrepreneur" a fancy word for the "businessman?"

I know. There's always a catch, right? Choice B is wrong for two reasons! First, the incongruity with the question-stem. Make sure your answer belongs to the same category with the question-stem: "chronicle," "history," and the correct answer A) "epoch," "era" are all conceptual synonyms in the same category. Choice B, albeit using the Synonym Pattern, may belong to the human vs. nonhuman pattern. Therefore, they are not the same analogy with the question-stem.
For choice C, "Dancer," just like choice B, is a human while "choreography" is an act performed by a dancer. So they are basically not synonyms.

Jimin: How about choices D and E?

Choice D is the Antonym Pattern. Choice E is the Homophony, a similar sound, that we'll discuss later.

Q2-2: Antipathy is antonym for sympathy; Love is antonym for (A) abhor.

Jimin: I didn't know what the "abhor" was, so I chose B. why not B?

If some difficult words are seen, don't be shy. Just divide the words into meaningful fractions like ab/hor. (Oh! Horror). So, next time, when you see words you've never heard before, just divide them and make sense out of them. You can at least feel whether the word meaning is negative or positive.
Choice B is wrong because "love" is not the antonym for "dislike," but "like" is. Remember, the term "synonym" used in the Analogy Pattern has a broader sense than a simple literal synonym between the words. It always includes a conceptual synonym as well.

12 Patterns for the Analogy Section

Pattern 3. The Purpose (Tool) Pattern
Find Relationship between the Purpose or Function of Individual or Thing

Q3 Stopwatch is to time as

A) oxygen tank is to breathe
B) swim fins is to fast
C) swim vest is to heavy
D) beach is to vacation
E) security guard is to safeguard

The correct answer is A

The purpose of stopwatch is to measure a time as the purpose of oxygen tank is to breathe in the water. Jimin: Still don't get it. This is how I think.
For choice B, the purpose of swim fins is to swim fast.
For choice C, when we use swim vest, we feel heavy.
For choice D, the purpose of going to beach is to enjoy vacation.
Finally for E, the purpose of security guard is to safeguard the area.
Then, no other answers are less correct than the correct answer.

A stopwatch is a tool to check the time. You must follow this same category with the question-stem

What I mean is that you should look for a pair of words that show the similar function or purpose.

For choice B, the purpose of swim fins is to SWIM fast, not "fast." "Fast" is a degree, not the purpose.

For choice C, the purpose of a swim vest is to float on the water. "Heavy," is a degree just like "fast"

For choice D, the word "beach" is a location not a tool like the stopwatch in the question.

For choice E, it is correct to say the purpose of a security guard is to safeguard areas. However, a security guard is a human, not a tool. Therefore, it is incongruent with question-stem.

Both the stopwatch and the oxygen tank are tools, not a human.

SSAT 8 Reading & Verbal Elementary Level

12 Patterns for the Analogy Section

Pattern 4. The Characteristic Pattern
Find the Characteristic of Person, Place, Object, or Idea

Q4 Embarrassment is to time as

A) gift is to cake

B) conceal is to fleeting

C) arrow is to mistake

D) permanent is to happiness

E) birthday is to celebration

The correct answer is B

We tend to conceal "embarrassment." and we feel "time" seems to fleeting.
The other choices are not associated with each other or with the question-stem.

Jimin: So the word "embarrassment" goes straight down to "conceal" and "time" goes straight down to "fleeting." For this question, the answer itself wasn't that difficult. But the question was quite out of place.

Jimin: I wasted a lot of time figuring out the relationship between "embarrassment" and "time."
I finally chose C thinking that a mistake causes an embarrassment and time is as fast as an arrow.

Remember, some question-stem may act as the answer for the correct answer choice by switching their locations. Or, as you can observe from this question, each word in the question-stem works as the half of the correct answer.

Choice C is incorrect because the word "arrow" indicates a thing, but "embarrassment," "mistake," and "time" are all intangible concept in our mind. Therefore, It does not follow the question-stem. Whereas, the words "conceal" and "fleeting" are concept.

You'll soon get used to distinguish intangible from tangible word. So that you can remove choices like A and C quickly.

Choices D and E are intangible concept just like the question-stem. However, we can't find any relations from these words, therefore they are incorrect.

UNAUTHORIZED COPYING OR REUSE OF ANY PART OF THIS PAGE IS ILLEGAL

12 Patterns for the Analogy Section

Pattern 5. The Degree Pattern
Find the Degree and Shape in person, place, thing, and emotion

Q5-1. Dime is to cent as
- A) yard is to area
- B) meter is to centimeter
- C) sea is to sky
- D) phone is to communication
- E) big is to great

Q5-2. Round is to bottle as
- A) bottle is to glass
- B) indication is to sign
- C) coffee is to caffeine
- D) monitor is to square
- E) monitor is to flat

(Q5-1) The correct answer is B

A dime is bigger than a cent, and a meter is longer than a centimeter. They all belong to the measurement category, in which we can find their degrees and values—which are shrinking in this question type.

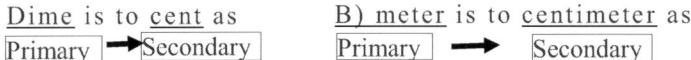

Seen above, In both the question-stem and choice B, the primary word is greater than the secondary word.

Jimin: How about choice A? A yard is used to measure an area and it follows the same question-stem.

Does choice A express any degree that is shrinking? No. There's no degree between yard and area. The most visible characteristic we can find from the question-stem is the Degree. Therefore, you must find the choice with the degree pattern.
Did you notice choice E has also the degree pattern but moves backward stating small concept (big) to big concept (great)?

Q5-2 A "Round" is a shape of a "bottle," and a "monitor" a shape of "square." Therefore, the correct answer is D.   The Shape Pattern quite often comes along with the Degree Pattern because it visualizes the degree of things or measurement.

Jimin: How about Choice E)?

It's incorrect because flat is not a shape. The compatible shape to the "round" has to be a 'square,' not a 'flat.'

SSAT ABSOLUTE PATTERNS

12 Patterns for the Analogy Section

Pattern 6. The Definition Pattern

Find the Definition/Concept of person, place, thing, and emotion

Q6. Love is to confession as
A) declaration is to independence
B) announcement is to news
C) rudeness is to apology
D) phone is to communication
E) error is to mistake

The correct answer is C

We confess to love, and apologize for rudeness.

Jimin: How about choices A and B?
We declare independence and announce news. Aren't they excellent definitions too?

Choices A and B have the error called the "flipping," a technique that switches the word orders. That is, the primary word "Love" acts like a noun and the secondary word "confession" acts like a verb as if "I confess love." Therefore, we must find the same Noun-Verb arrangement from the potential answers. "We declare independence" or "we announce news," not the other way around.

Jimin: Then, how about choice D?
We communicate through the phone. It follows the same word-order with the question-stem.

Love, confession, rudeness, and apology are all concepts that are intangible. But phone is a tangible object. To sum up, beneath this question-stem lie the definition pattern, tangible vs. intangible pattern, and verb vs. noun pattern.

HOW TO USE THIS BOOK

 **12 Patterns for the Analogy Section**

Pattern 7. The Mental (Emotion) Pattern
Find the Feeling or Emotion

Q7. Veneration is to Queen as
   A) prince is to royal family
   B) princess is to elegance
   C) apple is to poison
   D) weakness is to old lady
   E) king is to kingdom

The correct answer is D

This question basically asks how we feel about a certain word. That is, the question-stem contain the emotional word "veneration." That's what we need to focus on when we look for the answer.
To "Queen" we feel veneration as we feel weakness from an old lady.

 Identifying the mental (emotional) concept from the question-stem is the key point in this pattern.
Because the word "veneration" is certainly not a thing, the answer must be not a thing either such as C) apple.

Jimin: How about choice B? The word "elegance" represents human's emotion.

 The word-order is flipped over. To follow the question-stem and choice D, It should be elegance is to princess.

Choice A) royal family and E) kingdom do not directly represent human emotion. Although they represent concept, they are not our emotion.

SSAT ABSOLUTE PATTERNS

12 Patterns for the Analogy Section

Pattern 8. The Production Pattern
Find the Cause-and-Effect in Person, Concept, and Object

Q8. Fire is to heat as
A) job is to money
B) waiter is to restaurant
C) lamp is to bulb
D) shower is to bathroom
E) meal is to chef

The correct answer is A

Fire produces heat just as a job produces money. No other potential answers meet the question-stem category.

Jimin: What about choice E? A chef produces meal.

It is incorrect because the primary word "meal" and the secondary word 'chef" are flipped over. That can be a problem because in most cases the cause-and-effect relation gets mixed when viewed from the question-stem.
The question-stem states "What produces what?" Choice A follows the same order—the primary word produces the secondary word—as shown in the question-stem.
You can't pick choice E, in which the secondary word produces the primary word, and say Choice A is wrong.
Also note that the question-stem and choice A have no words that indicate human while choice E "chef" is a human. They cannot be mixed.

Jimin: Then, if the pair of words are flipped over, would that be always wrong?

It depends. In this question, "YES." It's because Choice E can't replace Choice A.
If choice A were not there in this question, which one would you choose? You should Inevitably choose E because there's no other alternative, but to follow the question-stem.

12 Patterns for the Analogy Section

Pattern 9. The Syntax Pattern
Find the Homophony, Contraction, Verb, Adjective, Tense, Confusing words

Q9-1. Seven is to Sandwiches as
A) sunny is Sunday
B) rainy is to umbrella
C) study is to lazy
D) dig is to tunnel
E) supermarket is to grocery

Q9-2. There's to There is as
A) he's is his
B) if I were to were I
C) she's to she will
D) we're to we were
E) they'd is to they have

(Q9-1) The correct answer is A

Q9-1 is all about the sound of the words. That's all there is. No concept or logic is involved.
Just as "seven" and "sandwiches" make the same sound, so do "sunny" and "Sunday."
if the question-stem does not make sense at all, then suspect it could be the Homophony Pattern.

Q9-2 is the Contraction Pattern. Choice B is the answer. The contraction form "There's" indicates There is/ There has. The contraction form "were I" indicates "If I were".
A) The contraction form "he's" indicates "he is/he has," not his.
C) The contraction form "she's" indicates "she is/she has."
D) The contraction form "we're" indicates "we are"
E) The contraction form "they'd" indicates "They had/they would."

Is that all in the Syntax Pattern? What does syntax even mean?

In fact, there are some more. This pattern basically relies on grammar, but is limited to the word usage, not to the clause or phrase usage.
Syntax means the grammatical arrangement and this pattern will ask such as a contraction, homophony, noun vs. verb, adjective vs. adverb, and tense.

12 Patterns for the Analogy Section

Pattern 9. The Syntax Pattern

Find the Homophony, Contraction, Verb, Adjective, Tense, Confusing words

Q9-3. Departure is to go as computer is to
A) calculate
B) calculator
C) electronics
D) expensive
E) computation

Q9-4. Blow is to blew as cut is
A) cut
B) cutted
C) cutting
D) cuts
E) get cut

(Q9-3) The correct answer is A

Q9-3: The primary word is the noun "departure" which is comparable to the verb "go." The primary word "computer" is also a noun which is comparable to the verb "calculate." It may appear to be the Synonym Pattern at first glance, but the correct answer will not be found from the Synonym Pattern because it consists of noun vs. verb pattern within the synonym relation. The question-stem "Departure is to go" is more than a synonym. If you understand the question from the category pattern or synonym pattern because departure and go belong to the same category or they are synonyms to each other, you cannot avoid choice A, B, C, and E altogether.

The correct answer for Q9-4 is (A). The question-stem asks what is the past tense for the word "cut," which was identified through the words "Blow" and "blew." That is, the question asks for the present tense vs. the past tense. "blow" is the present tense. "blew" is the past tense of "blow." The word "cut" is used for both the present tense and the past tense.

Jimin: Is there any other type of questions in the Syntax Pattern?

Yes! It may ask you to distinguish between adjective and adverb or the usage of adjective. Adjective will appear a lot on your test because it represents the concept or idea.

Jimin: How about spelling? Do they ask spelling too?

Not really! But they will ask you some confusing words like the difference between "there" and "their;" "allusion" and "illusion;" "ascent" and "assent."

12 Patterns for the Analogy Section

Pattern 10. The Positive vs. Negative Pattern
Find the Positive vs. Negative Value from the Antonym Category

Q10. Evil is to God
   A) north is to south
   B) lion is to zebra
   C) dark is to light
   D) medicine is to poison
   E) man is to woman

The correct answer is C

Evil is a negative value and God is a positive value and so too is dark a negative value, and light is a positive value.

This pattern appears to be the Antonym Pattern at first glance, but, in fact, it is one level higher than that. Choices A, B, and E are definitely opposite words but have no clear positive vs. negative Value as seen in the question-stem. That what went wrong with them.

Take a look at choice A for instance.

North and South are definitely antonyms to each other, but there is no negative vs. positive value in it. A big difference between evil and god, on the other hand, comes from their clear negative vs. positive polarity. That's the deciding factor that separates the correct answer C from all the rest. That's what we are looking for.

Don't forget Choice D is using the Positive vs. Negative Pattern but is incorrect because the word medicine refers to a tangible object. Worse yet, the word order is flipped over.

12 Patterns for the Analogy Section

Pattern 11. The Subjective *vs.* Objective Pattern
Find the Quality vs. Quantity, Tangible *vs.* Intangible Association

Q11-1. Temperature is to 10°F degree as
  A) Jane is to tall
  B) the movie is to good
  C) student is to school-uniform code
  D) last year is to 2019
  E) happiness is to money

Q11-2. Book is to knowledge
  A) age is to wisdom
  B) dime is to ten cents
  C) friend is to *friendship*
  D) centennial is to 100 years
  E) boiling point is to 100 degree

(Q11-1) The correct answer is D

The question-stem contains "10°F degree"—the numerical quantifier. That is, the question-stem that contains a number such as year, dollar (monetary value), degree, and so on would expect the same thing from the correct answer, containing value that can be quantified or counted. Only Choice D has the same numerical quantifier.

Jimin: How about E? Money can be counted too!

"Money" refers to a medium. To make it the correct answer it must show the definite amount. That is, the definite data, figures, values, or years... all of which can be quantified by numbers. In broad sense, it can include objective concept. too.

Jimin: Objective concept? What do you mean?

Take a look at choice C. School-uniform code has no exact numbers, yet still it is an objective concept as it can be measured. For instance, school-uniform code can be a blue color, or a nylon in type of fabric, or 30 inches below waistline, and so on. When you compare choice C) "school uniform code" with choice A) "tall" and B) "good," you'll immediately notice choices A and B are subjective concept. that cannot be measured like choice C. Therefore, choice C is closer to the answer than choice A or B. If there were no D in this question

12 Patterns for the Analogy Section

Pattern 11. The Subjective *vs.* Objective Pattern
Find the Quality vs. Quantity, Tangible *vs.* Intangible Association

Remember, almost all adjectives are subjective concept such as tall, fast, cheap, quick, expensive, beautiful.

One more thing!

Subjective concept and mental value can be further subcategorized into the passive *vs. a*ctive value. We will discuss this in the following pattern.

Do you know the answer for Q11-2?

Jimin: Is it A?

The correct answer is C.

A book is a tangible object. Knowledge is an Intangible concept.

A friend is tangible. Friendship is intangible.

A book produces knowledge, just as friend produces friendship.

Jimin: I thought it was choice A) age produces wisdom. Isn't "age" an Intangible concept too?

If it were a simple production pattern, virtually every choice would be the correct answer.

Underneath the Production Pattern is one more layer: the tangible vs. intangible.

Choice A "age" and "wisdom" are both intangible concept differing from "book"—the tangible object in the question-stem.

Choice B, D and E are incorrect because they have numerical quantifiers unlike the question-stem that cannot be measured.

12 Patterns for the Analogy Section

Pattern 12. The Human-Nonhuman Pattern
Find the Active vs. Passive/Human vs. Nonhuman Association

Q12-1. Goalie is to Champion as
- A) zebra is to stripe
- B) beaver is to dam
- C) thief is to police
- D) host is to guest
- E) bee is to sting

Q12-2 Baby is cute as battery is
- A) dead
- B) discharged
- C) gone
- D) deceased
- E) lifeless

(Q12-1) The correct answer is C

First of all, the question-stem indicates that it uses the human vs. nonhuman pattern. Find the word that uses a human from the possible answers. That's the good starting point. Thus, choices A, B, and E can be eliminated first because they are all animals. Between choice C and D, there is a subset under the human category. That is, "Goalie" is the passive concept compared to "champion." Choice C "thief" is also the passive concept compared to "police."

For choice D, although it is the human vs. nonhuman pattern, the word "host" is an active concept taking "active" role compared to the word "guest." In other words, the word-order is flipped over. Thus, it is critical to find the subset of the question-stem to the minimal level. This idea should be applied to the entire analogy patterns.

For Q12-2, Choice B is the answer.   Baby is cute; battery is discharged.
We often use the word "dead" when the battery is discharged. However, the proper word between the human vs. nonhuman pattern must strictly be crisscrossed.

Jimin: We use euphemism or metaphor though.

No! The entire Analogy questions use the first definition stated in dictionary.
Unless the question-stem contains such a nuance as metaphor or euphemism, you should never euphemistically interpret the question-stem. For instance, the word "fire" should be defined as a pure chemical reaction by friction," not as "love" or "passion."

SSAT Analogy Pattern Summary

Pattern 1. The Category Pattern
Find the Part and Whole Relation, the Same Type or Association

Pattern 2. The Synonym/Antonym
Find the similar or opposite meaning between the words

Pattern 3. Purpose (Tool) Pattern
Find the Purpose of Individual and the Goal, the Function of Tool

Pattern 4. The Characteristic Pattern
Find the Characteristic of Person, **Place**, Object, or Idea

Pattern 5. The Degree Pattern
Find the Degree (Increase or Decrease), Find the Shape of place or thing

Pattern 6. Definition Pattern
Find the Definition (Literal or Conceptual) of person, thing, and emotion

Pattern 7. Mental (Emotion) Pattern
Find the Human Emotion or the Word related to Mentality

Pattern 8. The Production Pattern
Find What Produces What and the Cause and Effect Relation

Pattern 9. Syntax Pattern
Find the Homophony, Contraction, Verb, Adjective, Tense, Confusing Words

Pattern 10. Positive vs. Negative Pattern
Find the Positive vs. Negative Value or Concept from the Antonym

Pattern 11. Subjective vs. Objective Pattern
Find the Quality vs. Quantity, Tangible vs. Intangible Concept

Pattern 12. Human-Nonhuman Pattern
Find the Human vs. nonhuman, the Active vs. passive Action

SSAT ANALOGY SUMMARY

Pattern 1. The Category Pattern
Find the Part and Whole Relation, the Same Type or Association

1. Sky is to cloud as
   A) mother is to father
   B) boy player is to girl player
   C) land is to sea
   D) breeze is to hurricane
   E) mountain is to tree

2. City is to building as
   A) male is to female
   B) teacher is to student
   C) cold is to colder
   D) internet is to computer
   E) road is to car

3. Root is to August as
   A) tree is to year
   B) December is to November
   C) friendship is to love
   D) branch is to nest
   E) family is to relative

Q1. E is the best answer.
'Cloud' is a part of the whole 'sky', just as 'tree' is a part of the whole 'mountain.' Also, they are all grouped in "nature" category. Choices A, B, and C use the Antonym Pattern.
Choice D is the Degree Pattern

Jimin: I thought it's C because "sky," "cloud," "land," and "sea" are all parts of nature.

Choice D and E are part of the nature too. The deciding factor is identifying the subset of the question-stem. In this question, the secondary word cloud directly belongs to the primary word sky.

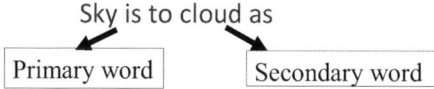

Q2. E is the best answer.
A 'building' is part of the whole 'city' as a car is part of the 'road' in the 'city'. They are all interconnected.
Choices A and B use the Antonym Pattern; Choice C is the Degree Pattern. Choice D is the Purpose Pattern as the purpose of the computer is to use internet.
Jimin: I thought it's D because people use internet as a part of function for computer.
The correct answer should be based on the question-stem. That is, choice D is less related to the question-stem than choice E.

Q3. A is the best answer.
A 'root' is part of whole 'tree' as 'August' is part of whole 'year'. Choices B and E are the Degree Pattern. Choice C is the Mental Pattern. Choice D is the Purpose (tool) pattern.
Jimin: I thought it's C or E. For C, "friendship" grows into "love." just as "tree" grows from "root." and choice E....

First of all, using metaphor is not accepted in the Analogy section. Second, choice E uses human concept, unlike the question-stem

SSAT ANALOGY SUMMARY

Pattern 2. The Synonym/Antonym
Find the similar or opposite meaning between the words

4. Country is to nation as pen is to

   A) writing instrument
   B) keyboard
   C) text message
   D) contract
   E) write

Q4. A is the best answer.
This question asks synonym or a similar concept between the words.
'Country' is synonym to 'nation' as a 'pen' is synonym to 'writing instrument'.
All the other incorrect answers do not follow the question-stem pattern. That is, they are related words with "pen," yet not the synonyms. Choice E is the Purpose Pattern as the purpose of pen is to write.

5. Rock is to boulder as

   A) water is to fire
   B) road is to street
   C) book is to knowledge
   D) internet is to information
   E) apple is to computer

Q5. B is the best answer.
'Rock' is synonym to 'boulder' and so, too, is a 'road' to 'street'. All four words belong to the same "land" category.
Choice A is the Antonym Pattern.
Choices C and D are the Production or Purpose Pattern.
Book produces knowledge. Internet produces information

6. Prevent is to think as

   A) consider is to avoid
   B) attract is to tracker
   C) scheduled is to unplanned
   D) contain is to exclude
   E) cling is to detach

Q6. A is the best answer.
'Prevent' is synonym to 'avoid,' just as 'consider' is synonym to 'think'.
Choice B is the Homonym Pattern.
Choices C, D, and E are the Antonym Pattern

SSAT ANALOGY SUMMARY

Pattern 2. The Synonym/Antonym
Find the similar or opposite meaning between the words

7. Safe is to danger as

A) important is to significant
B) secure is to hazard
C) black is to brown
D) odd is to even
E) late is punishment

Q7. B is the best answer.
'Safe' is antonym to 'danger' as 'secure' is an antonym to 'hazard'. Combined, they make synonyms.
Choice A is the Synonym Pattern. Choice C is the Degree Pattern. Choice D is the Antonym pattern but incorrect because it does not follow the question-stem pattern as B does. That is, the words 'safe,' 'danger,' 'secure,' and hazard' belong to the same category and they are conceptual synonyms to each other. Choice E is the Cause and Effect Pattern.

8. Fresh is to rotten as

A) often is to frequent
B) sometimes is to from time to time
C) always is to never
D) once is to twice
E) daily is to monthly

Q8. C is the best answer.
'Fresh' is antonym to 'rotten' as 'always' is antonym to 'never'
Choices A, B are the Synonym Pattern
Choices D, E are the Degree Pattern
Jimin: I thought the correct answer should be either D or E because they, along with the question-stem, belong to the Degree Pattern.

Pattern No. #11 the Subjective vs. Objective Pattern defines quality vs. quantity as different entities. That is, choices D and E both contain numbers and quantifiers. We cannot measure the question-stem in the same manner.
The question stem, which is based on subjective value, should not be understood as a degree pattern like choice D or E.

9. Shiny is to dark as

A) pen is to paper
B) nice is to rich
C) funny is to laugh
D) heavy is to light
E) now is to noon

Q9. D is the best answer.
'Shiny' is an antonym to 'dark' as 'heavy' is an antonym to 'light.'
Choice A is the Category Pattern. Both pen and paper are the same writing staples. Choices B is mental pattern.
Choice C is the Synonym Pattern or the production pattern.
Choice E belongs to the same "time" category.

SSAT ANALOGY SUMMARY

Pattern 3. The Purpose (Job/Tool) Pattern
Find Relationship between the Purpose of person, Object, Function

10. Gun is to shoot as bomb is to

A) T.N.T
B) war
C) damage
D) soldier
E) blow

Q10. E is the best answer.
The purpose of 'gun' is to 'shoot' as the purpose of 'bomb' is to 'blow.'
Choice A T.N.T. is synonym to bomb.
Choices B, C, and D are the words associated with bomb, yet do not follow the question-stem pattern. That is, not a synonym.
Another way to find the answer in this case is searching for a verb. Both "shoot" and "blow" are verbs.

11. Pencil is to read as book is to

A) cover
B) title
C) library
D) look
E) write

Q11. E is the best answer.
The purpose of 'pencil' is to 'write' as the purpose of 'book' is to 'read.'
Choices A, B, and C are the Category Pattern as they are all related with "book." but they are not related with the "purpose" of book.

12. Office is to work as restaurant is to

A) waiter
B) cook
C) eat
D) meal
E) take-out

Q12. C is the best answer.
The purpose of 'office' is to 'work' as the purpose of 'restaurant' is to 'eat'.
All the other incorrect answers are associated with "restaurant" but not with its "purpose."
As stated in Q10, finding a verb can also be a solution. "work" is the verb and so is "eat."

SSAT ANALOGY SUMMARY

Pattern 4. The Characteristic Pattern
Find the Characteristics of Person, Place, Object, or Idea

13. Sweet is to sugar as
A) legend is to book
B) leaves is to grass
C) ice is to winter
D) water is to snow
E) salty is to salt

Q13. E is the best answer.
The question asks about a sensory concept (touch, smell, taste, see, hear)
'Sugar' has a 'sweet' taste as 'salt' has a 'salty' taste.
Only choice E applies the same sensory concept.

14. Lion is to brave as
A) tiger is to animal
B) wolf is to pack animal
C) polar bear is to white
D) dog is to smart
E) ant is to small

Q14. D is the best answer.
The question is asking how we feel or think about something. The question "Lion is brave" is the way we think about lion. Or the word brave symbolizes lion. Only choice D) "smart" represents the characteristic of 'dog'. Choices A, B, C, and E contain no such a characteristic. For choice B, the word "pack animal" is the literal definition for social animal, not a symbol like "brave," or "smart."

15. Wedding dress is to happy as
A) Thanksgiving is to November
B) school is to principal
C) comedy is to funny
D) father is to head of the family
E) sister is to female

Q15. C is the best answer.
This question asks how we feel about something. 'Wedding dress' makes us feel 'happy' as choice C 'comedy' creates 'funny' mood.
The question-stem and choice C contain human's emotion or feelings. In that respect, this question can also be solved with the Mental (Emotion) pattern that separates the incorrect answers A, B, D, and E.

SSAT ANALOGY SUMMARY

Pattern 5. The Degree Pattern
Find the Degree and a Shape in person, place, thing, and emotion

16. Chick is to chicken as

A) brown is to black
B) sand is to witch
C) homework is to assignment
D) bird is to wing
E) meat is to fish

17. A+ is to F as warning is to

A) alphabet
B) classroom
C) expel
D) exam
E) arrest

18. 10 degree is to 20 degrees as million is to

A) a lot
B) luxury
C) thousand
D) rich
E) billion

Q16. A is the best answer.
'Chicken' is bigger than a 'Chick' as choice A) 'black' is darker than 'brown'.
As you can see, the Degree Pattern comes with many different styles, size, strength, length, and value, and so on.
Jimin: isn't it grey, not brown, that is lighter than black?

It is important to use approximation when there's no better answer.

Jimin: I thought the correct answer was choice C as both the question-stem and C are the Synonym.

The question-stem contains a strong indication that it uses the degree pattern. We cannot say baby and mother are synonyms because they both are humans.

Jimin: how about D. just as chick is part of chicken so as wing is part of bird.

Choice D is incorrect because "wing" is part of bird whereas the question-stem 'chick' and 'chicken' are two different entities. Choice E is the Category (food) Pattern

Q.17 C is the best answer.
'A+' is the higher score (degree) than 'F'; as 'expel' is more severe penalty (degree) than 'warning.' Choices A, B, and D show no degree with the question-stem "warning." Choice E has no relation with the question "A+ is to F."

Q18. E is the best answer.
'10 degree' is lower than '20 degree' as a 'million' is less than a 'billion.' Choices A, B, D are not measurable values. Choice C uses the Degree Pattern but in reverse order.

SSAT ANALOGY SUMMARY

Pattern 7. The Syntax Pattern
Find the Homophony, Contraction, Verb, Adjective, Tense, Confusing Words

19. To is two as wear is to

A) under
B) socks
C) three
D) pants
E) ware

Q19. E is the best answer.
Both "To" and "two" make the same sound as both "wear" and "ware" make the same sound.
Seen from the question-stem, this pattern considers little about the meanings of the words.
Choices A, B, C, and D are incorrect because they are not the homonym of the question-stem.

Jimin: I thought it's A "underwear."

20. Back is to neck as

A) principle is to principal
B) tail is to nail
C) hands is to feet
D) cow is to calf
E) body is to soul

Q20. B is the best answer.
"Back" and "neck" make the same sound as "tail' and "nail" make the same sound.
Jimin: How about choice A. it is homophony as well.

Choice A does not follow the question-stem category. The question-stem and the correct answer B are all parts of body.
Choice D is the Degree Pattern. Choices C and E are the Antonym Pattern

21. Idiom is to Medium as reign is to

A) power
B) king
C) country
D) rain
E) land

Q21. D is the best answer.
Both "idiom" and "medium" make the same sound as both "reign" and "rain" make the same sound.
Choice A is the synonym to "reign." Choices B, C, and E are either characteristics or definition of "reign" yet all of them do not follow the question-stem pattern.

SSAT ANALOGY SUMMARY

Pattern 8. The Production Pattern
Find the Cause-and-Effect in Person, Concept, and Object

22. Mother is to egg as bird is to

A) fly
B) sing
C) baby
D) wood
E) beak

Q22. C is the best answer.
'Mother' produces 'baby' as 'bird' produces 'eggs'.
Choices A, B, and D are Characteristic (Association) Pattern. Choice E is the Part-Whole Pattern. None of them reflects "mother produces baby" concept, which implies what bird can produces.

23. Lemon is to vitamin C as

A) water is to thirsty
B) fire is to heat
C) movie is to ticket
D) school is to boring
E) father is to mother

Q23. B is the best answer.
'Lemon' produces 'vitamin C' as 'fire' produces 'heat.'
Choices A and C are the Purpose (Tool) Pattern.
Choice D is the Characteristic Pattern.
Choice E is the Antonym Pattern

24. Sleep is to dream as bedroom is to

A) bathroom
B) sing
C) bed
D) relax
E) pillow

Q24. D is the best answer.
'Sleep' produces 'dream' as 'bedroom' produces 'relaxation.'
Choices C and E are the Part/Whole Pattern.

SSAT ABSOLUTE PATTERNS

SSAT

Chapter 1

The Official SSAT Test Analysis

THE *REAL* SSAT PATTERNS

SSAT OFFICIAL TEST ANALYSIS
ELEMENTARY LEVEL G.3 & G.4
view the test from google "official ssat elementary test pdf."

https://ssat.org/images/documents/test-prep/2018-19TOG-ElementaryGrade3Final.pdf

https://portal.ssat.org/SAP/Practice#/dashboard

SSAT OFFICIAL TEST DOES NOT ENDORSE, RECOMMEND, OR MAKE REPRESENTATIONS WITH RESPECT TO THE TEST ANALYSIS DESCRIBED IN THIS BOOK.

> Unable to locate the official SSAT test materials? Request through email at: satvancouver@gmail.com I will send you the link.

CAUTION

SSAT Official test analysis does not focus on every detail in the reading passage. Nor should you.
It rather focuses on how to analyze the questions, where to find the answers from the passages, and how to find the incorrect answers without even reading the passages.

.

Problem-Solving Strategy

All the questions that you see in the Reading section are divided into two categories: the Universal type and the Local type. There are subset categories lay under these two categories. For example, questions can be further subdivided into the Content question and the Technique question. Every single question that you solve is under this overarching set of principles.

The Universal-type questions such as the Main idea or Tone questions: here in these G3. official SSAT questions 1, 3,5, 6,9, 12 ask mainly about the overall passage comprehension. In this case, the correct answers can be usually found through the title, topic sentence, and the conclusion. Find from them the key words the genre of the passage and the dominant tone.

The Local-type question such as questions 2, 3, 4, 8, 10 focus more on the specific details of the passage. In this case, knowing the specific terminology and vocabulary used in the question is important. <u>Yet still, through the identified genre of the passage, the tone, and the main theme, you would be surprised to find at least a couple of incorrect answers., of course, without reading the passage!!!</u> Jimin: How do I know if the question is the universal-type or the local type?

The following chapter describes in details. To briefly introduce here, the Universal-type questions use cliché, general phrase, such as "what is the main idea of the passage?" The Local-type questions, on the other hand, use very specific words that make each question very unique.

Problem-Solving Strategy

Question 1. Try to understand the five alternatives through logic and common sense. For example, ask yourself "is there a place in the world that is warmer at night in the winter?" And then, apply logic. Choice E, for instance, uses the "mother" to the question that asks about the author. The correct answer has to focus on the question, not someone else.
DO YOU SEE NOW HOW TO FIND THE ANSWER WITHOUT EVEN READING THE PASSAGE?

Question 2. Follow the same procedure as you did in question 1. Apply logic. Eliminate the incorrect answers accordingly. The key phrase "not recently written" asks us to identify the approximately when the poem was created.

Jimin: To be honest, I still don't get it. Why should I know which one is the universal and which one is the local-type question?
I think I should just solve so many questions until I improve scores.

Of course, you can improve you scores by solving so many questions. It will take just about 700 years. If you know the type of questions, you can find the answer with very minimum information from the passage. You can see exactly where you must read, and many times, you can solve questions without even reading the passages.

If you want to practice more using the official tests analysis like this one, request for more materials through this email: satvancouver@gmail.com

If you need further private instructions, more comprehensive, private, step-by-step tutoring, I will provide you private tutoring sessions at a very reasonable rate.

Problem-Solving Strategy: The Elementary Level G3

Question 3. Maintain the same tonality found in question 1 and 2 about the boy (the speaker). Focus only on the positive and active tone from the alternatives, and eliminate the rest.

Question 4. Through the preceding three questions, we gathered enough information about the poem. The boy is unhappy for going to bed in the summer while it is still bright enough to play.

Question 5. The question 'What did the king want from the miller's daughter?" is very straightforward question. It asks the main idea of the passage. Go to the topic sentence and focus on the keywords "straw" and "gold."

Question 6. Apply the mirroring technique. (See chapter 1). Find the clue words from the sentence and from the alternatives find the synonym to the clue word.

Questions 7. This question can be solved by reviewing the previous question 5. No reading is necessary.

Question 8. The word "vanished" is a difficult word. If the word is difficult, the question asks for its literal definition. Apply the mirroring technique. Find the clue words from the sentence and from the alternatives find the synonym to the clue word.

Question 9. This is the main idea question. Focus on the topic sentence. Eliminates the alternatives with too specific information such as numbers or years.

Question 10. The question basically asks about the term "illegally," which means "without permission of the law" Some questions contain the keyword that, by itself, discloses the correct answer.

Question 11. The question asks specific information in the passage. The answer to the specific question must be located very close to each other. That is, the incorrect answers tend to be true statements but dripped away from the question sentence.

Question 12. This type of question—Understanding attitude (Tone) question—can be easily solved by identifying the main character's tonality. Find the most meaningful phrase from the sentence in question and think whether the tone is positive or negative.

THE OFFICIAL SSAT TEST ANALAYSIS

ELEMENTARY LEVEL OFFICIAL TEST G3.

Q1. AP 2: Summary Question: Read just one more line.

Genre: Poetry
- **Question Keyword/Key phrase:** "gets up, night"
- **Incorrect Pattern:** A) school—NI   B) warmer—DC/GE   C) factory—NI   **D) dark**   E) mother—NI
- **We Already Found the answer:** It's D. The answer was found before reading the passage. We all know that "in the winter, it is still dark in the morning." Therefore, we can guess that "the author thinks he gets up at night in the winter"
- **What Does The Question Really Ask?** The question starts with "Why." From the five alternatives find the most suitable phrase that best fits the "because" phrase. That is called "the cause-and-effect" logic. Start eliminating choices—before reading the passage (the poem in this case)—that sound awkward or not even remotely answering to the question.
- **Relevancy Check:** Choice B can be eliminated through a common sense. It is impossible to think of a place where night time is warmer during winter. Choice E is highly likely to be incorrect because the main subject is "His mother," not "Him (the author)." Think of the question again: "why does the speaker has to wake up at night in winter time?" Bringing a new character (mother) in one question becomes too complex in elementary level SSAT.   *SSAT Upper level and SAT, on the contrary, frequently use multiple characters in one question.

Answer Summary: After reading it through, we can imagine that the author gets up in the morning while outside is still dark. Why would he get up at night in winter? It's because in winter, it is still dark in the morning.

Incorrect Answer Explanation

Choices A and C are irrelevant information not stated in the passage.

Q2. AP 7: Inference Question   Find the indirect suggestion behind the sentence
- **Question Keyword/Key phrase:** "written"
- **Incorrect Pattern:** A) sky—IW   **B) candlelight**   C) parents—IW   D) people—IW   E) birds—IW
- **What Does The Question Really Ask?** The question starts with " We can assume." It, in other words, asks what can be inferred (guessed). Without reading the poem, but using information obtained from question 1, we can start eliminating incorrect answers that sound awkward.
- **Relevancy Check:** Choice C is incorrect for the same reasoning as choice E in Q1. That is, choice C is highly unlikely because the main subject should be "him" not "his parent." The question asks nothing about his parents.

Answer Summary: Choice B is stated in line 2, in which he describes "dress by candlelight" implying that the poem was written when there was no electricity. Choices A, D, and E are descriptions about bed in summer.

Q3. AP 2: Summary Question: Read just one more line.

- ■ **Question Keyword/Key phrase:** "why, bed, day"
- ■ **Incorrect Pattern:** A) allowed—DC(TI)   B) get up early—NI   C) misbehaved—DC(TI)   **D) not dark**   E) sick—NI
- ■ **We Already Found the answer:** It's D. The answer was found before reading the passage.
- ■ **What Does The Question Really Ask?** The question can be solved through information obtained from questions 1 and 2, in which we've already learned that evening in winter is not yet dark.
- ■ **Relevancy Check:** Choice A is incorrect because the phrase "He isn't allowed" implies the speaker under the parents' permission. Through information from question 1 and 2, we've learned that the poem does not contain 'parents.' Choice C "misbehaved" is a negative word. It should not be the answer because the poem does not put the speaker (the boy) into the negative tone.

Answer Summary: In line 4 "I have to go to bed by day," or in line 12" To have to go to bed by day?," the author clearly indicates that the evening in winter is not yet dark.
Choices B and E are not stated in the passage and they also distract the poem's main point.

Q4. AP 2: Summary Question: Read just one more line.

- ■ **Question Keyword/Key phrase:** "unhappy"
- ■ **Incorrect Pattern:** A) tired—NI   **B) play**   C) birds—IW   D) can't sleep—NI   E) people—IW
- ■ **We Already Found the answer:** It's B. The answer was found before reading the passage.
- ■ **What Does The Question Really Ask?** This question asks about the rhetorical question in lines 9-12. The rhetorical question does not expect the answer. Instead, it emphasizes the speaker's argument.
- ■ **Reading Tip:** Pay attention to strong indicators in the passage. A rhetorical question is one of the major indicators

Answer Summary: "And does it not seem hard to you...I should like so much to play?"
Above is the rhetorical question signifying the speaker's desire—his wanting to play in summer night as written in 11.

Incorrect Answer Explanation

Choice A is probable but incorrect. The speaker (the boy) complains for going to bed while outside is still bright enough to play. Choice C) "birds" and E) "people walking" are irrelevant information that used meaningful words from the passage but not related with the question. Choice D is incorrect. It didn't say he can't sleep unless it's dark.

Q5. AP 2: Summary Question: Read just one more line.

- ■ **Question Keyword/Key phrase:** "king want"
- ■ **Incorrect Pattern: A) gold**   B) necklace—IW   C) straw—IW   D) little man—IW   E) little man—IW
- ■ **What Does The Question Really Ask?** The question reveals, by itself, two important things: first, it suggests that the "king" and the "miller's daughter" should be the main characters of the passage; second, their relation is based on the King's demands from the miller's daughter.
- ■ **Reading Tip:** The first paragraph (lines 1-5 in this passage) normally begins with the character descriptions and their desires (the King's demands.)
- ■ **Relevancy Check:** Choice D and E are highly unlikely to be the answer because, as we have already practiced from question 1 and 2, bringing a new character ("the little man") other than the main characters becomes too complex.

Answer Summary: Line 3 states "spun this straw into gold"
The king demands the miller's daughter turn straw into gold.
Choices B "necklace" and C "straw" are irrelevant information not spoken by the king.

Q6. AP 8: Understanding Attitude (Tone) Find the character tonality: positive vs. negative, mental vs. physical
■ **Question Keyword/Key phrase:** "king" ■ **Incorrect Pattern: A) mean**   B) tricky—DC   C) boring—NI   D) nervous—NI   E) sneaky—NI ■ **We Already Found the answer:** It's A. The answer was found before reading the passage. ■ **What Does The Question Really Ask?** The question asks the king's personality, which is obviously negative. The test creator asks whether a "mean" person can also be "tricky person," "boring person," "nervous person," and "sneaky person." It can't be. Just like "happy" person cannot be automatically "handsome" or "rich" person. ■ **Reading Tip:** This question focuses on the first paragraph (lines 1-5) that normally describes the character descriptions and their desires—the King's unreasonable demands.
Answer Summary: Line 3 states "spun this straw into gold" The king's tone of voice is demanding and absurd. He is just a mean person. All the rest are negative words but not related with the king's character.
Q7. AP 2: Summary Question   Summarize the sentence or the entire paragraph
■ **Question Keyword/Key phrase:** "crying because" ■ **Incorrect Pattern:** A) alone—IW   B) unlock—IW   C) little man—IW   D) necklace—IW   **E) gold** ■ **We Already Found the answer:** It's E. The answer was found before reading the passage. If you could solve question 5, this wouldn't be hard either because, as you can see from the similarity between the two answers, they draw the same situation. ■ **What Does The Question Really Ask?** Pay attention to the word "because" in the question. Try to connect "The girl was crying" with each phrase in the alternatives by using "because". That will make you feel more comfortable in understanding logic between the phrases. ■ **Relevancy Check:** Choice C is, as clarified several times, highly likely to be incorrect for using a character "the little man" other than the king and the girl.
Answer Summary: [EFFECT] She began to cry [BECAUSE] She had no idea how to spin straw into gold. As stated above, choice E clearly states the cause and effect situation. She couldn't turn straw into gold. Choices A) "alone" B) "door" D) "necklace" are irrelevant to the cause and effect situation.
Q8. AP 4: Word-In-Context Question   Find the clue words and keywords from the sentence
■ **Question Keyword/Key phrase:** "vanished" ■ **Incorrect Pattern: A) disappeared**   B) finished—NI   C) helped—NI   D) called—NI   E) cried—NI ■ **We Already Found the answer:** It's A. The answer was found before reading the passage. ■ **What Does The Question Really Ask?**   The word "vanished" is a difficult word. If the word is difficult, the question asks for its literal definition.
Answer Summary: "So it went until morning, and then...and all....and the little man had vanished." The last sentence describes a series of incidents. Naturally, it's time for the little man to disappear. Choices B and C are incorrect because "the little man has already finished and helped the girl by morning. Now, it's time for him to disappear. Choices D and E are incorrect because these two words are bound to continue the story instead of ending it. Therefore, they don't fit the sentence.

Q9. AP 1: Main Idea (Focus Shifts) Question   Find the main idea of the entire passage or the paragraph
■ **Question Keyword/Key phrase:** "main"
■ **Incorrect Pattern:** A) people—NI/GE   B) U.S.Mint—IS   C) 1913—IS   D) 1913—IS   **E) rare coins**
■ **What Does The Question Really Ask?** This is the main idea question. Keep in mind that the main idea question seeks general information. It does not ask specific information such as specific year, number, a name or place.
■ **Reading Tip:** If the topic sentence is still unclear, go to the ending parts of the passage.
■ **Relevancy Check:** Choice A is general information (GE). General information is a statement that is applicable at any type of question because, generally speaking, it is largely true statement. However, such information cannot represent the unique information of the passage. Choices B, C, and D use too specific information that is unsuitable to describe the entire passage. We call them Insufficient Information (IS).

Answer Summary: Choice E contains the key words "rare coins," which is all about of the passage. Choices B and C are true statements but are Insufficient Information to be called "the main idea." Choice D is incorrect. Of course, the author spent a considerable amount of time describing the fifth coin. The phrase, however, must further describe why finding the coin is the main idea. Choice E describes this.

Q10. AP 5: Understanding the True Purpose   Find the explicitly stated true purpose of the sentence
■ **Question Keyword/Key phrase:** "illegally"
■ **Keyword in Each Choice:**   A) government—DC   B) museums—DC   C) collectors—EX   D) request—DC   **E) without permission**
■ **We Already Found the answer:** It's E. The answer was found before reading the passage.
■ **What Does The Question Really Ask?** The question basically asks about the term "illegally," which means "without permission of the law"
■ **Reading Tip:** Some questions contain the keyword that, by itself, discloses the answer.
■ **Relevancy Check:** If you knew the meaning "illegally" you would know choices A, B, and D are direct contradiction.

Choice C is incorrect because the phrase "only to coin collectors" is too extreme. The test creator focuses on the term "illegally" in the question, not to where would the illegally made coins be sold.

Q11. AP 2: Summary Question   Summarize the sentence or the entire paragraph
■ **Question Keyword/Key phrase:** "another name" ■ **Incorrect Pattern:** A) 1913—IW   B) Walton—IW   **C) Buffalo**   D) Liberty—IW   E) Danneruther—IW ■ **What Does The Question Really Ask?** The question asks a specific detail about "Indian Head nickel"

Answer Summary: "replaced the Liberty Head nickel with the Indian Head, or Buffalo"
As stated above, another name for the "Indian Head" is "Buffalo"

Incorrect Answer Explanation

A) "1913," B) "Walton," D) "Liberty," and E) "Danneruther" are all located further away from "Indian Head nickel."
The answer to the specific question must be located very close to each other.

Q12. AP 8: Understanding Attitude (Tone) Find the tonality: positive vs. negative, mental vs. physical
■ **Question Keyword/Key phrase:** "John feels" ■ **Incorrect Pattern:** A) tired—DC   **B) pleased**   C) uncertain—DC   D) thoughtful—IW   E) disappointed—DC(TI) ■ **What Does The Question Really Ask?** This type of question—Understanding attitude (Tone) question—can be easily solved by identifying the main character's tonality. Find the most meaningful phrase from the sentence in question and think whether the tone is positive or negative.

Answer Summary: "it's *been missing for so long*....And there it is."
As stated above, John's speech is definitely positive; therefore, only choice B becomes the answer.

Incorrect Answer Explanation

Choices A, C, and E are all negative words that contradict the key phrase "there it is" which is a positive tone.
Choice D "thoughtful" means showing a very careful attention, an Irrelevant word to this sentence.

ELEMENTARY LEVEL OFFICIAL TEST G4.

Q1. AP 2: Summary Question   Summarize the sentence or the entire paragraph
■ **Question Keyword/Key phrase:** "where, tree"
■ **Incorrect Pattern:** A) mill—IW   B) sand—IW   C) one side—DC   D) in, river—NI   **E) both sides**
■ **What Does The Question Really Ask?** This question asks specific information about the "tree"
■ **Reading Tip:** Unless the "tree" is the main theme of the poem appearing everywhere, try to focus on the word "tree" but don't read too far from the word "tree."
■ **Relevancy Check:** Many incorrect answers can be found not through the passage, but by commonsense. Choices B "in the sand" and D "in the river" are highly unlikely to be the answer. Plants could be found in the river or in the sand, but not trees.

Answer Summary: "with trees on either hand." "either hand" refers "both sides"

Incorrect Answer Explanation

Choice A "mill" is stated too far away from the "tree," giving little relevance to be the answer.
Choice C contradicts the poem. "either hand" refers "both sides," not one side. Choice D, unlike the answer E, focuses on the appearance "dark brown" of the river. The question asks about the location, not the appearance.

Q2. AP 2: Summary Question   Summarize the sentence or the entire paragraph
■ **Question Keyword/Key phrase:** "poet"
■ **Incorrect Pattern:** A) home—NI   B) cruise—NI   C) castle—IW   **D) floating boats**   E) journey—IW
■ **What Does The Question Really Ask?** The question asks what the poet (the boy speaker) is doing.
■ **Reading Tip:** Just as any other passages, read the ending part of the poem to find out the consequence or the main argument of the poet.
■ **Relevancy Check**: Choice B is incorrect because the word "cruise," knowing the speaker is a boy, is absurd.

Answer Summary: "Other little children Shall bring my boats ashore."
As stated above, the last line clarifies that the poet (speaker) is a boy and is floating the paper boats in the river.

Incorrect Answer Explanation

Choice s A "home," C "castle," and E "hundred miles" are irrelevant information that used meaningful words from the passage but not related with the question.

Q3. AP 4: Word-In-Context Question   Find the clue words and keywords from the sentence
■ **Question Keyword/Key phrase:** "lines, together" ■ **Incorrect Pattern:** A) epic—NI   B) verse—NI   C) simile—NI   **D) stanza**   E) idiom—NI ■ **What Does The Question Really Ask?** The question asks about the meaning of the literary device. It requires not the reading skills, but vocabulary skills.
Answer Summary: Choice D) "stanza" is a group of lines in a poem like the lines 9-12. <center>**Incorrect Answer Explanation**</center>Choice A) "epic" means a long poem. B) "verse" means a metrical rhythm in a poem. C) "simile" means a figure of speech involving the comparison. Choice E) "idiom" is a group of words having one meaning.
Q4. AP 4: Word-In-Context Question   Find the clue words and keywords from the sentence
■ **Question Keyword/Key phrase:** "hand" ■ **Incorrect Pattern:** A) sky—NI   **B) side**   C) boat—IW   D) river—IW   E) valley—IW ■ **We Already Found the answer:** It's B. The answer was found before reading the passage. ■ **What Does The Question Really Ask?** When the word-in-Context question asks such an easy word as "hand," it almost certainly asks for the figurative meaning, not the literal meaning. To be sure, the word "hand" in this question does obviously not mean a human hand. To understand the figurative meaning of the word, always find a clue word. Finding a clue word is most important step to find the answer. ■ **Reading Tip:** Even without reading the passage, some alternatives are almost guaranteed to be incorrect. Irrespective of what type of figurative meaning it is, the word "hand" can never be understood as choice C, D, or E. They are not even close to the word "hand"
Answer Summary: "With **trees** on either hand [side]" With "trees" as a clue word, "side" is the only suitable word that can replace "hand." <center>**Incorrect Answer Explanation**</center>A) With trees on either [sky] —X   B) With trees on either [side]   C) With trees on either [boat] —X D) With trees on either [river] —X   E) With trees on either [valley] —X
Q5. AP 2: Summary Question   Summarize the sentence or the entire paragraph
■ **Question Keyword/Key phrase:** "best known" ■ **Incorrect Pattern:** A) shoes—IW   B) children—DC   C) family—IW   **D) magician**   E) Jewish—IW ■ **What Does The Question Really Ask?** The key words "best known" indicates that the question focuses on the topic sentence. The reasoning behind this idea is that the topic sentence usually contains the best known facts of the main character such as his or her achievement. ■ **Reading Tip:** Focuses on the topic sentence. If the topic sentence does not provide information, read the conclusion. ■ **Relevancy Check:** Choice C is highly likely to be incorrect. As we've observed several times in the previous questions, bringing another character ("family") other than the main character "Harry Houdini" is too complex for the SSAT elementary level. Focus, therefore, on the key words "Harry Houdini" and what he is best known for.

Answer Summary: "Houdini was well known as the greatest magician"
As stated above, the first line gives the answer.

Incorrect Answer Explanation
Choice A) "shoes" and E) "Jewish" are irrelevant information that used meaningful words from the passage but not related to the question. Choice B contradicts the passage. The last sentence states "never tell how you do a trick!"

Q6. AP 2: Summary Question   Summarize the sentence or the entire paragraph

- ■ **Question Keyword/Key phrase:** "so good"
- ■ **Incorrect Pattern:** A) books—NI   B) lessons—NI   C) circus—IW   D) powers—DC   **E) practice**
- ■ **What Does The Question Really Ask?** If the previous question 5 is about finding the main idea of the passage, this question relies on logic. Whereas question 5 asks about general idea or "best known fact," this question asks about the cause-and-effect situation as was indicated as "because" in the question.
- ■ **Reading Tip:** Never miss the Important transition word: "despite" (line 3) rolls out the cause-and-effect situation.

Answer Summary: "Despite what some people thought,...He worked long and hard..."
The word 'because" in the question implies the cause-and-effect situation. Here "Despite" in line 3 is the important transition word for the cause-and-effect situation. The question states the [EFFECT] "he became so good at trick"
The clause starting with the word "despite" stresses the [CAUSE].
Houdini became so good at tricks because he worked long and hard."

Incorrect Answer Explanation
Choices A and B are not stated in the passage. Choice C "circus" is irrelevant information that used meaningful words from the passage but not related with the question. Choice D contradicts the original statement in line 3 "Despite what some people thought..."

Q7. AP 2: Summary Question   Summarize the sentence or the entire paragraph

- ■ **Question Keyword/Key phrase:** "first rule"
- ■ **Incorrect Pattern:** A) trapeze—IW   **B) secret**   C) family—IW   D) audience—IW   E) Prince—IW
- ■ **We Already Found the answer:** It's B. The answer was found before reading the passage.
- ■ **What Does The Question Really Ask?** The question asks some specific detail related to the "first rule" as a magician.
- ■ **Reading Tip:** When the answer for the specific detail question is hard to find, focus on the last sentence, where contains the author's main idea and the tone that can give either the direct or indirect support for the specific detail.

Answer Summary: "He already knew the first rule of magic—never tell how you do a trick."
As stated above, the last sentence describes the answer.

Incorrect Answer Explanation
All the rest are irrelevant information that used meaningful words from the passage but not related with the question.

Q8. AP 8: Understanding Attitude (Tone) Find the tonality: positive vs. negative, mental vs. physical
■ **Question Keyword/Key phrase:** "Houdini" ■ **Incorrect Pattern:** A) shy—DC   B) silly—DC(TI)   C) stubborn—DC(TI)   D) thoughtful—DC(TI)   **E) determined** ■ **We Already Found the answer:** It's E. The answer was found before reading the passage. ■ **What Does The Question Really Ask?** This question basically asks about the main character (Houdini). The passage (or the author) maintains the positive tone about Houdini. Therefore, the answer should also be positive. Be careful not to choose negative words that contradict the passage. ■ **Relevancy Check:** Choices A, B, and C are not positive but more close to negative.

Answer Summary: "He studied and worked long and hard..."
As stated above and as learned from question 6, he practiced a great deal, which can be expressed as "determination."

Incorrect Answer Explanation

Choice A the word "shy" shows direct contradiction to line 18 "He loved the clapping and the cheering"
Choice D "thoughtful" contradicts the character description. For Houdini mainly uses his body.

Q9. AP 2: Summary Question   Summarize the sentence or the entire paragraph
■ **Question Keyword/Key phrase:** "don't like" ■ **Incorrect Pattern:** A) don't know   B) savage—DC   C) pets—IW   D) stories—DC   E) livestock—NI ■ **What Does The Question Really Ask?** The question asks the cause-and-effect logic using the word "because" ■ **Reading Tip:** Find the meaningful transition: In this question the rhetorical question (lines 7-8), and with it the word "because" completes the cause-and-effect logic. ■ **Relevancy Check:** Many questions can be solved through commonsense: choice C and D are absurd and unrealistic.

Answer Summary: "Most people are afraid of wolves because they do not really know"
As stated above, people's ignorance about wolves make them scared of wolves.

Incorrect Answer Explanation

Choice B contradicts the original statement. "Are they really savage?" emphasizes the fact that they actually aren't.
Choice E is plausible but not stated in the passage.

Q10. AP 1: Main Idea (Focus Shifts) Question Finding the main idea of the entire passage
■ **Question Keyword/Key phrase:** "agree"
■ **Incorrect Pattern:** A) pets—NI   B) scary—DC   C) everybody—DC   D) tales—IW   **E) learn**
■ **We Already Found the answer:** It's E). The answer was found before reading the passage.
■ **What Does The Question Really Ask?** This question is almost identical with the previous question 9 that leads to the same answer. As seen in question 9, people's ignorance about wolves make them scared of wolves.
■ **Reading Tip:** The author emphasizes his main idea through the meaningful words or phrase: one of them is using the rhetorical questions—"Or are they just misunderstood?" in this passage.
■ **Relevancy Check:** Choices A and D are very absurd therefore incorrect even without reading the passage.

Answer Summary: "Most people are afraid of wolves because they do not really know"
As stated above, the transition word "because" leads to the answer.
"When people learn about wolves" (line 14) solidifies the answer E.

Incorrect Answer Explanation

Choices B and C contradict the passage. The statement in line 9 "Most people are afraid of wolves" is what the author disagree about. Therefore, seemingly true statements though, these are inconsistent with the author's argument.

Q11. AP 4: Word-In-Context Question   Find the clue words and keywords from the sentence
■ **Question Keyword/Key phrase:** "creepy"
■ **Incorrect Pattern:** A) sad—DC(TI)   B) angry—NI   C) happy—DC(TI)   **D) frightening**   E) embarrassed—DC(TI)
■ **We Already Found the answer:** It's D. The answer was found before reading the passage.
■ **What Does The Question Really Ask?** When the Word-in-Context question asks a relatively difficult word, it normally asks the literal meaning. In this question, knowing the definitions of choice D and E should be the key in finding the answer.
■ **Relevancy Check:** All the remaining answers are irrelevant to the word "creepy."

Q12. AP 7: Inference Question   Find the indirect suggestion behind the sentence
■ **Question Keyword/Key phrase:** "where, wolf"
■ **Incorrect Pattern: A) forests**   B) prairies—NI   C) Everglades—NI   D) frozen tundra—NI   E) swamps—NI
■ **We Already Found the answer:** It's A. The answer was found before reading the passage.
■ **What Does The Question Really Ask?** The question asks to "imagine" the location where you might hear a wolf. The answer is written in the first sentence.
■ **Reading Tip:** The first sentence describes the location wherein you might hear a wolf.
■ **Relevancy Check:** All the rest of the places are absurd. Wolf can't live in B) "prairies"—a large open grassland, or in C) Everglades, or D) swamps—under water, or D) tundra—a permanently frozen Artic region.

Answer Summary: "Imagine standing alone in the forests...All you hear is the sound of ..."
As stated above, you might hear a wolf in the forests.

SSAT Official Analogy Question Elementary Grade 3 Level

AP3. Purpose (Tool) Pattern Finding Relationships between the Purpose of Individual

Q8. D is the best answer. The question-stem uses the Purpose (Tool) Pattern.
The purpose of music is to 'listen' as the purpose of book is to read.
Another way to find the correct answer is by identifying the word arrangements: the verb 'Listen' is placed before the noun 'music.' Only choice D uses the verb before the noun. That is, both the question-stem and choice D use verb as the primary word. Choice A is the Category Pattern. Choices B, C, and E use the Purpose (Tool) Pattern but the words orders between the primary and secondary are flipped over.

AP8. Production Pattern Find What Produces What and the Cause and Effect Relation

Q9. E is the best answer. The question-stem uses the Production Pattern. 'wheat' produces 'bread' as 'milk' produces 'cheese.' Both the question-stem and choice E belong to the same food category.
Choice A 'cow' is related to the word "milk" but not to the entire question-stem. To correct the error, "cow" should be placed before "milk" to say "cow produces milk." not the other way around. Choice B is incorrect for the same reasoning as choice A. Choices C and D are related to the word "milk" but not to the entire question-stem.

AP2. Synonym/Antonym Find the similar or opposite meaning between the words

Q10. E is the best answer.   The question-stem uses the antonym Pattern. 'happy' is antonym to 'sad' as 'laugh' is antonym to 'cry.'   Choices A, C, and D use the Synonym Pattern Choice B uses the homophony category. That is, the primary word "hop" and the secondary word "pop" make the same sound.

AP4. Characteristic Pattern Find the Characteristic of Person, Place, Object, or Idea

Q11. A is the best answer. The question-stem uses the Characteristic Pattern. Sun is hot as ice is cold.
Choices B, C, D, and E are related to "ice" but not to the entire question-stem.

AP1. Category Pattern Find the Part and Whole Relation, the Same Type or Association

Q12. E is the best answer. "The question-stem uses a part and whole relation in the Category Pattern .
'blue' is part of 'color' as 'rabbit' is part of 'animal.' The primary word "blue" belongs to the secondary word "color." The correct answer must maintain the same sequence.
Choice A is incorrect for two reasons: first, although maintained the part and whole relation, it uses 'human,' unlike the question-stem. Second, the words order between the primary and secondary is flipped.
Choice B is the Purpose (Tool) Pattern. Choices C and D are the Category Pattern, but not held in the part and whole relation between the primary and secondary words.

AP9. Syntax Pattern Find the Homophony, Contraction, Verb, Adjective, Tense, Confusing Words

Q13. B is the best answer. The question-stem uses the Syntax Pattern. Both 'pane' and 'pain' make the same sound. Both 'weigh' and 'way' make the same sound. Keep in mind that the question-stem do not concern for the meaning behind the words. All the rest are related to the word "weigh" but not to the sound in the question-stem.

AP2. Synonym/Antonym Find the similar or opposite meaning between the words

Q14. D is the best answer. The question-stem uses the antonym Pattern. 'find' is antonym to 'lose' 'build' is antonym to 'demolish' Choices A, B, and E are related to the word "build" but not to the entire question-stem. Choice C is related to the secondary word "lose" but not to the entire question-stem.

THE OFFICIAL SSAT TEST ANALAYSIS

SSAT Official Analogy Question
Elementary Grade 4 Level

AP3. Purpose (Tool) Pattern Finding Relationships between the Purpose of Individual

Q8. D is the best answer. The question-stem uses the Purpose (Tool) Pattern.
The purpose of music is to 'listen' as the purpose of book is to read.
Another way to find the correct answer is by identifying the word arrangements: the verb 'Listen' is placed before the noun 'music.' Only choice D uses the verb before the noun. That is, both the question-stem and choice D use verb as the primary word. Choice A is the Category Pattern. Choices B, C, and E use the Purpose (Tool) Pattern but the words orders between the primary and secondary are flipped over.

AP2. Synonym/Antonym Find the similar or opposite meaning between the words

Q9. D is the best answer. The question-stem uses the antonym Pattern. 'simple' is antonym to 'complex.'
'miniature' is antonym to 'massive.' All the rest are held in synonyms between the primary and secondary words.

AP3. Purpose (Tool) Pattern Finding Relationships between the Purpose of Individual

Q10. C is the best answer. The question-stem uses the Purpose (Tool) Pattern. 'teacher' teaches at 'school.'
'coach' instructs in the 'field.' Both the question-stem and the correct answer use the same human concept and they perform similar job.
Choices A, B, and D use the Purpose (Tool) Pattern but they use nonhuman concept. Therefore, they don't match with the question-stem. Choice E uses the Category Pattern.

AP 9. Syntax Pattern Find the Homophony, Contraction, Verb, Adjective, Tense, Confusing Words

Q11. D is the best answer. The question-stem uses the Syntax pattern. With the words 'apple' and 'pie,' it becomes an apple pie. With the words 'chocolate' and 'cake,' it becomes a chocolate cake. This is called, in grammar, a compound noun. Only the answer D follows the question-stem in this sense. All the rest do not follow the question-stem.

AP3. Purpose (Tool) Pattern Finding Relationships between the Purpose of Individual

Q12. C is the best answer. "The question-stem uses the Purpose (Tool) Pattern. 'carpenter' uses 'hammer' as 'painter' uses 'brush' Choices A and B are irrelevant words to the question-stem. Choice D is related to "hammer" and choice E is related to "carpenter," but they are not related to the entire question-stem.

AP1. Category Pattern Find the Part and Whole Relation, the Same Type or Association

Q13. B is the best answer. The question-stem uses the Category Pattern. 'orange' is part of 'fruit.' 'poodle' is part of 'dog' category. Choice A is incorrect because it is tiger' not 'lion' that lives in 'jungle.' Also, it does not respond to the question-stem relation. Choice C, although related to each other, fork is not part of dinner. Thus, it does not follow the question-stem. Choice D is Irrelevant words to each other. Choice E is the Purpose (Tool) Pattern.

AP3. Purpose (Tool) Pattern Finding Relationships between the Purpose of Individual

Q14. D is the best answer. The question-stem is Purpose (Jobl) Pattern. 'captain' operates 'ship' as 'pilot' operates 'airplane' No other choices contains human. Therefore, they are all irrelevant to the question-stem.
Choice A is the Characteristic Pattern. Choices B, C, and E use the Category Pattern.

SSAT ABSOLUTE PATTERNS

SSAT

Chapter 2

- Answer Explanations for Test 1
- Test 1
- Test 2-8
- Answer Explanations for Test 2-7

THE *REAL* **SSAT** **PATTERNS**

SSAT ELEMENTARY LEVEL

Reading & Verbal Section

Test 1

Answer Explanations

&

The Pattern Analysis

CAUTION

The Reading Section

The answer explanations in this book do not scrutinize the reading passage. It rather focuses mostly on the patterns analysis. For that is the only way to improve your guessing skills.

The Analogy Section

The question-stems in test 1 focuses on the fundamental pattern. You may find multilayer patterns from the question-stems. But keep an eye on the fundamental pattern. The following tests will gradually expand the analysis to meet your eye level.

The secret in achieving high scores—within a very short time:

Focus on the questions—question patterns, question key phrases, and focus on five potential answers.
Master 10 Absolute Patterns, 5 Common Incorrect Answer Patterns, and 12 Analogy Patterns, based upon which develop the question-analyzing skills. For instance, you should be able to immediately identify the type of questions—whether the question belongs to the universal type or the local type. Through which you can instantly feel where to find the answer from the passage. Or—in many cases—you can feel whether reading the passage is necessary or not.
Most students focus 90% on reading passages. Most test creators focus 90% on questions.

# Test 1 Absolute Patterns for the Reading Section

Questions 1-6 are based on the following passage.

A Town Mouse once upon a time went on a visit to his cousin in the country. Beans and bacon, cheese and bread, were all he had to offer. The Town Mouse rather turned up his long nose and said: 'I cannot understand, (Q1 & Q2 & Q3.) **Cousin, how you can put up with such poor food as this, but of course you cannot expect anything better in the country**; come you with me and I will show you how to live. The two mice arrived at the Town Mouse's residence. Town Mouse took his friend into the grand dining-room. There they found the remains of a fine feast, and soon the two mice were eating up jellies and cakes and all that was nice. Suddenly they (Q6.) **heard growling and barking**. 'What is that?' said the Country Mouse. 'It is only the dogs of the house,' answered the other. 'Only!' said the Country Mouse. 'I do not like that **music** at my dinner. Good-bye, Cousin,' said the Country Mouse. (Q4. & Q5.)'**Better beans and bacon in peace than cakes and ale in fear.**

Q1. Question Pattern: The Town Mouse thinks that the Country Mouse
AP 8: Understanding Attitude (Tone) Find the tonality: positive vs. negative, mental vs. physical

- ■ **Question Keyword/Key phrase:** "The Town Mouse thinks"
- ■ **Incorrect Pattern:** A) does not appreciate the nature—DC   B) enjoys his life—DC
  C) understands town very well—DC   D) should expect the better world   E) does not live peacefully in a country—DC
- ■ **What Does The Question Really Ask?** Always check from whose point of view the question is created and being asked. The key phrase in the question "The Town Mouse thinks" asks you to find a certain tone or attitude of the Town Mouse.
- ■ **Reading Tip:** It is then important to find the keyword from the Town Mouse's speech, in which we can find whether the Town mouse is a positive or negative character. Also, focus on the contradictory conjunction "but" whenever it appears from the passage because it always provides the answer.

Answer Summary: D is the best answer.   "but of course you cannot expect anything better in the country"
The above phrase clearly reveals the arrogance—the negative character—of the Town Mouse. Therefore, the correct answer should also be negative. Choice D implies that the country is not a good place to live, and therefor the country mouse should expect the better world.

Incorrect Answer Explanation

All the rest incorrect answers contradict the passage. That is, The town mouse would say (A) "appreciating nature," or (C) understanding town" or (E) "living peacefully," is not enough compared to actually living in Town. Choice B contradicts the remark made by the arrogant Town Mouse. He believes the country mouse does not enjoy life.

Q2. Question Pattern: Town Mouse sees "**Beans and bacon,** cheese and bread" in line 2 as
AP 3: Example Question   Find the primary reason for using the example sentence

- ■ **Question Keyword/Key phrase:** "Beans and bacon"
- ■ **Incorrect Pattern:** A) a quality meal—DC   B) a luxurious living—DC   C) a healthy food—DC
  D) a unique and happy lifestyle—DC   **E) a poor living condition**
- ■ **We Already Found the answer:** It's E. The answer was found before reading the passage.

ANSWER EXPLANATIONS FOR TEST 1

- ■ **What Does The Question Really Ask?** You may already know that "Beans and bacon" is not the main topic of the passage. That is, this is an example-type question oriented from the arrogant Town Mouse's point of view, from which we should think his primary reason for using the "Beans and bacon, cheese and bread."
- ■ **Reading Tip:** Right above or below the example phrase you may find the answer for the example type of question. For that's where the main idea is found.

E is the best answer. "Cousin, how you can put up with such poor food as this,"
When the Town Mouse says Beans and bacon, he was referring to the poor living condition in which the Country Mouse is living.

Incorrect Answer Explanation

Choices A, B, C and D contradict the passage as they all contain positive tonalities. Choice A "a quality" means a good quality.

Q3. Question Pattern: The **attitude of the Town Mouse** is best characterized as one of
AP 8: Understanding Attitude (Tone) Find the tonality: positive vs. negative, mental vs. physical

- ■ **Question Keyword/Key phrase:** "attitude"
- ■ **Incorrect Pattern: A) arrogance**   B) uncertainty—DC   C) humility—DC(TI)   D) guilt—DC   E) sympathy—DC(TI)
- ■ **We Already Found the answer:** It's A. The answer was found before reading the passage.
- ■ **What Does The Question Really Ask?** The question basically asks the same thing with question 1 and therefore no further information from the passage is necessary.
- ■ **Reading Tip:** Finding attitude means finding tonality. We observed from Q1 that the Town Mouse possesses a negative attitude. Therefore, choice B, C, D, and E are incorrect.

A is the best answer.   "...but of course you cannot expect anything better in the country."
As stated above and shown in question 2 explanation, this sentence reveals the arrogance of the Town Mouse.

Incorrect Answer Explanation

Choice B is incorrect because the Town Mouse's attitude, when he says "poor food and poor living in country," was "certainly" negative. Choices C, D, and E are , under this circumstance, all positive tone.

Q4. Question Pattern: The **attitude of the Country Mouse** is best characterized as one of
AP 8: Understanding Attitude (Tone) Find the tonality: positive vs. negative, mental vs. physical

- ■ **Question Keyword/Key phrase:** "attitude "
- ■ **Incorrect Pattern:** A) proud—EX B) stupid—EX **C) realistic**   D) selfish—DC(TI)   E) smug—DC(TI)
- ■ **We Already Found the answer:** It's C. The answer was found before reading the passage.
- ■ **What Does The Question Really Ask?** This question asks the opposite character in the story, in which the Town Mouse is depicted as a negative character while the Country Mouse, a positive character. The answer, therefore, must contain the positive tone.
- ■ **Reading Tip:** As explained several times in the official test analysis, it is very helpful to read the concluding sentence when a clearer evidence is needed.

SSAT ABSOLUTE PATTERNS

C is the best answer. "Better beans and bacon in peace than cakes and ale in fear."
The country mouse—whether likes it or not—has nothing else to eat but beans and bacon. He, however, at least, finds peace of mind while living with beans and bacon. Therefore, we can call it the Town Mouse is realistic.

Incorrect Answer Explanation

Choices A and B are using extreme words. For neither is he proud nor stupid for eating beans.
Choices D and E represent the attitude of the Town mouse, not the Country Mouse.

Q5. Question Pattern: "**Country Mouse can see "beans and bacon" and "jellies and cakes"** " as a pair of
AP 9: Relationships Question Find the relationship between the cause and effect, characters, ideas

- ■ **Question Keyword/Key phrase:** "beans and bacon" and "jellies and cakes"
- ■ **Incorrect Pattern:** A) stupidity and wisdom—NI   B) time and money—NI   C) shame and proud—DC
  D) poor and rich—DC   **E) peace and fear**
- ■ **We Already Found the answer:** It's E. The answer was found before reading the passage.
- ■ **What Does The Question Really Ask?** The key phrase in this question is "beans and bacon" and "jellies and cakes." Remember, from whose point of view—"the Country Mouse's view in here—the question is presented.
- ■ **Reading Tip:** For the comparison questions—such as comparing two characters, two examples, or two comparable ideas—always focus on the latter—in this question "Jellies and cakes." It's because the former—"beans and bacon" —is relatively easier to identify, whereas the latter is tricky that usually determines the correct answer.

E is the best answer. "Better beans and bacon in peace than cakes and ale in fear."
Country Mouse compares "beans and bacon" as humble but peaceful country life; jellies and cakes "as affluent but fearful city life. Choice E correctly shows this positive vs. negative combination of the words.

Incorrect Answer Explanation

Choices A and B are Irrelevant words with the passage. Choices C and D shows the Town Mouse's point of view that contradict the Country Mouse's view.

Q6. Question Pattern: "**music**" mentioned in line 14 most nearly refers to a
AP 4: Word-In-Context Question   Find the clue words and keywords from the sentence

- ■ **Question Keyword/Key phrase:** "music"
- ■ **Incorrect Pattern:** A) dog—IS   B) lyric—IW   C) beans—IW   **D) barking**   E) song—IW
- ■ **What Does The Question Really Ask?** Remember, when the Word-in-Context question asks a very easy word, it does not ask for the literal meaning of the word. It is almost guaranteed that one could miss the question if he or she picked the literal meaning. It is because the test creators have a clear purpose when asking for such an easy word.
- ■ **Reading Tip:** Apply the mirroring technique: Read the designated sentence, Find the clue word, Remove the incorrect answers that do not match with the clue word.

D is the best answer. **"heard growling and barking.** 'What is that?' said the Country Mouse. 'It is only…'Only!' The Country mouse was referring the dog's barking to music euphemistically.

Incorrect Answer Explanation

Choice A is Insufficient Information because it should be "dog's barking" not the "dog." In other words, the phrase "I don't like that dog (music)" would completely change the meaning.

Choices B and E take the word "music" too literally. Choice C is Irrelevant word to this phrase.

Questions 7-11 are based on the following passage.

(Q7) **The Earth is the third planet** from the Sun and (Q8) **it is the only planet known to have life** on it. The Earth formed around 4.5 billion years ago. (Q9) **It is one of four rocky planets on the inside of the Solar System. The other three are Mercury, Venus, and Mars.** (Q10) **The large mass of the Sun makes the Earth move around it instead of falling**, just as the mass of the Earth makes the Moon move around it. The Earth also turns round in space, so different parts face the Sun at different times. The Earth goes around the Sun once for every 365¼ times (Q11) **it turns all the way around (one day).**

Q7. Question Pattern: **This passage** would most likely be **found** in the

AP 7: Inference Question Find the indirect suggestion behind the sentence

- ■ **Question Keyword/Key phrase:** "passage found"
- ■ **Incorrect Pattern:** A) student's journal-EX   B) Bible-NI   C) world map book-NI   D) traveling magazine-NI   **E) encyclopedia**
- ■ **What Does The Question Really Ask?** To answer this question, it requires a bit of imagination or common sense. As we solve more and more questions, we will see many more questions can be solved through common sense.
- ■ **Reading Tip:** The pattern that requires logical imagination is called the "inference." That is, the inference question asks logic behind the context. Unlike other types of questions that use direct reference from the passage, the correct answer for the inference question uses either unrelated word or indirectly mentioned words. That's why the inference question is considered difficult.

E is the best answer. The passage is about the Earth and some basic aspects of the Solar System that can be found in encyclopedia.

Incorrect Answer Explanation

Earth and some basic aspects of the Solar System cannot be seen in A) "student's journal," B) "Bible," C) "world map book" or D) "traveling magazine."

Q8. Question Pattern: The most **unique quality** of the Earth is that it

AP 2: Summary Question Summarize the sentence or the entire paragraph

- ■ **Question Keyword/Key phrase:** "unique"
- ■ **Incorrect Pattern:** A) is a planet—IS   **B) has living things**   C) is the oldest planet in the Solar System—DC
  D) is the only rocky planet—DC   E) is within the Solar System—IS
- ■ **What Does The Question Really Ask?** The phrase "…is that" in the question means "because" and seeking the cause-effect relations from the passage.
- ■ **Reading Tip:** Focus on the extreme word—"only" in this passage.

B is the best answer. "it is the only planet known to have life on it"
As stated above, the adverb "only" in the passage and the word "unique," meaning one and only, in the question indicate a strong connection to each other, hinting the answer "have life" as the unique quality.

Incorrect Answer Explanation

Choices A, D, and E are all common characteristics shared by eight planets in the Solar system, which make the Earth not so unique planet. Choice C is incorrect because the Sun is the oldest.

Q9. Question Pattern: When scientists study **Mercury**, Venus, and Mars, they would probably find from them
AP 7: Inference Question Find the indirect suggestion behind the sentence

- ■**Question Keyword/Key phrase:** "Mercury, Venus, and Mars,"
- ■**Incorrect Pattern:** A) different life forms—DC   B) their own Solar Systems—DC
  C) 4.5 billion years of history—NI   **D) rocks**   E) air—NI
- ■**What Does The Question Really Ask?** This question applies the technique called the "side-stepping." Students understandably focus on the main idea of the passage. Indeed, many questions are answered based on the main idea. The side-stepping, however, focuses on minor idea (In this question, the "Earth" is the main idea, whereas Mercury, Venus, and Mars are the minor idea.
- ■**Reading Tip:** Out of curiosity, what's the purpose of asking the minor idea instead of the main idea? In so doing, the test creators hope, students knowingly pick the incorrect answers based on information from the main idea.

D is the best answer. "It is one of four **rocky** planets" on the inside of the Solar System. The other three are Mercury, Venus, and Mars.

Incorrect Answer Explanation

Choices A and E are unique characteristics of the Earth, which is the main idea of the passage. Again, the question focuses on minor idea.
Choice B is incorrect because all eight planets belong to the solar system. Choice C is incorrect because we don't have this information. The passage indicates the earth is formed 4.5 billion years ago. However, there's no other comment indicating other planets' histories.

Q10. Question Pattern: The author describes that the **Earth does not fall** from the sky because
AP 2: Summary Question   Summarize the sentence or the entire paragraph

- ■**Question Keyword/Key phrase:** "not fall"
- ■**Incorrect Pattern:** A) the mass of the Sun makes the Earth moving
  B) the Earth circles the Sun for every 365¼ times—IW   C) the Earth is the third planet in the Solar System—IW
  D) the Earth has life form—IW   E) there's a string attached to the Sun—EX
- ■**What Does The Question Really Ask?** This question asks for the reason that the earth does not fall. Remember, many incorrect answers usually contain important key words in the passage, or even tell the true statements. What then make them wrong even with the correct key words? They may be telling the truth but speaking unrelated information to the question.
- ■**Reading Tip:** Find the key phrase that directly refers to the question, such as "The Earth does not fall."
- ■**Relevancy Check:** Choice E can be eliminated with common sense.

ANSWER EXPLANATIONS FOR TEST 1

A is the best answer. "The large mass of the Sun makes the earth move around it instead of falling,"
Just like two opposite magnets are pulling each other, the Sun makes the Earth keeps on spinning, so it does not fall from the sky.
Choices B, C, and D are true statements but referring to other issues.

Q11. Question Pattern: The Earth turns itself once completely for
AP 2: Summary Question   Summarize the sentence or the entire paragraph

---

- ■ **Question Keyword/Key phrase:** "turns"
- ■ **Incorrect Pattern:** A) forever—EX B) every 365¼ days—IW **C) every 24 hours** D) every hour—EX
  E) every 4.5 billion years—EX
- ■ **What Does The Question Really Ask?** The question asks for the specific detail related to the orbiting earth.
- ■ **Reading Tip:** Scan the passage and find the key phrase in the question—"earth turns"—that would eliminate all the unrelated statements.
- ■ **Relevancy Check:** Choices A, D, E are too extreme.

C is the best answer.   "it (EARTH) turns all the way around "(one day)" means every 24 hours.
Incorrect Answer Explanation
Choice B is incorrect because "every 365¼ " refers to the Earth goes around the Sun once.
Choice E refers to the earth's history.

Questions 12-16 are based on the following passage.
   The boy or girl who reads to-day may (Q12.) **know more about the real Lincoln than his own children knew.** The greatest President's son, Robert Lincoln, (Q14.) **discussing** a certain **incident** in their life in the White House, remarked to the writer, with a smile full of meaning: "I believe you know more about our
family matters than I do!" This is because (Q13.)"**all the world loves a lover**"--and Abraham Lincoln loved everybody.
With all his (Q15.) **brain and brawn,** (Q16.) **his real greatness was in his heart.**

Q12. Question Pattern: Which of the following **situation is most similar** to the sentence below?
AP 6: Analogy Question   Find the logically-supported similar situation

---

The boy or girl who reads to-day may know more about the real Lincoln than his own children knew.
- ■ **Question Keyword/Key phrase:** "may know more "
- ■ **Incorrect Pattern: A) A millionaire father learned from the newspaper that his son was kidnapped**
  B) A boy tells his mom that his father is sick—NI   C) A girl felt that she failed the test—IS
  D) A daughter of celebrity father told his fan that he is not her real father—DC
  E) A grandmother told her grandson about his father's secret life—NI
- ■ **What Does The Question Really Ask?** Just like in the analogy section, this type of question asks a similar situation from the passage. Just like the inference question, analogy question focuses more on logic behind the phrase but less on the context in the passage. So, don't be puzzled when you see completely unrelated phrases from each choice. The answer, that is, must contain a logical relation with the passage, not the content of the passage.

SSAT ABSOLUTE PATTERNS

A is the best answer. The author states that other people know more about his father Lincoln than Lincoln's own children and family do. The answer must contain people who are not the family members, yet still have better knowledge about Lincoln. The closest analogy for this situation is reflected in choice A.

Incorrect Answer Explanation

Choices B and E are incorrect because a boy, mother, father, and grandmother are all family members.

Choice C is incorrect because the sentence has only one person (a girl). It should have two people to make the analogy.

Choice D shows the opposite situation.

Q13. Question Pattern: Which of the following statements most closely supports the sentence below?

AP 9: Relationships Question Find the relationship between the cause and effect, characters, ideas

---

- **Question Keyword/Key phrase:** "With all his brain and brawn, **his real greatness** was in his heart."
- **Incorrect Pattern:** A) Lincoln had such a big size heart—EX

  B) It requires brain and brawn to have a great heart—DC   C) Brain and brawn are useless without a big heart—EX

  D) Heart is more important than brain and brawn—EX   **E) Lincoln was true humanitarian**
- **What Does The Question Really Ask?** Distinguish whether the word in question uses a figurative or literal meaning. The word "heart" in this question is figurative not referring to the human organ.
- **Relevancy Check:** "With all his brain and brawn" is called the prepositional phrase. "his real greatness was in his heart" is called the main clause. The prepositional phrase is usually secondary information whereas the main clause Is primary information. Most questions usually focus on the primary information, which means, in this question, any phrase that emphasizes "brain and brawn" is highly likely to be incorrect.

E is the best answer that represents "heart" as the Lincoln's humanitarianism.

Incorrect Answer Explanation

Choice A wrongly interprets the word "heart" as is used literally. For it does not refer to part of human organs. Choice B has significantly changed the original meaning. Choices C and D are incorrect because when the author says "his greatness was in his heart," it does not mean that "his brain and brawn" are inferior or useless. Take this example. If you prefer pizza to hamburger, does that mean you don't like hamburger? No. to be the answer, the focus has to be made on "pizza." In other words, any attempt to focus on "hamburger (the secondary issue) is wrong in the first place. Here, "brain and brawn" should not eclipse the author's emphasis on "heart."

Q14. Question Pattern: In lines 4 "all the **world loves a lover**" the author talks about **love between**

AP 9: Relationships Question Find the relationship between the cause and effect, characters, ideas

---

- **Question Keyword/Key phrase:** "love between "
- **Incorrect Pattern:** A) Abraham Lincoln and his family—IW   B) Abraham Lincoln and other countries—NI

  C) Robert Lincoln and Abraham Lincoln—IW   D) Abraham Lincoln and other people—DC

  E) other people and Abraham Lincoln
- **What Does The Question Really Ask?** One of the most challenging part in the reading passage is probably dealing with several characters in one question. Incorrect answers typically write true statements but use different character (i.e., A) Cindy ate the whole pizza.   B) Cindy's sister ate the whole pizza.)
- **Reading Tip:** Find the protagonist (the main character) in the passage and its tonality.

- **Relevancy Check:** All the alternatives contain the major character Abraham Lincoln, being referred to as "a lover." Now, find what the 'all the world' refers to. Choices A, B, C, and D are incorrect because "all the world" is the collective noun—in other words, it refers to a great many people. "Robert Lincoln" is a single individual.

E is the best answer. "All the world"—which is the plural—refers to other people, which is also the plural. Whereas, "love"—which is a singular—refers to "Abraham Lincoln," which is also a singular. This sentence describes love between Lincoln and all the world.

Incorrect Answer Explanation

Choice B is incorrect because "all the world" is used as a figurative meaning, not as literally as "other countries." Choice D is incorrect because the words order is flipped over.

Q13. Question Pattern: In line 2, "incident" most nearly means
AP 4: Word-In-Context Question   Find the clue words and keywords from the sentence

- **Question Keyword/Key phrase:** "incident"
- **Incorrect Pattern:** A) accident—NI B) chance—NI **C) story** D) problem—NI E) issue—NI
- **What Does The Question Really Ask?** This question uses a trick. And more importantly, this question reminds us the significance of applying the mirroring technique. The mirroring technique requires you to read the phrase in the passage before decide the answer. Through the mirroring technique, you should find a clue word from the sentence. Apply the clue word —like reflecting a mirror—into each alternative. During which the incorrect answers, that do not agree with the clue word in terms of tonality or meaning, should be removed.
- **Reading Tip:** Word-in-Context question does not ask overall understanding of the passage. It asks only a specific sentence in question. So it is not necessary to read several sentences, not to mention reading the entire passage.

C is the best answer.   Robert Lincoln, *discussing* a certain *incident in their life* in the White House.
We should first employ the mirroring technique to find the clue word. The words "discussing" and "in their life" are the clue words. For they are most meaningful words nearby the word "incident."
At this point, we can reach to the conclusion that—because the clue words, "discussing" and 'their life" are not in negative tone—the correct answer should not be the negative tone either. Therefore, only choice C becomes the legitimate answer. For the word "story" is a neutral tone.

Incorrect Answer Explanation

Choice A, D, and E are incorrect because they all contain negative connotations. If you didn't read the passage, the answer could have been A or E. As you have observed, a critical mistake can be made if the mirroring technique was not applied.

Q16. Question Pattern: The words "brain and brawn" in line 6 can also mean
AP 4: Word-In-Context Question   Find the clue words and keywords from the sentence

- **Question Keyword/Key phrase:** "brain and brawn"
- **correct Pattern:** A) love and friendship—NI   **B) intelligence and strength**
   C) education and sports—NI D) life and death—NI E) power and knowledge—DC
- **What Does The Question Really Ask?** This is the Word-in-Context question that requires your vocabulary skill

■ **Reading Tip:** Compared to the previous question 13—that used the easy word in figurative meaning—this question is based on a difficult word that normally asks its pure literal meaning. Frequently, reading the passage won't help much without knowing its exact meaning of the Word in question.

B is the best answer. Brain means intelligence; Brawn means strength, which are, of course, the most valuable qualities for President.

Incorrect Answer Explanation

Choice E has flipped the words order. All the rest incorrect answers are irrelevant information.

Questions 17-22 are based on the following passage.

Do you have hobbies? Many people do. I do. For some, it's computer games or wrestling or collecting things like stickers or stamps. Some people's hobbies become their whole life and some of them are just, well, hobbies and (Q18) **some of them are very, very weird. I discovered the other day** that **some people hold competitions for mooing like a cow** and there are people who make their dogs look like tigers. **Some people** lie down in public places and put a photo of it on-line. That's it. They don't do anything else, they just lie down. I don't mean they lie down in a pattern or wear some silly outfit, they just lie down.

(Q17 & Q19) **I guess in the end hobbies are like people -(QUESTION 22) they're all different** and not everyone will find yours interesting. (Q20) **I'm pretty certain not everyone finds my hobby interesting** (Q21) **but that's fine** with me. **I like robot.**

Q17. Question Pattern: The narrator thinks that people's hobbies are
AP 2: Summary Question   Summarize the sentence or the entire paragraph

■ **Question Keyword/Key phrase:** "people's hobbies"
■ **Incorrect Pattern: A) diverse   B) limited to only for a few people—DC
   C) dangerous—DC(TI)   D) affordable—NI   E) boring—DC(TI)
■ **What Does The Question Really Ask?** To find the correct answer to this question, the author's main tone—that represents his opinion about hobbies—needs to be identified. Stick to the same tonality with the passage. If the passage is positive, never choose a negative word.
■ **Reading Tip:** Treat this question as the main idea question. You may leave it for now and come back later after the author's tone about hobby is clearly identified.

A is the best answer. "I guess in the end hobbies are like people—they're all different."
"different" means "diverse."

Incorrect Answer Explanation

Because the narrator's tone about "hobby" is positive, choices B, C, and E that use the negative tone are incorrect. Choice D "affordable" means cheap. The author didn't say hobby is supposed to be affordable.

Q18. Question Pattern: The narrator sees the phrase "**some people hold competitions,...a cow**" in line 4 as
AP 8: Understanding Attitude (Tone) Find the tonality: positive vs. negative, mental vs. physical

■ **Question Keyword/Key phrase:** "cow"
■ **Incorrect Pattern:** A) witty—EX   B) cow-like—IW   **C) unusual**   D) people's nature—EX   E) awesome trick—EX
■ **What Does The Question Really Ask?** From the question key phrase we can verify the question type. Questions asking example sentence and the author's opinion about it usually place the answer in the previous sentence.

ANSWER EXPLANATIONS FOR TEST 1

■ **Reading Tip:** To find the author's tone or attitude about the examples sentence, we should find the main idea that uses the example, As we have seen a couple of times from the previous questions, the main idea cannot be found from the example sentence. Instead, it is located right next to the example sentence.

C is the best answer. "some are very, very weird. I discovered...some people hold competitions for mooing like a cow" "very weird" means unusual. As stated in the preceding sentence, the author finds the hobby very unusual.

Incorrect Answer Explanation

Choices A, B, D, and E are all incorrect for using too extreme expressions in one way or another.

Choice A and E are positive words that do not properly reflect the author's opinion when he says "very weird."

Choices B and D take the phrase too literally. "cow-like" or "people's nature" insinuates the negative way he sees with these people.

Q19. Question Pattern: The narrator **concludes hobbies** are
AP 5: Understanding the True Purpose   Find the explicitly stated true purpose of the sentence

■ **Question Keyword/Key phrase:** "concludes **hobbies**"
■ **Incorrect Pattern: A) individualized attempt**   B) serious job—DC   C) very weird acts—IS
   D) important way to make friends—DC   E) difficult process to master—DC
■ **What Does The Question Really Ask?** The key phrase in the question indicates that it is the main idea question asking the conclusion of the passage.
■ **Reading Tip:** Focus on the conclusion because the question asks you to do so.

A is the best answer.   "hobbies are like people they're all different"
Focus on the conclusion, find the right tonality and the key phrase: "hobbies are like people they're all different."
Thus, the author claims hobbies are individualized attempt.

Incorrect Answer Explanation

Choices B, D and E use too serious words, thereby making too heavy the narrator's opinion about "hobby," contradicting the narrator's lighthearted mood. Choice C is incorrect. The author did mention "very weird acts" in line 3. However, it was referring only the example concerning weird hobbies. We can't say, stamp collection—the author is fond of—is weird hobby.

Q20. Question Pattern: In line 9 "**I like robot.**" the narrator suggests that his hobby is
AP 8: Understanding Attitude (Tone) Find the tonality: positive vs. negative, mental vs. physical

■ **Question Keyword/Key phrase:** "I like robot."
■ **Incorrect Pattern:** A) the best—EX   B) sophisticated—EX   C) as important as is robot in our economy—EX
   D) his own favorite   E) very weird—DC   *sophisticated = complex and not simple

D is the best answer.   "that's fine with me."
The author thinks his hobby is just for himself regardless of whether people find it interesting or not.

Incorrect Answer Explanation

Choices A) "best," B) "sophisticated," and C) "in our economy" are incorrect because they are far too extreme expressions. Choice E contradicts the author's opinion about his hobby. He does not say his hobby is weird. He sees positive aspects from all hobbies including his own.

Q21. Question Pattern: How would the narrator **react if** other people said that his hobby is boring?
AP 7: Inference Question   Find the indirect suggestion behind the sentence

- ■ **Question Keyword/Key phrase:** "narrator **reply to boring** "
- ■ **Incorrect Pattern:** A) criticize that their hobbies are boring too—DC(TI)
  B) give them some lessons about robot assembly—NI   C) suggest them to join his hobby—NI
  D) appreciate their judgment   E) tell them there is no perfect hobby—NI
- ■ **What Does The Question Really Ask?** The answer for the inference question is not supposed to be written in the passage. For It asks for a logical assumption behind the written statement. In case when the answer is hard to find, focus on the last sentence of the passage and identify the tone of the last sentence.
- ■ **Reading Tip:** When you see "but" or similar contradictory conjunctions from the passage, pay attention to that area. The contradictory conjunction (or adverb) usually shows the answer in forms of tonality or keywords.

D is the best answer.   "**but that's fine** with me."
The author appreciates other people's negative view on his hobby. The answer was found after the word "but."

Incorrect Answer Explanation

Seen above, the author does not mind other people's judgment. Therefore, the negative choices such as A and E should be removed. Choices B and C are irrelevant information.

Q22. According to lines 3-5, which of the following **hobbies** would **the narrator most likely agree**?
AP 7: Inference Question   Find the indirect suggestion behind the sentence

- ■ **Question Keyword/Key phrase:** "narrator most likely agree "
- ■ **Incorrect Pattern:** A) Learning a foreign language like others do—DC
  B) Going to church as the Bible says—DC   C) Raising the same pet that his friend has—DC
  D) Taking a part time job at a grocery store—NI   **E) Participating in an insect-eating competition**

E is the best answer. In lines 3-5 the author emphasizes some of the weird hobbies: "some of them are very, very weird. I discovered."
Choice E that shows "participating in an insect-eating competition" expresses the similar weird characteristics of hobbies.

Incorrect Answer Explanation

Choices A, B, and C show some of the general hobbies. They are, however, do not reflect the main idea presented in lines 3-5. Choice D is not even a hobby.

Questions 23-27 are based on the following passage.

   A Wolf had been gorging on an animal he had killed, when suddenly (Q26.) **a small bone in the meat stuck in his throat and he could not swallow it**. **He soon felt terrible pain** in his throat, and ran up and down groaning and groaning and seeking for something to relieve the pain.
He tried to induce every one he met to remove the bone. 'I would give anything,' said he, 'if you would take it out.' (Q23.) **At last the Crane agreed to try,** and told the Wolf to lie on his side and open his jaws as wide as he could. Will you kindly give me the reward you promised?' said the Crane. (Q25.) **The Wolf grinned and showed his teeth** and said: '**Be content.** (Q.27.) **The Wolf grinned and showed his teeth** and said: (Q24.) **'Be content. You have put your head inside a Wolf's mouth and taken it out again in safety; that ought to be reward enough for you.'** Gratitude and greed go not together.

ANSWER EXPLANATIONS FOR TEST 1

Q23. Question Pattern: The Crane agreed to remove a bone from the Wolf's throat because
AP 5: Understanding the True Purpose Find the explicitly stated true purpose of the sentence

- ■ **Question Keyword/Key phrase:** "agreed to remove **a bone** "
- ■ **Incorrect Pattern: A) the crane expected a reward**   B) they were old friends to each other—DC
  C) the crane felt sympathy for the wolf—IS   D) the wolf was in pain—IS   E) the wolf couldn't swallow the bone—IS
- ■ **What Does The Question Really Ask?** The question asks the true purpose of the question. Remember, incorrect answers may contain true but insufficient Information to be the answer. Or they may consist of true statement but irrelevant to the question.
- ■ **Reading Tip:** Focus on transitional words—"At last" (line 5) in this passage: transitional words indicate a significant turning point of the story such as the cause-and-effect, the compare-and-contrast, or the contradiction.

A is the best answer. "I would give anything,' said he, 'if you would take it out.' At last the Crane agreed to try"
The above phrase clearly shows that the Crane helped the wolf because it expected a reward from the wolf. The transitional word "At last" represents the cause-and-effect logic.

Incorrect Answer Explanation

Choice B contradict the passage. Line 4 states that they met first time. It is not clear whether the Crane was sympathetic to help as stated in choices C, D or E.
" Will you kindly give me the reward you promised?" implies that the crane didn't help the wolf simply out of pity. Therefore, choices B, C, D, and E are, at best, insufficient information.

Q24. Question Pattern: By saying "be content" the **Wolf characterizes** the crane as
AP 8: Understanding Attitude (Tone) Find the tonality: positive vs. negative, mental vs. physical

- ■ **Question Keyword/Key phrase:** "be content"
- ■ **Incorrect Pattern:** A) stupid—EX   **B) greedy**   C) generous—DC D) friendly—DC   E) clever—DC
- ■ **What Does The Question Really Ask?** This question, to some, could be the Word-in-Context question because it asks the definition for the word "content" Knowing the word "content" is even more important than reading the passage.
- ■ **Relevancy Check:** Choice A is extreme expression which should be eliminated through commonsense.

B is the best answer. "You have put your head inside a Wolf's mouth and taken it out again in safety"
The Wolf, by saying "Be content (or be satisfied)," thinks the crane is greedy.

Incorrect Answer Explanation

Choices C, D, and E—because they are positive words—wouldn't be the proper expressions that represent the Wolf's negative character.

Q25. Question Pattern: The word **"teeth" (line 8)** serves as the
AP 5: Understanding the True Purpose Find the explicitly stated true purpose of the sentence

SSAT ABSOLUTE PATTERNS

- ■ **Question Keyword/Key phrase:** "teeth"
- ■ **Incorrect Pattern:** A) general symbol of wolf—NI (Generalization)   B) pain that wolf felt—IW   C) wolf's wisdom—NI (Generalization)   D) strength of the wolf—NI (Generalization)   **E) cunning instinct of the wolf**
- ■ **What Does The Question Really Ask?** The question asks the true purpose of using the word "teeth" The word "teeth" represent the wolf's negative characteristic.

E is the best answer. "The Wolf grinned and showed his teeth and said: Be content."
The word "teeth" is directly linked to the phrase "Be content." "teeth"—surrounded by the negative words "grinned and showed his"—symbolizes the wolf's cunning instinct.

Incorrect Answer Explanation

Choices A, C, and D are incorrect because they are general descriptions about wolf, whereas "teeth" contains explicitly negative tone. Choice B is irrelevant information to the word "teeth." For It's not the teeth but the bones that caused the pain.

Q26. Pattern: In **the real world**, which of the following choices would be similar to **"a small bone"** (line 1)?
AP 7: Inference Question   Find the indirect suggestion behind the sentence

---

- ■ **Question Keyword/Key phrase:** "a small bone"
- ■ **Incorrect Pattern:**
   A) a sadness—DC(IS)   B) a reward—DC   **C) an uncomfortable situation**   D) greed—NI   E) lying—NI
- ■ **What Does The Question Really Ask?** The question basically asks between choice A and C. That is, A describes the mental discomfort the wolf is experiencing, while C, a physical discomfort.
- ■ **Relevancy Check:** Choice A is incorrect because the word "sad" represents only the emotional stress. It must factor in the small bone that caused the wolf physical pain.

C is the best answer.   "He soon felt terrible pain in his throat"   "Bone" creates uncomfortable physical pain. Or physical discomfort.
Choice B reflects the Crane's desire. Choice D and E reflect the Wolf's character. Therefore, they are irrelevant words.

Q27. Question Pattern: The last sentence "**Gratitude and greed go not together.**" can be expressed as
AP 5: Understanding the True Purpose   Find the explicitly stated true purpose of the sentence

---

- ■ **Question Keyword/Key phrase:** "Gratitude and greed go not together"
- ■ **Incorrect Pattern:** A) absence makes the heart grow fonder —NI
   B) actions speak louder than words —NI   **C) a good speaker makes a good liar**
   D) a journey of a thousand miles begins with a single step—NI   E) a picture is worth a thousand words —NI
- ■ **What Does The Question Really Ask?** The question basically asks what proverb best explains the Wolf's attitude.

C is the best answer.   The Wolf grinned and showed his teeth and said: 'Be content'.
Choice C clearly shows the Wolf's cunning attitude depicted in the passage, especially the last sentence.

Incorrect Answer Explanation

Choice A means that being away from someone makes you appreciate that person more.
Choice B means that what you do is more important than what you say.
Choice D means that you must begin something with one step first.
Choice E means that an image can tell a story better than words.

ANSWER EXPLANATIONS FOR TEST 1

Test 1 ABSOLUTE PATTERNS for the analogy Section

AP 8. The Production Pattern Find What Produces What and the Cause and Effect Relation

16. Bread is to mold as iron is to   A) strong   B) silver   C) heavyweight   D) luster   **E) rust**

E is the best answer.   Bread produces mold as iron produces rust.
Jimin: "why not choices A, B, C, D? Iron produces strength or luster. Or we can even say that Iron produces silver color or heavy.

The question-stem
16. Bread is to mold as iron is to
Primary word   Secondary word

1. Identify the question-stem: Bread is to mold
2. Find the relation between the primary and secondary word: Bread & mold
3. The correct answer must reflect the entire question-stem

You must first use the question-stem as the stepping-stone to start with: It describes the condition of bread that grows mold. Therefore, you should expect the same condition created by iron.
Don't miss out the similar characteristics between 'mold' and 'rust.' The negative similarities between "mold" and "rust" and their deteriorating characteristics separate them apart from all the other choices. Despite your seemingly appropriate explanations, all the other incorrect answers do not work as the synonym to "mold."

AP4. Characteristic Pattern Find the Characteristic of Person, Place, Object, or Idea

17. Wood is to decay as
A) water is to vaporize   B) fire is to extinguisher   C) movie is to song   D) school is to boring   E) father is to mother
A is the best answer.   Wood decays as water vaporizes. "decay" and "vaporize" illustrate the same thermodynamic degradation of property. Characteristic similarity between the question-stem and choice A is not found in others.
Choice B is the purpose (TOOL) Pattern. The purpose of extinguisher (tool) is to put out fire.   Choice C is the Category Pattern. For 'movie' and 'song' are in the same entertainment category.   Choice D is the mental Pattern.
Choice E is the antonym Pattern.

AP3. Purpose (Tool) Pattern Finding Relationships between the Purpose of Individual

18. Human is to lung as fish is to   A) dinner   B) restaurant   C) expensive   **D) gill**   E) ocean

D is the best answer. Human has lungs to breathe as fish has gills to breathe. The secondary word "lung" in the question-stem and choice D share the same functionality. In that sense both are conceptual synonyms.
Choices A, B, and E are associated with "fish" but not with the entire question-stem. Choice C is Irrelevant word to the question-stem

AP1. Category Pattern Find the Part and Whole Relation, the Same Type or Association

19. Cat is to tiger as whale is to   A) bird   B) frog   **C) octopus**   D) wolf   E) lion

C is the best answer.   Cat and tiger are land animal category; whale and (C) octopus are ocean animal.
The rest animals do not follow the question-stem that relates between the land animals and the sea animals.

SSAT ABSOLUTE PATTERNS

AP9. Syntax Pattern Find the Homophony, Contraction, Verb, Adjective, Tense, Confusing Words

20. She's is to she is as it's is to   A) its   **B) it is**   C) it had   D) it is going to   E) it will

B is the best answer. "It's" is the contraction (the reduced form) of "It is" as "she's" is the contraction of "she is." The question basically asks between choices A and B. Choice A) "its" is a possessive pronoun. Ex) The cruise canceled its schedule. The rest are Irrelevant words to the question-stem

AP9. Syntax Pattern Find the Homophony, Contraction, Verb, Adjective, Tense, Confusing Words

21. He is to him as she is to   A) its   B) she's   C) hers   **D) her**   E) she is

D is the best answer. "He" is the subjective form while 'him' is the objective form. "She" is the subjective form while 'her' is the objective form. The question basically asks between choice C and D. "hers" is the possessive pronoun. Ex) I couldn't find my hat, so I brought hers. The rest become Irrelevant words to the question-stem

AP1. Category Pattern Find the Part and Whole Relation, the Same Type or Association

22. Ice skating is to Hang gliding as   A) mother is to father   B) female player is to male player   C) cheap is to expensive   **D) polar bear is to eagle**   E) North Pole is to South Pole

D is the best answer. Both Ice skating and Polar bear are associated with cold temperature.
Both Hang gliding and eagle are associated with the Sky.

Don't be misled by the question-stem, presuming it could be the antonym pattern. If you did, as you can notice immediately, everything will be the answer. Remember, the question-stem must be the stepping-stone upon which the answer is build. Choices A and B are incorrect because the relations between the primary and secondary words are Antonym. They also use humans unlike the question-stem. Choice C and E show no relation to the question-stem.

AP 7. Syntax Pattern Find the Homophony, Contraction, Verb, Adjective, Tense, Confusing Words

23. Flour is to flower as

A) bread is to delicious   B) rose is to fragrance   **C) red is to bed**   D) bread is to bakery   E) plant is to spring

C is the best answer. Flour and flower make the same sound as red and bed make the same sound. That is, the question stem and choice C are homophony. The answer is not decided by the meaning or the characteristics of the question-stem. Choices B and E are Production Pattern: Rose produces fragrance and spring produces plant. Choice D is the Category Pattern.

AP 2. Synonym/Antonym Find the similar or opposite meaning between the words

24. Happy is to fast as glad is to   **A) quick**   B) feast   C) marathon   D) Usain Bolt   E) good

A is the best answer. Happy is synonym to glad as fast is synonym to quick. Choice C is incorrect because 'marathon' is associated with the secondary word 'fast,' but not with the entire question-stem.
Some students may choose D because "Usain Bolt," the world fastest sprinter, conjures up an image of being fast. 'Usain Bolt' is a human, not a synonym to 'fast' and again does not correspond to the entire question-stem.
Jimin: Why not choice E? I thought it's E because all four words are adjectives.

No! If you go by the adjective, choice A is adjective too. Therefore, you should find more than adjective relation from the question-stem.

ANSWER EXPLANATIONS FOR TEST 1

AP 2. Synonym/Antonym   Find the similar or opposite meaning between the words

25. Big is to small as sleep is to   A) dream   **B) wake**   C) my sister   D) homework   E) danger

B is the best answer. Big is antonym to small as sleep is antonym to wake. Choice A becomes the Production Pattern. For sleep produces dream. All the rest are Irrelevant words to the question-stem.

P4. Characteristic Pattern   Find the Characteristic of Person, Place, Object, or Idea

26. Team is to captain as fan is to   A) ticket   **B) cheerleader**   C) football   D) free   E) watching

B is the best answer. Captain leads the team as a cheerleader leads the fan.

The question-stem and B) share the same characteristics in terms of their leading roles in a game.

Choice D is irrelevant word to the question-stem. Choices A and E are related only to the word "fan" but not to the entire question-stem. Choice C is associated with the words "team" and "captain" but not with the word "fan."

AP1. Category Pattern   Find the Part and Whole Relation, the Same Type or Association

27. Goalie is to catcher as hockey is to   A) hitter   **B) baseball**   C) boring   D) receive   E) striker

B is the best answer. The question-stem and choice B share the similar sports category and positions in sports. Both goalie and catcher share the similar functionality in each of their games.

Choices A and E are antonym to "goalie" and 'catcher," and are not following the synonym patterns held in the question-stem. Choice C is Irrelevant word.

Choice D is incorrect. The word "receive" describes a job of both 'goalie' and 'catcher,' but it does not follow the question-stem that shows the game "hockey."

AP1. Category Pattern   Find the Part and Whole Relation, the Same Type or Association

28. Ocean is to salty

A) fire is to dangerous   B) tomatoes is to vegetable   C) mother is to father   D) east is to south   **E) candy is to sweet**

E is the best answer. The question-stem and choice E share the same five-sensory category.

Choice A uses the Mental (Emotion) Pattern. Choice B uses part and whole in the Category pattern. Choices C and D are the antonym Pattern.

AP8. Production Pattern Find What Produces What and the Cause and Effect Relation

29. Ant is to tunnel as beaver is to   A) big teeth   B) animal   C) rodent   **D) dam**   E) fence

D is the best answer. Ant makes the tunnel as beaver makes the dam.

Both the question-stem and D) share the same production pattern.

Choices A, C, and E are associated with "beaver" but not with the entire question-stem.

Choice B is associated with "ant" and "beaver" but not with the entire question-stem.

AP1. Category Pattern   Find the Part and Whole Relation, the Same Type or Association

30. Aunt is to uncle as

A) nephew is to niece   B) brother is to brothers   C) friend is to family   D) family is to relative   E) young is to old

A is the best answer.

If you were thinking of a simple antonym pattern, you may have found more than one answer here.

The question-stem and choice A share several similarities to each other not found in other choices. First of all, they are all antonyms; second, all humans; and third, all family members.

Choice E is, on the other hands, a simple antonym and cannot be further related to the question-stem like A does.

Choice B refers to the singular vs. plural relation. Choice C "friend" is irrelevant word to the question-stem. Choice D is too vague in description.

SSAT ELEMENTARY LEVEL

Reading & Verbal Section

Test 1

Try to solve all the questions in Test 1
within 30 minutes with 100% accuracy

Test 1 Reading Section
Time: 30 Minutes, 27 Questions

Directions: Each reading passage is followed by questions about it. Answer the questions that follow a passage on the basis of what is stated or implied in that passage.

Questions 1-6 are based on the following passage.

Line   A Town Mouse once upon a time went on a visit to his cousin in the country. Beans and bacon, cheese and bread, were all he had to offer. The Town Mouse rather turned up his long nose and said: 'I cannot understand, Cousin, how you can put up with such poor food as this, but of course you cannot expect anything better in the country; come you with me and I will
5   show you how to live. The two mice set off for the town and arrived at the Town Mouse's residence. 'You will want some refreshment after our long journey,' said the polite Town Mouse, and took his friend into the grand dining-room. There they found the remains of a fine feast, and soon the two mice were eating up jellies and cakes. Suddenly they heard growling and barking. 'What is that?' said the Country Mouse. 'It is only the dogs of the house.' 'Only!' said
10   the Country Mouse. 'I do not like that **music** at my dinner.' 'Good-bye, Cousin,' said the Country Mouse. 'Better beans and bacon in peace than cakes and ale in fear.

1
The Town Mouse thinks that the Country Mouse

A) does not appreciate the nature
B) enjoys his life
C) understands town very well
D) should expect the better world
E) does not live peacefully in a country

2
The Town Mouse sees "Beans and bacon, cheese and bread" in line 2 as

A) a quality meal
B) a luxurious living
C) a healthy food
D) a unique and happy lifestyle
E) a poor living condition

3
The attitude of the Town Mouse is best characterized as one of

A) arrogance
B) uncertainty
C) humility
D) guilt
E) sympathy

*arrogance=being stuck up, bragging
* sympathy=being kind

Questions 7-11 are based on the following passage.

Line

The Earth is the third planet from the Sun and it is the only planet known to have life on it. The Earth formed around 4.5 billion years ago. It is one of four rocky planets on inside of the Solar System. Other three are Mercury, Venus, and Mars. The large mass of the Sun makes the Earth move around it, just as the mass of the Earth makes the Moon move around it instead of
5 falling. The Earth also turns round in space, so different parts face the Sun at different times. The Earth goes around the Sun once for every 365¼ times when it turns all the way around (one day).

7

This passage would most likely be found in the

A) student's journal
B) Bible
C) world map book
D) traveling magazine
E) encyclopedia

8

The most unique quality of the Earth is that it

A) is a planet
B) has living things
C) is the oldest planet in the Solar System
D) is the only rocky planet
E) is within the Solar System

9

When scientists study Mercury, Venus, and Mars, they would probably find from them

A) different life forms
B) their own Solar Systems
C) 4.5 billion years of history
D) rocks
E) air

10

The author describes that the Earth does not fall from the sky because

A) the mass of the Sun makes the Earth moving
B) the Earth circles the Sun for every 365¼ times
C) the Earth is the third planet in the Solar System
D) the Earth has life form
E) there's a string attached to the Sun

11

The Earth turns itself once completely for

A) forever
B) every 365¼ days
C) every 24 hours
D) every hour
E) every 4.5 billion years

Questions 12-16 are based on the following passage.

Line   The boy or girl who reads to-day may know more about the real Lincoln than his own children knew. The greatest President's son, Robert Lincoln, discussing a certain incident in their life in the White House, remarked to the writer, with a smile full of meaning: "I believe you know more about our family matters than I do!" This is because "all the world loves a lover"--
5 and Abraham Lincoln loved everybody. With all his brain and brawn, his real greatness was in his heart.

12

Which of the following situation is most similar to the first sentence ("The boy or girl... children knew.") ?
A) A millionaire father learned from the newspaper that his son had been kidnapped
B) A boy tells his mom that his father is sick
C) A girl felt that she failed the test
D) A daughter of a celebrity father told his fan that he is not her real father
E) A grandmother told her grandson about his father's secret life

13

Read the sentence from line 5 in the box below.

With all his brain and brawn, his real greatness was in his heart.

Which statement most closely supports the above sentence?
A) Lincoln had such a big size heart
B) It requires brain and brawn to have a great heart
C) Brain and brawn are useless without a big heart
D) Heart is more important than brain and brawn
E) Lincoln was true humanitarian

"humanitarian" means a person who is seeking to promote human welfare and happiness.

14

In lines 4 "all the world loves a lover" the author talks about love between
A) Abraham Lincoln and his family
B) Abraham Lincoln and other countries
C) Robert Lincoln and Abraham Lincoln
D) Abraham Lincoln and other people
E) other people and Abraham Lincoln

15

In line 2, "incident" most nearly means
A) accident
B) chance
C) story
D) problem
E) issue

16

The words "brain and brawn" in line 5 can also mean
A) love and friendship
B) intelligence and strength
C) education and sports
D) life and death
E) power and knowledge

Questions 23-27 are based on the following passage.

Line   A Wolf had been gorging on an animal he had killed, when suddenly a small bone in the meat stuck in his throat and he could not swallow it. He soon felt terrible pain in his throat, and ran up and down groaning and groaning and seeking for something to relieve the pain.
    He tried to induce every one he met to remove the bone. 'I would give anything,' said he, 'if you
5 would take it out.' At last the Crane agreed to try, and told the Wolf to lie on his side and open his jaws as wide as he could. Then the Crane put its long neck down the Wolf's throat, and with its beak loosened the bone, till at last it got it out. 'Will you kindly give me the reward you promised?' said the Crane. The Wolf grinned and showed his teeth and said: 'Be content. You have put your head inside a Wolf's mouth and taken it out again in safety; that
10 ought to be reward enough for you.' Gratitude and greed go not together.

23

The Crane agreed to remove a bone from the Wolf's throat because

A) the crane expected a reward
B) they were old friends to each other
C) the crane felt sympathy for the wolf
D) the wolf threatened the crane
E) the wolf couldn't swallow the bone

24

By saying "Be content" (line 9) the Wolf characterizes the crane as

A) stupid
B) greedy
C) generous
D) friendly
E) clever

25

The word "teeth" (line 8) serves as the

A) general symbol of wolf
B) pain that wolf felt
C) wolf's wisdom
D) strength of the wolf
E) cunning instinct of the wolf

26

In the real world, which of the following choices would be similar to "a small bone" (line 1)?

A) a sadness
B) a reward
C) an uncomfortable situation
D) greed
E) lying

27

The last sentence "Gratitude and greed go not together." can be expressed as

A) absence makes the heart grow fonder
B) actions speak louder than words
C) **a** good speaker makes a good liar
D) a journey of a thousand miles begins with a single step
E) a picture is worth a thousand words

Verbal Test 1
20 MINUTES, 30 QUESTIONS

Directions: the synonym questions ask you to find the most appropriate synonym to the question.

The analogy questions ask you to find the most appropriate analogy to the question. Select the answer that best matches to the question.

Synonyms

Each of the following questions consists of one word followed by five words or phrases. You are to select the one word or phrase whose meaning is closest to the word in capital letters.

Sample Question:

ABILITY

A) mistake
B) **talent**
C) abandon
D) best student
E) late

1. EXPLORE
A) mistake
B) talent
C) abandon
D) feeling sorry
E) curiosity

2. GRACE
A) beauty
B) big
C) best
D) great
E) god

3. ADVICE
A) adult
B) advance
C) information
D) teacher
E) positive

4. FORTUNATE
A) fortune teller
B) money
C) furniture
D) example
E) lucky

5. AVERAGE
A) less
B) equal
C) good
D) score
E) Ordinary

6. HARSH
A) hard
B) sharp
C) remark
D) decision
E) soft

7. RECALL
A) memory
B) cell phone
C) communication
D) clear
E) reject

8. ARCTIC
A) North Pole
B) bear
C) frosty
D) artistic
E) often

9. REMARK
A) feeling
B) refer
C) sign
D) fact
E) saying

10. STARVE
A) happy
B) cease
C) remember
D) benefit
E) Assignment

11. THEORY
A) project
B) idea
C) chemistry
D) principle
E) situation

12. WIT
A) with
B) delay
C) worry
D) fun
E) lying

13. COWARD

A) chicken

B) wimp

C) brave

D) cow-like

E) bad behavior

14. WISDOM

A) old man

B) enlightenment

C) book

D) study

E) math

15. DEFEND

A) pencil

B) attack

C) deft

D) rely

E) shield

Analogies

The following questions ask you to find relationships between words. For each question, select the answer choice that best completes the meaning of the sentence.

SAMPLE QUESTION
Q: River is to Ocean as:

A) better is to good

B) rain is to cloud

C) father is to mother

D) city is to country

E) fork is to spoon

This question is Degree Analogy question (small to big movement).

Ⓓ is the correct answer. Just as river is smaller than Ocean, so is city to the country.

Ⓐ is incorrect because the order is flipped over.

Ⓑ is incorrect because this is 'Production Analogy—what-produce-what.'

Ⓒ and Ⓔ are incorrect because there are no big and small relations between mother and father, so does fork to spoon.

16. Bread is to mold as iron is to

A) strong

B) silver

C) heavyweight

D) luster

E) rust

17. Wood is to decay as

A) water is to vaporize

B) fire is to extinguisher

C) movie is to song

D) school is to boring

E) father is to mother

18. Human is to lung as fish is to

A) dinner

B) restaurant

C) expensive

D) gill

E) ocean

19. Cat is to tiger as whale is to

A) bird

B) frog

C) octopus

D) wolf

E) lion

20. She's is to she is as it's is to

A) its

B) it is

C) it had

D) it is going to

E) it will

21. He is to him as she is to

A) its

B) she's

C) hers

D) her

E) she is

22. Ice skating is to Hang gliding as

A) mother is to father

B) female player is to male player

C) cheap is to expensive

D) polar bear is to eagle

E) North Pole is to South Pole

23. Flour is to flower as

A) bread is to delicious

B) rose is to fragrance

C) red is to bed

D) bread is to bakery

E) plant is to spring

24. Happy is to fast as glad is to

A) quick

B) feast

C) marathon

D) Usain Bolt

E) good

25. Big is to small as sleep is to

A) dream

B) wake

C) my sister

D) homework

E) danger

SSAT ABSOLUTE PATTERNS

26. Team is to captain as fan is to
A) ticket
B) cheerleader
C) football
D) free
E) watching

27. Goalie is to catcher as hockey is to
A) hitter
B) baseball
C) boring
D) receive
E) striker

28. Ocean is to salty
A) fire is to dangerous
B) tomatoes is to vegetable
C) mother is to father
D) east is to south
E) candy is to sweet

29. Ant is to tunnel as beaver is to
A) big teeth
B) animal
C) rodent
D) dam
E) fence

30. Aunt is to uncle as
A) nephew is to niece
B) brother is to brothers
C) friend is to family
D) family is to relative
E) young is to old

TEST 1

SYNONYM QUESTIONS
TEST 1 NO.1 ~ 15

1	E
2	A
3	C
4	E
5	E
6	B
7	A
8	C
9	E
10	B
11	B
12	D
13	B
14	B
15	E

ANALOGY QUESTIONS
TEST 1 NO. 16 ~30

Please refer to the analogy AP Analyses

TEST 1
READING SECTION

Please refer to the Reading Section AP Analyses

SSAT

Reading & Verbal Section

Test 2

Test 2 Reading Section
Time: 30 Minutes, 29 Questions

Directions: Each reading passage is followed by questions about it. Answer the questions that follow a passage on the basis of what is stated or implied in that passage.

Questions 1-5 are based on the following passage.

> The Lion went once a-hunting along with the Fox, the Jackal, and the Wolf. They hunted and they hunted till at last they surprised a Stag, and soon took its life. Then came the question how the spoil should be divided. 'Quarter me this Stag,' roared the Lion; so the other animals cut it into four parts. The first quarter is for me in my capacity as King of
> 5 Beasts; the second is mine as arbiter; another share comes to me for my part in the chase; and as for the fourth quarter, well..., as for that, I should like to see which of you will dare to lay a paw upon it.' 'Humph,' grumbled the Fox in a low growl .'You may share the labours of the great, but you will not share the spoil.'

1

The other three animals may call the Lion as the

A) King of Beasts
B) Judge
C) Chaser
D) Hunter
E) Cheater

2

"the spoil" in line 3 most nearly means

A) unduly behavior
B) hunted animal
C) useless animal
D) rotten animal
E) skinned animal to eat

3

The lesson from the passage can be described as

A) All's Well that Ends Well
B) All That Glitters is Not Gold
C) Always Put your Best Foot Forward
D) An Apple a Day Keeps the Doctor Away
E) Don't bite the hand that feeds you

4

Read the phrase from line 6 in the box below.

| well...., as for that, |

Why did the Lion say in such a way?

A) he could not create another excuse immediately
B) he was worried other animals might be hungry too
C) he was so righteous to his behavior
D) he wanted to be fair to everyone
E) he was patient to tell the last reason

5

When the Lion said "Quarter me this Stag," (line 3), the other animals thought the Lion

A) was not hungry
B) considered the stag was not delicious
C) had no right to have all four parts
D) was spoiled
E) would divide the Stag equally with them

Questions 6-11 are based on the following passage.

Line
    Archaeology is the study of the past by looking for the remains and artifacts (historical things) left by the people who lived long ago. These remains can include old coins, tools, buildings, and garbage. Archaeologists, the people who study archaeology, use these remains to understand how people lived.
5   When archaeologists do fieldwork, they look for remains, often by digging deep in the ground. When things are found, or even when nothing is found, the results of the fieldwork are taken back to the place where the archaeologist's base is, maybe a university or museum.
    They record everything they found by writing down on paper or entering the information into a computer. As settlements change and grow, old buildings are often buried to make space for new
10 buildings. Ancient Rome, for example, is now up to 40 feet (12 metres) below the present city. This is why archaeological fieldwork is expensive and why it takes a long time.

6
The main function of paragraph 1 is to
A) compare the study of the present and the future
B) describe a well-known archaeological site
C) praise Ancient Rome's achievement
D) introduce what the archaeology is
E) see how people will live in the future.

7
The author's description of "Ancient Rome" (line 10) is to
A) show the importance of ancient Rome
B) tell why archeological work takes a long time
C) describe the elevation (height) of the city
D) show how old the Ancient Rome is
E) show how dirty archeological work is

8
Which of the following statements is true?
A) Archeologists carefully remove ancient garbage and destroy them
B) To protect the site, archeologists do not touch the area but use computers
C) All the discoveries must go to the museum first for recording purpose
D) Archeologists no longer use handwriting,
E) When nothing is discovered, archeologists move to another site immediately.

9
The tone of the passage is
A) informative
B) playful
C) persuasive
D) critical
E) anecdotal

"informative" means providing useful information. "Critical" means disproval. :Anecdotal" means personal short story

10

Read this statement from lines 3-4

> Archaeologists, the people who study archaeology, use these **remains** to understand how people lived.

In which sentence below does the word **remains** mean the same as in the sentence above?

A) Ancient people often **remained** in the same places where they were born.

B) Cindy **remains** silent when others are singing

C) Canned food **remained** unopened can last ten years.

D) The **remaining** five kids are sleeping now

E) After the bomb explosion the **remains** were taken by the FBI agent.

11

Which of the following items would the author most likely add to "These remains" (line 2)?

A) broken umbrella
B) old battery
C) a newspaper before WWII
D) diary
E) arrow spear made of stone

Questions 12-17 are based on the following passage.

Line

> Iceland is a little country far north in the cold sea. Men found <u>it</u> and went there to live more than a thousand years ago.
>
> During the warm season they used to fish and make fish-oil and hunt sea-birds and gather feathers and tend their sheep and make hay. But the winters were long and dark and cold.
>
> 5 Men and women and children stayed in the house and carded and spun and wove and knit.

12

The first sentence describes Iceland as

A) the country that has no summer
B) the coldest country in the world
C) the country located far south on earth
D) the country surrounded by the sea
E) the land covered with ice all year

13

Read the sentence from line 1 in the box below.

> Men found **it** and went there to live more than a thousand years ago

Based on the story, **it** refers to

A) Cold sea
B) Iceland
C) Fish
D) Fish oil
E) Seabird

14

The probable disadvantage of living in Iceland is

A) hunting seabirds
B) weaving garment
C) using fish oil
D) having long winters
E) tending sheep

15

Unlike the first paragraph (lines 1-2), second paragraph (lines 3-5) is primarily concerned with

A) seasonal routines and chores
B) geographical location
C) people's need to make fish-oil
D) people's desire to live in warmer seasons
E) people's tendency to stay in the house

16

The primary purpose of the passage is to show the

A) harsh living condition
B) history of Iceland
C) reliance on fish for living
D) basic understanding of living in Iceland
E) effective survival guide in cold weather

17

During winter, which of the followings would boys in Iceland probably do

A) sheep herding
B) fishing
C) hay drying
D) bird hunting
E) weaving clothes

Questions 18-23 are based on the following passage.

Line

    In the very beginning of all things, when the gods were creating the world, at last the time came to separate the earth from the heavens.

    This was hard work, and if it had not been for the coolness and skill of a young goddess all would have failed. This goddess was named Lu-o. She had been idly watching the growth of the
5 planet, when, to her horror, she saw the newly made **ball** slipping slowly from its place. In another second it would have shot down into the bottomless pit. Quick as a flash Lu-o stopped it with her magic wand and held it firmly until the chief god came dashing up to the rescue.

    But this was not all. When men and women were put on the earth Lu-o helped them greatly by setting an example of purity and kindness. After she had left the world and gone into the
10 land of the gods, beautiful statues of her were set up in many temples to keep her image always before the eyes of sinful people.

18

The word "ball" in line 5 refers to

A) the Sun
B) the Moon
C) the Earth
D) a playball
E) Lu-o

19

Read this statement from lines 4-7

> This goddess was...the rescue.

Lu-o's feeling in the above statement shifts from horror to

A) anger
B) excitement
C) sadness
D) relief
E) confusion

20

Read this statement from lines 8-9

> But this was not all. When men and women were put on the earth Lu-o helped them greatly by setting an example of purity and kindness.

Lu-o's character can be described as one of

A) pessimistic
B) godlike
C) mildly oppressive
D) sinful
E) innocent and generous

21

The main reason for setting up the statues (line 10) was to

A) provide a playground
B) warn sinners
C) display how beautiful she is
D) forgive sinners
E) remind people that she created the earth

22

Which of the following statements is true?

A) The earth and the heavens were once not separated.
B) Lu-o was the only human in heaven
C) Lu-o destroyed the earth
D) Once the earth was made of a ball
E) Men and women on the earth were all pure and kind

23

Which of the following words best describes the atmosphere of the story?

A) sad
B) fantastic
C) comical
D) surprising
E) witty

Questions 24-29 are based on the following passage.

Line   Once upon a time a Wolf was lapping at a spring on a hillside, when, looking up, what should he see but a Lamb just beginning to drink a little lower down. 'There's my supper,' thought he, 'if only I can find some excuse to seize it.' Then he called out to the Lamb, 'How dare you muddle the water from which I am drinking?' 'Nay, master, nay,' said
5   Lambikin; 'if the water be muddy up there, I cannot be the cause of it, for it runs down from you to me.' 'Well, then,' said the Wolf, 'why did you call me bad names this time last year?' 'That cannot be,' said the Lamb; 'I am only six months old.' 'I don't care,' snarled the Wolf; 'if it was not you it was your father;' and with that he rushed upon the poor little Lamb and WARRA WARRA WARRA WARRA WARRA ate her all up. But before she died she
10 gasped out. 'Any excuse' will serve a tyrant.

24
The Author characterizes that the Lamb
A) was greedy like the Wolf
B) showed sympathy to the Wolf
C) was deeply concerned by the Wolf's hardship
D) reasonably argued with the Wolf
E) essentially agreed with the Wolf's complaints

25
In line 3, the term **"seize"** refers to
A) cutting
B) persuading
C) stealing
D) killing
E) buying

26
Line 4 (How dare...I am drinking) shows that the Wolf wants to
A) build a friendship with the Lamb
B) make an excuse to kill the Lamb
C) ask for the reason for the Lamb's past misconduct
D) make a sincere apology to the Lamb
E) make a final warning not to contaminate water

27
"Any excuse" in line 10 reveals the
A) Lamb's innocent character
B) Wolf's wicked nature
C) Lamb's apologetic behavior
D) Wolf's guilt-ridden confession
E) strong friendship

28
Which of the followings best describes the Lamb's reaction?
A) She was impressed by the Wolf's speech
B) She understood that the Wolf has its own concern
C) She admitted his father's faults last year
D) She apologized for the wrong doings
E) She denied the Wolf's argument

29
The repetition of the capitalized words "WARRA" is intended to show
A) physical description
B) sound effect
C) traditional practice
D) visual exaggeration
E) first-hand information

Verbal Test 2
20 MINUTES, 30 QUESTIONS

Directions: the synonym questions ask you to find the most appropriate synonym to the question.

The analogy questions ask you to find the most appropriate analogy to the question. Select the answer that best matches to the question.

Synonyms

Each of the following questions consists of one word followed by five words or phrases. You are to select the one word or phrase whose meaning is closest to the word in capital letters.

Sample Question:

ABILITY

A) mistake
B) **talent**
C) abandon
D) best student
E) late

1. ABSORB

A) same
B) base
C) remove
D) sorrow
E) soak up

2. CHARM

A) charge
B) alarm
C) character
D) attraction
E) symptom

3. ACCUSE

A) excuse
B) inquiry
C) blame
D) information
E) praise

4. RARE

A) abound
B) plenty
C) nothing
D) few
E) great

5. SENSITIVE

A) emotional

B) sense

C) touch

D) feeling

E) Joy

6. RESPONSIBLE

A) answer

B) question

C) reliable

D) liable

E) doubtful

7. CLEVER

A) stupid

B) intelligent

C) diligent

D) friendly

E) clear

8. DOZE

A) nap

B) dozen

C) many

D) a few

E) activity

9. REVERSE

A) repeat

B) turn

C) very

D) sincere

E) version

10. VOLUNTEER

A) value

B) violin

C) cost

D) money

E) offer services

11. ORIGIN

A) base

B) advance

C) expensive

D) oral

E) old

12. MISERY

A) Mrs.

B) penny-pincher

C) Mr.

D) heartache

E) mistake

13. REVIVE

A) victory

B) repeat

C) restore

D) rend

E) respect

14. AMBITION

A) amble

B) vision

C) ample

D) desire

E) greed

15. PRIVILEGE

A) town

B) city

C) towners

D) special

E) before

Analogies

The following questions ask you to find relationships between words. For each question, select the answer choice that best completes the meaning of the sentence.

SAMPLE QUESTION
Q: River is to Ocean as:

A) better is to good

B) rain is to cloud

C) father is to mother

D) city is to country

E) fork is to spoon

This question is Degree Analogy question (small to big movement).

Ⓓ is the correct answer. Just as river is smaller than Ocean, so is city to the country.

Ⓐ is incorrect because the order is flipped over.

Ⓑ is incorrect because this is 'Production Analogy—what-produce-what.'

Ⓒ and Ⓔ are incorrect because there are no big and small relations between mother and father, so does fork to spoon.

16. Breeze is storm as bicycle is to

A) walk

B) run

C) car

D) bird

E) boy

17. Pen is to paint as

A) brush is to write

B) coin is to save

C) date is to calendar

D) computer is to laptop

E) mouse is to microphone

18. Autumn is to leaves as spring is to

A) mountain

B) river

C) wood

D) heart

E) sprout

19. Fish are to pack as

A) wolf is to lone

B) geese are to flock

C) rat is to smart

D) poppy is to cute

E) cat is to shy

20. Hat is to socks as head is to

A) fingers

B) toes

C) feet

D) arms

E) nose

21. Roof is to house as lid is to

A) coffee

B) juice

C) tea

D) candy

E) cup

22. Finger is to hand as

A) leave is to tree

B) girl is to boy

C) baby is to adult

D) bus is to engine

E) hand is to foot

23. Striker is to soccer as

A) hitter is baseball

B) male is to female

C) puck is to hockey

D) pitcher is to baseball

E) fan is to game

24. Bacon is to pig as milk is to

A) supermarket

B) drink

C) cow

D) mom

E) baby

25. Frog is to tadpole as
A) prince is to fairy tale
B) green is to color
C) lady is to girl
D) candy is to chocolate
E) dessert is to appetizer

26. Snow is to moon as
A) chicken is to egg
B) December is cold
C) white is to silver
D) black is to coal
E) green is to frog

27. Calculator is to add as boxer is to
A) subtract
B) calculate
C) math
D) solve
E) fight

28. Sunrise is to 7 am as sunset is to
A) 7:30 pm
B) beautiful
C) evening
D) west
E) fantastic

29. Printer is to print as **meal** is to
A) restaurant
B) wood
C) stove
D) water
E) direction

30. Car is to engine as **pedal** is to
A) bicycle
B) tire
C) handlebars
D) spokes
E) chain

SSAT ELEMENTARY LEVEL

Reading & Verbal Section

Test 2

Answer Explanations

The Pattern Analyses

ALL THE LOGIC AND RULES BEHIND EVERY SINGLE SSAT QUESTION

TEST 2
READING SECTION

Please refer to the Reading Section AP Analyses

SYNONYM QUESTIONS   ANALOGY QUESTIONS
TEST 2 NO.1 ~ 15   TEST 2 NO. 16 ~30
                    Please refer to the Reading Section AP Analyses

1   E
2   D
3   C
4   D
5   C
6   D
7   B
8   A
9   B
10 E
11 A
12 B
13 C
14 D
15 D

ANSWER EXPLANATIONS FOR TEST 2

Test 2 Absolute Patterns for the Reading Section

Questions 1-5 are based on the following passage.
   The Lion went once a-hunting along with the Fox, the Jackal, and the Wolf.
Then came the question how (Q3.) **the spoil should be divided.** 'Quarter me this Stag,' roared the Lion; **so the other animals cut it into four parts,** and as for the fourth quarter, (4.) **well..., as for that,** I should like to see which of you will dare to lay a paw upon it.' 'Humph,'
grumbled the Fox as he walked away with his tail between his legs; but he spoke in a low growl .
(Q1 & 2.& Q5.) **'You may share the labours of the great, but you will not share the spoil.'**

Q1. Question Pattern: The other three animals may **call the Lion** as a
AP 7: Inference Question   Find the indirect suggestion behind the sentence

---

- ■ **Question Keyword/Key phrase:** "call the Lion "
- ■ **Incorrect Pattern:** A) King of Beasts—DC   B) Judge—DC   C) Chaser—DC   D) Hunter—DC   **E) Cheater**
- ■ **What Does The Question Really Ask?** This question asks about the character description (personality) of the lion.
   Keep in mind that it asks about "the other three animals' point of view, not the Lion's.
- ■ **Reading Tip:** Focus on the last sentence to find the character personality either through the main keyword or tone.

E is the best answer. 'You may share the labours of the great, but you will not share the spoil.'
The above sentence reveals that the Lion cheated the other animals and their grudge against the Lion.
Incorrect Answer Explanation
All the remaining alternatives A, B, C, and D directly contradict the lion's personality depicted negatively in the story.
The Lion in the story may think of himself as a justifiable character, but the other animals would disagree.

Q2. Question Pattern: "the spoil" in line 3 most nearly means
AP 4: Word-In-Context Question   Find the clue words and keywords from the sentence

---

- ■ **Question Keyword/Key phrase:** "spoil"
- ■ **Incorrect Pattern:** A) unduly behavior—NI   **B) hunted animal**   C) useless animal—NI
   D) rotten animal—NI   E) skinned animal to eat—NI
- ■ **What Does The Question Really Ask?** A seemingly easy Word-in-Context question tends to play a trick. For an easy word in question, always read the sentence before choosing the answer.
   Apply the mirroring technique and find the clue words from the passage.

B is the best answer. "the spoil should be divided."
The sentence states how the spoil should be divided. The clue word "divided" implies that the word "spoil" refers to the hunted animal.
Incorrect Answer Explanation
Choice A is incorrect because the clue word "divided" implies the physical division of the word "spoil." Therefore, it couldn't be a behavior. The other alternatives are irrelevant to the word "spoil."

Q3. Question Pattern: The **lesson** from the passage can be described as
AP 5: Understanding the True Purpose Find the explicitly stated true purpose of the sentence

- **Question Keyword/Key phrase:** "lesson"
- **Incorrect Pattern:** A) All's Well that Ends Well—NI   B) All That Glitters is Not Gold—NI
  C) Always Put your Best Foot Forward—NI   D) An Apple a Day Keeps the Doctor Away—NI
  E) Don't bite the hand that feeds you
- **We Already Found the answer:** It's E. The answer was found before reading the passage.
- **What Does The Question Really Ask?** All the phrases in alternatives are composed of proverbs. It asks the most suitable proverb to the passage.
- **Reading Tip:** Focus on the last sentence because the keyword "lesson" in the question implies the "conclusion" of the passage.

E is the best answer. The last sentence describes the Lion's deceiving other animals that had been hunting together. The lion did not want to share the hunted animal. The main theme, therefore, is most clearly reflected in choice E "Don't bite the hand that feeds you" meaning that "don't hurt someone if he is helping you."

Incorrect Answer Explanation

Choice A) "All's Well that Ends Well" means that if the consequence is good, then the problems that come up in between do not really matter.

Choice B) "All That Glitters is Not Gold" means that anything which attracts you because of its external appearance may not be that worthwhile to use.

Choice C) "Always Put your Best Foot Forward" means that one must always try to give the best shot.

Choice D) "An Apple a Day Keeps the Doctor Away" means that in order to keep healthy, a healthy diet is required.

Q4. Question Pattern: Based on the story, **why did the Lion say** in such a way?
AP 7: Inference Question Find the indirect suggestion behind the sentence

- **Question Keyword/Key phrase:** "well…., as for that"
- **Incorrect Pattern: A) he could not create another excuse immediately**
  B) he was worried other animals might be hungry too—DC(TI)   C) he was so righteous to his behavior—DC
  D) he wanted to be fair to everyone—DC   E) he was patient to tell the last reason—DC
- **What Does The Question Really Ask?** The question asks why the lion hesitated before telling the last reason. Find the keyword that expresses the personality of the lion and within it the narrator's tone.
- **We Already Found the answer:** It's A. The answer was found before reading the passage.
- **Relevancy Check:** it is obvious, based on information from the previous questions, that the lion is depicted as a negative character. All the rest alternatives are definitely positive. Therefore, they are all incorrect.

A is the best answer. The Lion, went on to say "well....as for that" because it could not come up with any other excuse, so he paused for a moment to think of the last excuse.

Incorrect Answer Explanation

Choices B, C, and D contradict the story. The passage illustrates the Lion as a greedy cheater. Choice E contradicts the Lion's behavior. He was "impatient" to come up with an excuse.

ANSWER EXPLANATIONS FOR TEST 2

Q5. Question Pattern: When the Lion said "Quarter me this Stag," (line 3), **the other animals thought** the Lion
AP 7: Inference Question   Find the indirect suggestion behind the sentence

■ **Question Keyword/Key phrase:** "the other animals thought "
■ **Incorrect Pattern:** A) was not hungry—NI   B) considered the stag was not delicious—NI
   C) had no right to have all four parts—DC   D) was spoiled—IW   **E) would divide the Stag equally with them**
■ **What Does The Question Really Ask?** The question basically asks about the character personality.

E is the best answer. "'You may share the labours of the great, but you will not share the spoil."
When the Lion said "Quarter the Stag," the other animals divided it into four parts, believing they would have each part equally.

Incorrect Answer Explanation

Choices A and B are not stated in the passage. Choice C contradicts the story. The other animals didn't dare to think of the lion that way. Choice D is incorrect. The word "spoil" in the passage refers to the hunted animal, not the bad character of the lion.

Questions 6-11 are based on the following passage.

(Q6. & Q9) **Archaeology is the study of the past** by looking for the remains and artifacts (historical things) left by the people who lived long ago. (Q11) **These remains** can include old coins, tools, buildings, and garbage. Archaeologists, the people who study archaeology, use (Q10.) **these remains** to understand how people lived.

When archaeologists do fieldwork, they look for remains, often by digging deep in the ground. When things are found, or even when nothing is found, (Q8) **the results of the fieldwork are taken back to the place where the archaeologist's base is, maybe a university or museum.**

They record everything they found by writing down on paper or entering the information into a computer. As settlements change and grow, old buildings are often buried to make space for new buildings. Ancient Rome, for example, is now up to 40 feet below the present city. (Q7) **This is why archaeological fieldwork is expensive and why it takes a long time.**

Q6. Question Pattern: The **main function** of paragraph 1 is to
AP 10: Structural Pattern of the Passage   Find the structural pattern of the paragraph or the entire passage

■ **Question Keyword/Key phrase:** "function"
■ **Incorrect Pattern:** A) compare the study of the present and the future—NI
   B) describe a well-known archaeological place—IS   C) praise Ancient Rome's achievement—IW
   D) introduce what the archaeology is   E) understand how people will live in the future—NI
■ **What Does The Question Really Ask?** Keep an eye on the key phrase "the main function." In other words, it does not ask the content of the paragraph. For instance, the main function of automobile is to drive. Descriptions of the car such as yellow, long, expensive, heavy are content, not the function of the car. The question illustrates how important it is to understand correctly the question pattern.
■ **Reading Tip:** 1st paragraph

D is the best answer. The function of the first paragraph is always to introduce the passage. The first sentence starting with "Archeology is the study...." introduces what the archeology is. Thus, paragraph 1 functions as the introduction of the passage about archaeology.

Incorrect Answer Explanation

Choices A and E are incorrect because archeology is the study of ancient times, not of the present nor of the future. Choices B and C are incorrect because they are—irrespective of whether true or false statement—content of the passage. As explained, the phrases describing content of the passage cannot be the answer for the function question.

Q7. Question Pattern: The author's description of **"Ancient Rome" in line 11** is to show
AP 3: Example Question The reason for using the example sentences

- ■ **Question Keyword/Key phrase:** "Ancient Rome"
- ■ **Incorrect Pattern:** A) the importance of Ancient Rome—NI(GE)   B) why archeological work takes a long time
  C) the elevation (height) of the city—IW   D) how old the Ancient Rome is—NI(GE)
  E) how dirty archeological work is—DC(TI)
- ■ **What Does The Question Really Ask?** "Ancient Rome" is an example of the passage. We know this because the passage focuses on archeology, not on Ancient Rome. From this perspective, we should eliminate the incorrect answers that focus on the Ancient Rome.
- ■ **Reading Tip:** The answer for the example type of question is usually found right above or below the example sentence where the main idea for that example sentence is located.
- ■ **Relevancy Check:** Choices A and D are called "generalization." Generalization refers to the phrase that is generally true and therefore seems to be correct in any situation. Generalization, however, does not directly answer the question. Therefore, they cannot be the correct answer. We can frequently identify the generalization through a common sense, not through the passage reading. Choice C, just as choice A and D, focuses on the Ancient Rome, therefore, incorrect.

B is the best answer. "This is why archaeological fieldwork is expensive and why it <u>takes a long time</u>." The author explains, right after referring to the Ancient Rome, how expensive and time consuming archeological fieldworks are.

Incorrect Answer Explanation

Choice C is incorrect because, although "40 feet" is stated in the passage, It only supports the description about Rome, therefore is not the main purpose. Choice E "dirty" is negative tone. The author's tone about archeology is neutral.

Q8. Question Pattern: Which of the following **statements is true**?
AP 2: Summery Question Summarize the sentence or the entire paragraph

- ■ **Question Keyword/Key phrase:** "true"
- ■ **Incorrect Pattern:** A) Archeologists carefully remove Ancient garbage and destroy from the artifacts-DC
  B) To protect the site, archeologists do not touch the area but use computers—DC
  C) All the discoveries must go to the museum first for recording purpose
  D) Archeologists no longer use handwriting, but use computer system—DC
  E) When nothing is discovered, archeologists move to another site immediately—DC
- ■ **What Does The Question Really Ask?** The question asks about the overall understanding of the passage.
- ■ **Relevancy Check:** Choice D is absurd. We can eliminate it through common sense.

ANSWER EXPLANATIONS FOR TEST 2

C is the best answer. The passage clearly states that the results are taken to the museum to record everything they found.

Incorrect Answer Explanation

All other alternatives contradict the passage. Choice A is incorrect because even ancient garbage is artifacts to be preserved. They therefore shouldn't be destroyed. Choices B, D and E contradict the passage: Choice B "often by digging deep in the ground…" D) "by writing down on paper…" E) "move to another site." clearly contradict the passage descriptions.

Q9. Question Pattern: The **tone** of the passage is

AP 8: Understanding Attitude (Tone) Find the tonality: positive vs. negative, mental vs. physical

- ■ **Question Keyword/Key phrase:** "tone"
- ■ **Incorrect Pattern:** A) informative   B) playful—NI   C) persuasive—NI   D) critical—NI   E) anecdotal—NI
- ■ **We Already Found the answer:** It's A. The answer was found before reading the passage.
- ■ **What Does The Question Really Ask?** The passage describes "archeology," which is science genre, therefore it should be informative.
- ■ **Relevancy Check:** Choices B and E are incorrect because archeology is science that can't be written in playful or anecdotal tone.

A is the best answer. This passage briefly describes archaeology. We call it the informative passage.

Incorrect Answer Explanation

Choices C and D are incorrect because the author does not persuade the readers nor criticizes anything.
Choice E is incorrect. The word "anecdotal" means a personal short story which cannot represent the scientific passage

---

Q10. Question Pattern: In which sentence below does the word **remains mean the same as** in the sentence below?

AP 4: Word-In-Context Question   Find the clue words and keywords from the sentence

*Archaeologists, the people who study archaeology, use these **remains** to understand how people lived.*
- ■ **Question Keyword/Key phrase:** "remains"
- ■ **Incorrect Pattern:** A) Ancient people often remained in the same places where they were born—NI
    B) Cindy remains silent when others are singing—NI   C) Canned food remained unopened can last ten years—NI
    D) The remaining five kids are sleeping now—NI
    E) After the bomb explosion the remains were taken by the FBI agent
- ■ **We Already Found the answer:** It's E. The answer was found before reading the passage.
- ■ **What Does The Question Really Ask?** The word "remains" was used as a noun.
- ■ **Relevancy Check:** Choices A and B use the word "remain" as a verb. Choices C and D are used as an adjective.

E is the best answer. The "remains" in the passage is used as a noun meaning whatever leftover.

Q11. Question Pattern: Which items would the author most likely **add to "These remains"** (line 2)?

AP 3: Example Question   The reason for using the example sentences

---

SSAT ABSOLUTE PATTERNS

- ■ **Question Keyword/Key phrase:** "remains"
- ■ **Incorrect Pattern:** A) broken umbrella—NI   B) old battery—NI   C) a newspaper before WWII—NI
  D) diary—NI   **E) arrow spear made of stone**
- ■ **We Already Found the answer:** It's E. The answer was found before reading the passage.
- ■ **What Does The Question Really Ask?** Find the item that belongs to the Ancient times.
- ■ **Relevancy Check:** All the rest items in the alternatives are modern objects.

E is the best answer.   Only choice E 'arrow spear' belongs to the Ancient period.

Questions 12-17 are based on the following passage.

(Q16) **Iceland is a little country far north** (Q12) **in the cold sea**. Men found **it** and (Q13) **went there** to live more than a thousand years ago. (Q9 &Q15) **During the warm season they used to fish and make fish-oil and hunt sea-birds and gather feathers and tend their sheep and make hay.** (Q14) **But the winters were long** and dark and cold. (Q17) **Men and women and children stayed in the house and** carded and spun and wove and knit.

Q12. **Question Pattern:** The **first sentence** describes Iceland as
AP 2: Summery Question   Summarize the sentence or the entire paragraph .

- ■ **Question Keyword/Key phrase:** "first sentence"
- ■ **Incorrect Pattern:** A) the country that has no summer—DC   B) the coldest country in the world—NI
  C) the country located far south on earth—DC   **D) the country surrounded by the sea**
  E) the land covered with ice all year—IW
- ■ **Relevancy Check:** Choice C can be eliminated through a common sense. "far south on earth" refers to the hot region

D is the best answer.   The passage states it is in the cold sea. In other words, it is surrounded by the sea.
Choice A contradicts the passage that states "During the warm season." Choices B and E are probable but unknown information.

Q13. **Question Pattern:** Based on the story, **it** refers to
AP 2: Summery Question   Summarize the sentence or the entire paragraph

- ■ **Question Keyword/Key phrase:** "it"
- ■ **Incorrect Pattern:** A) Cold sea—IW   **B) Iceland**   C) Fish—IW   D) Fish oil—IW   E) Seabird—IW
- ■ **We Already Found the answer:** It's B. The answer was found before reading the passage.
- ■ **What Does The Question Really Ask?** The question asks what "it" in the sentence refers to. This type of question, called the "amplifier," frequently appears on the tests. The amplifier questions pinpoints out the most meaningful (or important) keyword within the phrase and convert it into a pronoun such as "it" or "this" or "these." In amplifier question, words written far away from the pronoun—"it" in this question—rarely becomes the answer.
- ■ **Reading Tip:** The answer is normally located at the previous sentence of the pronoun (the amplifier).

B is the best answer.   Men found **it** and *went there* to live more than a thousand years ago.
"went there" refers to Iceland.   All the rest incorrect answers do not refer to "it" or the "Iceland."

ANSWER EXPLANATIONS FOR TEST 2

Q14. Question Pattern: The probable **disadvantage of living in** Iceland is
AP 2: Summery Question   Summarize the sentence or the entire paragraph

- **■ Question Keyword/Key phrase:** "disadvantage"
- **■ Incorrect Pattern:** A) hunting seabirds—DC   B) weaving garment—DC   C) using fish oil—DC
  D) having long winters   E) tending sheep —DC
- **■ We Already Found the answer:** It's D. The answer was found before reading the passage.
- **■ What Does The Question Really Ask?** The question keyword "disadvantage" hints that the answer should be negative.
- **■ Reading Tip:** Keep an eye on the conjunction "but" from the passage because it always gives an important clue, if not the answer. In most Reading questions, contradictory conjunction such as "But" plays an important role. Test creators create many logical questions using the contradicting conjunctions.
- **■ Relevancy Check:** All the rest incorrect answers can be eliminated through common sense. For they are obviously advantages in the cold place like Iceland.

D is the best answer. The "But" phrase starts with negative "But the winters were long and dark and cold."

Q15. Question Pattern: Unlike the first paragraph (lines 1-2), **second paragraph** (lines 3-5) is primarily concerned with
AP 7: Inference Question   Find the indirect suggestion behind the sentence

- **■ Question Keyword/Key phrase:** "second paragraph"
- **■ Incorrect Pattern: A) seasonal routines and chores**   B) geographical location—IW
  C) people's need to make fish-oil—IS   D) people's desire to live in warmer seasons—NI
  E) people's tendency to stay in the house—IS
- **■ What Does The Question Really Ask?** In the question the phrase "Unlike the first paragraph" is a bait. Many students, by a pure mistake, almost knowingly pick the wrong choice that belongs to paragraph 1. Test creators seem to encourage students to make such a mistake. To prevent it, always use a pencil and cross out irrelevant information.
- **■ Relevancy Check:** Choice D uses a generalization, which sounds appropriate in common sense. It, however, is not at all stated in the passage, therefore incorrect.

A is the best answer. "During the warm season...But the winters"
The second paragraph mainly describes seasonal routines and chores.

Incorrect Answer Explanation

Choice B is true statement but belongs to the first paragraph. Choices C and E are Insufficient Information. For they are only the examples, not the primary concerns. Choice D is incorrect because the passage didn't mention people's desire to live in warmer seasons.

Q16. Question Pattern: The primary purpose of the passage is to show the
AP 5: Understanding the True Purpose   Find the explicitly stated true purpose of the sentence

SSAT ABSOLUTE PATTERNS

- ■ **Question Keyword/Key phrase:** "primary purpose"
- ■ **Incorrect Pattern:**   A) harsh living condition—IS   B) history of Iceland—NI   C) reliance on fish for living—IS
   D) basic understanding of living in Iceland   E) effective survival guide in a cold weather—NI
- ■ **What Does The Question Really Ask?** The primary purpose question requires a through understanding of the passage. To do that, find the key phrases and the main tone of the passage.
- ■ **Relevancy Check:** The answer to the primary purpose question usually uses a broad term and the keyword—Iceland in this passage—that represents the entire passage. It also does not rely on detailed information such as choices A and C. Choice E, while having no keyword "Iceland," relies on a general statement therefore incorrect.

D is the best answer.   The passage is about Iceland. And It briefly introduces inhabitants' living in Iceland.

Incorrect Answer Explanation

Choices A and C are examples stated in the passage. That is, they support the primary purpose of the passage, not by themselves the primary purpose. Choice B is not stated in the passage.

Q17. Question Pattern: During winter, which of the followings would boys in Iceland probably do
AP 7: Inference Question   Find the indirect suggestion behind the sentence

- ■ **Question Keyword/Key phrase:** "During winter, boys"
- ■ **Incorrect Pattern:** A) sheep herding—DC   B) fishing—DC   C) hay drying—DC   D) bird hunting—DC
   E) weaving clothes
- ■ **We Already Found the answer:** It's E. The answer was found before reading the passage.
- ■ **What Does The Question Really Ask?** The question asks about the indoor activities boys can do during winter.
- ■ **Relevancy Check:** All the other incorrect answers are outdoor activities during the warmer-seasons.

E is the best answer.   **But the winters** were long and dark and cold. Men and women and children stayed in the house and carded and spun and **wove and knit.**

Questions 18-23 are based on the following passage.
   In the very beginning of all things, when the (Q23) **gods** were creating the world, (Q22) **at last the time came to separate the earth from the heavens.**
   This was hard work, and if it had not been for the coolness and skill of a young goddess all would have failed. This goddess was named Lu-o. (Q18) **She had been idly watching the growth of the planet, when, to her horror, she saw the newly made ball** slipping slowly from its place. In another second it would have shot down into the bottomless pit. (Q19) **Quick as a flash Lu-o stopped it with her magic wand and held it firmly until the chief god came dashing up to the rescue.**
   But this was not all. When men and women were put on the earth Lu-o helped them greatly by setting an example of (Q20) **purity and kindness**. Every one loved her and pointed her out as the one who was always willing to do a good deed. After she had left the world and gone into the land of the gods, **beautiful statues of her** were set up in many temples to keep her image always (Q21) **before the eyes of sinful people.** The greatest of these was in the capital city. Thus, when sorrowful women wished to offer up their prayers to some virtuous goddess they would go to a temple of Lu-o and pour out their broken hearts in life journey before her shrine.

Q18. Question Pattern: The word **"ball" in line 5** refers to
AP 4: Word-In-Context Question   Find the clue words and keywords from the sentence

ANSWER EXPLANATIONS FOR TEST 2

- ■ **Question Keyword/Key phrase:** "ball"
- ■ **Incorrect Pattern:** A) the Sun—IW   B) the Moon—IW   **C) the Earth**   D) a playball—IW   E) Lu-o—IW
- ■ **Reading Tip:** Compared to the primary purpose question that requires the overall understanding of the passage, this type asks specific word stated in the passage. The answer is usually found not far from the question sentence.

C is the best answer. "She had been idly watching the **growth of the planet,** when, to her horror, she saw the newly made **ball**..." The ball refers to the planet earth.
All the rest are irrelevant information used meaningful words from the passage but not related with the question.

Q19. Question Pattern: Lu-o's feeling in the above statement shifts **from horror to**
AP 8: Understanding Attitude (Tone) Find the tonality: positive vs. negative, mental vs. physical

- ■ **Question Keyword/Key phrase:** "This goddess was...the rescue."
- ■ **Incorrect Pattern:** A) anger—EX   B) excitement—EX   C) sadness—DC   **D) relief**   E) confusion—DC(TI)
- ■ **What Does The Question Really Ask?** The technique called "focus shift" relies on tonality change. A character's emotion may change in the passage. Find from the passage the most meaningful keyword that represents "horror" that eventually leads to focus shift.
- ■ **Relevancy Check:** Choice A is incorrect because "anger" is too far extreme to be the overall theme of the passage.

D is the best answer. Quick as a flash Lu-o stopped it with her magic wand and held it firmly until the chief god came dashing up to the **rescue.**
Lui-o felt horror when she saw the ball (the earth) was slipping away, then was relieved when the chief god rescued.

Incorrect Answer Explanation

Choice B is extreme. Relief from peril does not create any excitement.
Choices A, C, and E are negative words; therefore, can't be the answer in this situation.

Q20. Question Pattern: Lu-o's character can be described as one of
AP 8: Understanding **Attitude (Tone)** Find the tonality: positive vs. negative, mental vs. physical

"But this was not all. When men and women were put on the earth Lu-o helped them greatly by setting an example of purity and kindness."
- ■ **Question Keyword/Key phrase:** "purity and kindness"
- ■ **Incorrect Pattern:**   A) pessimistic—DC(TI)   B) godlike—DC   C) mildly oppressive—DC(TI)
  D) sinful—DC(TI)   **E) innocent and generous**
- ■ **We Already Found the answer:** It's E. The answer was found before reading the passage.
- ■ **What Does The Question Really Ask?** The question asks Lu-O's personality.
- ■ **Relevancy Check:** Lu-o represents the goddess in the passage, and therefore, should be the positive character. Choices A, C, and D are negative words. Choice B is incorrect because she is goddess.

E is the best answer. The following sentence "Every one loved her...good deed." explicitly states Lu-o's positive character. The words "purity" and "kindness" in the passage are used in the answer as E) "innocent," and "generous."

Q21. Question Pattern: The main **reason for setting up the statues** (line 13) was to
AP 7: Inference Question Find the indirect suggestion behind the sentence

SSAT ABSOLUTE PATTERNS   148

- **Question Keyword/Key phrase:** "statues"
- **Incorrect Pattern:** A) provide a playground—EX **B) warn sinners** C) display how beautiful she is—NI(GE)
  D) forgive sinners—IW E) remind people that she created the earth—IW
- **Relevancy Check:** Choice A sounds absurd compared to other alternatives. Choice C relies on the general statement not stated in the passage. We can cancel these two through common sense.

B is the best answer. "to keep her image always before the eyes of sinful people."
The above phrase clearly suggests the reason for setting up her statues: It was built to warn sinners.

Incorrect Answer Explanation

Choice C is incorrect because the passage uses the word "beautiful" to describe the statues, not Lu-o herself.
Choice D is not stated in the passage. Choice E is incorrect because the question "statues" and the creation of the earth are two different issues. That is, choice E has merely used some meaningful words from the passage unrelated to the question.

Q22. Question Pattern: Which of the following **statements is true**?
AP 2: Summery Question Summarize the sentence or the entire paragraph

- **Question Keyword/Key phrase:** "true"
- **Incorrect Pattern: A) The earth and the heavens were once not separated**
  B) Lu-o was the only human in heaven—DC C) Lu-o destroyed the earth—DC
  D) Once the earth was made of a ball—IW E) Men and women on the earth were all pure and kind-IW
- **Relevancy Check:** Choices B and C can be easily eliminated through information obtained from the previous questions. We have learned that Lu-O was a goddess. And she saved the earth.

A is the best answer. The passage tells that "the gods at last separated the earth from the heavens," which implies that the earth and heavens were once not separated. Choices B, C, and E are incorrect for the following reasons: Lu-o was B) goddess, who (C) saved the earth, and (E) was pure and kind.
Choice D is incorrect. It uses the word "ball" too literally. The passage describes the earth as a ball.

Q23. Question Pattern: Which of the following words best describes **the atmosphere of the story**?
AP 8: Understanding Attitude (Tone) Find the tonality: positive vs. negative, mental vs. physical

- **Question Keyword/Key phrase:** "atmosphere of the story"
- **Incorrect Pattern:** A) sad—IS **B) fantastic** C) comical—NI D) surprising—IS E) witty—NI
- **We Already Found the answer:** It's B. The answer was found before reading the passage.
- **What Does The Question Really Ask?** The question asks about the atmosphere (the overall mood) of the story.
- **Reading Tip:** The story about 'gods" and "goddess" is literally "fantastic."
- **Relevancy Check:** Incorrect answers may contain true but incomplete statement. For example, choices A and D are true but incomplete because "sad" and "surprising" represent Lu-o's emotion when she saw the earth slipping away. However, these two words do not represent the entire passage. Therefore, they are true, but incomplete, not representing the entire atmosphere of the story. Choices C and E are irrelevant words to the story.

B is the best answer. The story is not real, but filled with fantasy. Or, we can call it "fantastic."

ANSWER EXPLANATIONS FOR TEST 2

Questions 24-29 are based on the following passage.

Once upon a time a Wolf was lapping at a spring on a hillside, when, looking up, what should he see but a Lamb just beginning to drink a little lower down. (Q25) **'There's my supper,'** thought he, 'if only I can find some excuse to <u>seize</u> it.' Then he called out to the Lamb, (Q26) **'How dare you muddle the water from which I am drinking?'** 'Nay, master, nay,' said Lambikin; 'if the water be muddy up there, I cannot be the cause of it, for it runs down from you to me.' 'Well, then,' said the Wolf, 'why did you call me bad names this time last year?' (Q24. & Q28) **"That cannot be,' said the Lamb**; 'I am only six months old.' 'I don't care,' snarled the Wolf; 'if it was not you it was your father;' and with that he rushed upon the poor little Lamb and (Q29) **WARRA WARRA WARRA WARRA WARRA** ate her all up. But before she died she gasped out. (Q27) **'Any excuse will serve a tyrant.**

Q24. Question Pattern: The author characterizes that the Lamb
AP 8: Understanding Attitude (Tone) Find the tonality: positive vs. negative, mental vs. physical

---

- **Question Keyword/Key phrase:** "characterizes, lamb"
- **Incorrect Pattern:** A) was greedy like the Wolf—DC   B) showed sympathy to the Wolf—DC
   C) was deeply concerned by the Wolf's hardship—DC   **D) reasonably argued with the wolf**
   E) essentially agreed with the Wolf's complaints—DC
- **What Does The Question Really Ask?** The question asks about the lamb's attitude.
- **Reading Tip:** Find the key speech made by the Lamb and with it its tone.
- **Relevancy Check:** Choice A can be solved through common sense. For being "greedy" refers to the wolf's character, not the lamb.

D is the best answer.   "That cannot be,' said the Lamb."
As stated above, the author characterizes the Lamb as a smart one, reasonably arguing against the predator Wolf.
All the other choices contradict the Lamb's character who is in peril.

Q25. Question Pattern: In line 3, the term **"seize"** refers to
AP 4: Word-In-Context Question   Find the clue words and keywords from the sentence

---

- **Question Keyword/Key phrase:** "seize"
- **Incorrect Pattern:** A) cutting—NI   B) persuading—DC   C) stealing—NI   **D) killing**   E) buying—DC
- **We Already Found the answer:** It's D. The answer was found before reading the passage.
- **What Does The Question Really Ask?** The word-in-Context can be either figurative or literal. Here the word "seize" definitely represents the Wolf's vicious characteristic.
- **Relevancy Check:** Choice B contradicts the original meaning of "seize"

D is the best answer.   The wolf says "that's my supper. if only I can find some excuse to seize it."
As stated above, the wolf saw the lamb as his supper. "seize," with the clue word "my supper," must be understood as "killing" Other alternatives such as "cutting" (lamb) or "stealing" (lamb) do not make sense.
.

SSAT ABSOLUTE PATTERNS

Q26. Question Pattern: Line 4 (**How dare...I am drinking**) shows that the wolf wants to
AP 5: Understanding the True Purpose Find the explicitly stated true purpose of the sentence

- ■ **Question Keyword/Key phrase:** "How dare...I am drinking"
- ■ **Incorrect Pattern:** A) build a friendship with the Lamb—DC   **B) make an excuse to kill the Lamb**
  C) ask for the reason for the Lamb's past misconduct—DC   D) make an sincere apology to the Lamb—DC
  E) make a final warning not to contaminate water—DC
- ■ **We Already Found the answer:** It's B. The answer was found before reading the passage.
- ■ **What Does The Question Really Ask?** As seen from the previous questions, the Wolf's false accusation actually didn't happen. The Lamb did not contaminate the water.
- ■ **Relevancy Check:** Choices A, C and D are positive tone that contradict the Wolf's character described in the story.

B is the best answer. Line 4 shows the debate between the wolf and the lamb wherein the wolf is making an excuse to kill the Lamb. Only choice B contains the negative tone.
Choice E is incorrect. The muddy water is only a made-up story by the wolf in order to kill the lamb.

Q27. Question Pattern: "**Any excuse**" in line 10 reveals the
AP 7: Inference Question Find the indirect suggestion behind the sentence

- ■ **Question Keyword/Key phrase:** "any excuse"
- ■ **Incorrect Pattern:** A) Lamb's innocent character—DC   **B) Wolf's wicked nature**
  C) Lamb's apologetic behavior—DC   D) Wolf's guilt-ridden confession—DC   E) strong friendship—DC
- ■ **What Does The Question Really Ask?** The last sentence—which normally summarizes the story—clarifies the tonality of the main characters that leads to the answer.
- ■ **Relevancy Check:** Choice A, C, and E are incorrect. The word in the last sentence "excuse" is pointing at the wolf, not the lamb. Therefore, the answer must be centered on the Wolf. Thus, choices A and C must be eliminated. Choices D and E contradict the wicked nature of the wolf.

B is the best answer. The "excuse" is seen as the Wolf's wicked instinct.

Q28. Question Pattern: Which of the followings best describes **the Lamb's reaction?**
AP 9: Relationships Question Find the relationship between cause and effect, between characters

- ■ **Question Keyword/Key phrase:** "reaction"
- ■ **Incorrect Pattern:** A) She was impressed by the Wolf's speech—DC
  B) She understood that the Wolf has its own concern —NI   C) She admitted his father's faults last year—DC
  D) She apologized for the wrong doings—DC   **E) She denied the Wolf's accusation**
- ■ **We Already Found the answer:** It's E. The answer was found before reading the passage.
- ■ **What Does The Question Really Ask?** This question asks the same response as seen in the Q24.
- ■ **Relevancy Check:** The Lamb, throughout the passage, tried to fight against the false accusation from the wolf. Therefore, choices A, B, C and D with the positive tone are all incorrect.

E is the best answer. "I cannot be the cause of it" "That cannot be,' said the Lamb;"
The Lamb reasonably denied the Wolf's accusation.

ANSWER EXPLANATIONS FOR TEST 2

> **Q29. Question Pattern:** The repetition of the capitalized words "WARRA" is intended to suggest
>
> **AP 5:** Understanding **the True Purpose** Find the explicitly stated true purpose of the sentence

- ■ **Question Keyword/Key phrase:** "capitalized word "
- ■ **Incorrect Pattern:** A) physical description— NI   **B) sound effect**   C) traditional practice— NI
  D) visual exaggeration— NI   E) first-hand information— NI
- ■ **We Already Found the answer:** It's B. The answer was found before reading the passage.
- ■ **What Does The Question Really Ask?** The question asks for the function of the capitalized words.
- ■ **Relevancy Check:** "WARRA," an onomatopoeia, creates sound effect and therefore it is not A) physical description or D) visual exaggeration. Nor does it show C) tradition or E) first-hand information.

B is the best answer.   The repetition of capitalized word "WARRA" is onomatopoeia (sound similarity) exaggerating the moment of the wolf swallowing the lamb.

Test 2 ABSOLUTE PATTERNS for the analogy Section

AP1. Category Pattern   Find the Part and Whole Relation, the Same Type or Association

16. Breeze is storm as bicycle is to   A) walk   B) run   **C) car**   D) bird   E) boy

C is the best answer. The question-stem quite frequently has more than one pattern. This question, for instance, can be understood as the Degree pattern. 'Breeze' is weaker than 'storm' and 'bicycle' is slower than 'car.' However, it can also be understood as the category pattern as 'breeze' and 'storm' belong to the same weather category just as both 'bicycle' and 'car' belong to the same vehicle category.
Choice A, if considered the Degree Pattern, has flipped over the primary word to the secondary word. For walk is slower than bicycle. Choice B, same as choice A, is a relevant word only to "bicycle" but not to the entire question-stem. Choices D and E are Irrelevant words.

AP3. Purpose (Tool) Pattern   Finding Relationships between the Purpose of Individual

17. Pen is to paint as

A) brush is to write   B) coin is to save   C) date is to calendar   D) computer is to laptop   E) mouse is to microphone

A is the best answer. The purpose of pen is to write as the purpose of brush is to paint. In respect to their writing and drawing functionality, both "pen" and "brush" are conceptual synonym.
Choice B is not related to the question-stem. Choice C applies the purpose pattern. However, its purpose is not as close as that of "pen" and "brush." Choice D is the Synonym Pattern. Choice E is irrelevant word to the question.

AP8. Production Pattern   Find What Produces What and the Cause and Effect Relation

18. Autumn is to leaves as spring is to   A) mountain   B) river   C) wood   D) heart   **E) sprout**

E is the best answer. Autumn produces (falling) leaves as the spring produces (E) sprout
Choices A and C are associated with "leaves," the secondary word in the question stem but not with the entire question-stem. Choices B and D are Irrelevant words to the question-stem.

AP1. Category Pattern   Find the Part and Whole Relation, the Same Type or Association

19. Fish are to pack as   A) wolf is to lone   **B) geese are to flock**   C) rat is to smart   D) poppy is to cute   E) cat is to shy

B is the best answer. Fish are grouped in a pack; geese are grouped in a flock. The question-stem and choice B are group animals. Choice A is the Mental (Emotion) Pattern. Choices C, D, and E are the Subjective-Objective Pattern

AP3. Purpose (Tool) Pattern   Finding Relationships between the Purpose of Individual

20. Hat is to socks as head to   A) fingers   B) toes   **C) feet**   D) arms   E) nose

C is the best answer. Hat is used to head; socks are used to feet.
Choices A, B, D, and E are associated with "head." For all of them are parts of body. But they are not associated with "Hat" or 'socks' In other words, they are not entirely associated with the question-stem.

ANSWER EXPLANATIONS FOR TEST 2

AP3. Purpose (Tool) Pattern Finding Relationships between the Purpose of Individual

21. Roof is to house as lid is to   A) coffee   B) juice   C) tea   D) candy   **E) cup**

E is the best answer. A Roof covers up the house as a lid covers up the cup.
Choices A, B, and C are associated with choice E "cup," but not with the entire question-stem. Choice D is Irrelevant word.

AP1. Category Pattern Find the Part and Whole Relation, the Same Type or Association

22. Finger is to hand as

A) leave is to tree   B) girl is to boy   C) baby is to adult   D) bus is to engine   E) hand is to foot

A is the best answer. Finger is part of hand as leave is part of a tree. Choices B, C, and E are the antonym Pattern. Choice D is part-whole relation but its words order is flipped over.

AP4. Characteristic Pattern Find the Characteristic of Person, Place, Object, or Idea

23. Striker is to soccer as

A) hitter is baseball   B) male is to female   C) puck is to hockey   D) pitcher is to baseball   E) fan is to game

A is the best answer. Both striker in the soccer and hitter in the baseball share the same position in each of his/her sport; they attack the opponents. Choice B is the antonym Pattern. Choice C is a part-whole relation, choice E is the Category Pattern. Choice D is incorrect because "pitcher" defends, not attacks.

AP8. Production Pattern Find What Produces What and the Cause and Effect Relation

24. Bacon is to pig as milk is to   A) supermarket   B) drink   **C) cow**   D) mom   E) baby

C is the best answer.   Pig produces bacon as cow produces milk.
Choice A is associated with 'bacon' and 'milk' but not with the entire question-stem. That is, "supermarket" cannot be related to "pig." Choices B, D, and E are associated with "milk" but not with the entire question-stem.

AP5. Degree Pattern Find the Degree (Increase or Decrease), Find the Shape of place or thing

25. Frog is to tadpole as

A) prince is to fairy tale   B) green is to color   **C) lady is to girl**   D) candy is to chocolate   E) dessert is to appetizer

C is the best answer. Tadpole becomes frog as a girl becomes a lady. Choice A is associated with "frog" but not with the entire question-stem.   Choice B uses the part-whole relation in the Category Pattern. Choice E is the antonym pattern.

AP4. Characteristic Pattern Find the Characteristic of Person, Place, Object, or Idea

26. Snow is to moon as

A) chicken is to egg   B) December is to cold   **C) white is to silver**   D) black is to coal   E) green is to frog

C is the best answer. The question-stem and choice C express the representative colors of each object. Snow is white as (C) moon is silver. Only with choice C the question-stem can be completed.
Choice A is Production Pattern. Choice B is associated with "snow" but not with "moon." Therefore it is not associated with the question-stem. Choices D and E are incorrect because they cannot complete the question-stem.

AP3. Purpose (Tool) Pattern Find the Purpose of Individual and the Goal, the Function of Tool

27. Calculator is to add as boxer is to   A) subtract   B) calculate   C) math   D) solve   **E) fight**

E is the best answer. The purpose of calculator is, among many, to add as the purpose of boxer is to fight.
The rest are associated with "calculator" but not with 'boxer." Therefore, they do not follow the entire question-stem.

AP 11. Subjective vs. Objective Pattern   Find the Quality vs. Quantity, Tangible vs. Intangible Concept

28. Sunrise is to 7 am as sunset is to   **A) 7:30 pm**   B) beautiful   C) evening   D) west   E) fantastic

A is the best answer. the question-stem "Sunrise is to 7 am" contains number. The answer therefore should also contain number as does in A) "7:30pm." We call this a "quantifier." The quantifier uses specific numbers such as kilograms, year, amount of money, distance, and so on.
The other choices, as you may have noticed already, are not using any numbers. Therefore, they are not quantifiers. Choice B and E are subjective, and choice C and D use objective terms referring "sunset."

AP 3. Purpose (Tool) Pattern   Find the Purpose of Individual and the Goal, the Function of Tool

29. Printer is to print as meal is to   A) restaurant   B) wood   **C) stove**   D) water   E) direction

C is the best answer. The purpose of Printer is to print as the purpose of stove is to cook meal.
Both 'printer' and 'stove' are used as tools. Choice A is incorrect. 'restaurant' is not a tool. Some students may say that just as the purpose of the printer is to print, and so too is the purpose of restaurant to serve meals. Albeit true, the functional similarity between 'printer' and 'stove' is much more close than of between 'printer' and 'restaurant.' That is, 'restaurant' is a place not a tool. Choice B is associated with "meal" in a sense that 'wood' can be a tool to cook meals. However, wood is not as close as that 'stove' is close to 'printer.' Choice D is associated with "meal" not with the entire question-stem. Choice E is an Irrelevant word.

AP1. Category Pattern Find the Part and Whole Relation, the Same Type or Association

30. Car is to engine as pedal is to   **A) bicycle** B) tire   C) handlebars   D) spokes   E) chain

A is the best answer. Both engine and pedal perform the same function: run vehicle. Choice B is associated with 'car,' the primary word in the question stem not with the entire question-stem. Choices C, D, and E are associated with (A) bicycle, not with the question-stem

SSAT ELEMENARY LEVEL

Reading & Verbal Section

Test 3

Test 3 Reading Section
Time: 30 Minutes, 28 Questions

Directions: Each reading passage is followed by questions about it. Answer the questions that follow a passage on the basis of what is stated or implied in that passage.

Questions 1-5 are based on the following passage.

Line   A Farmer one day came to the stables to see to his beasts of burden: among them was his favorite Ass, that was always well fed and often carried his master. With the Farmer came his Lapdog, who danced about and licked his hand and frisked about as happy as could be. The Farmer felt in his pocket, gave the Lapdog some dainty food, and sat down while he gave his
5   orders to his servants. The Lapdog jumped into his master's lap, and lay there blinking while the Farmer stroked his ears. The Ass, seeing this, broke loose from his halter and commenced prancing about in imitation of the Lapdog.
    The Farmer could not hold his sides with laughter, so the Ass went up to him, and putting his feet upon the Farmer's shoulder attempted to climb into his lap. The Farmer's servants rushed up
10 with sticks and pitchforks and soon taught the Ass that clumsy jesting is no joke.

1

The Ass's behavior to his master is seen as

A) foolish
B) spontaneous
C) witty
D) sly
E) sad

*spontaneous = happening at the same time

2

The master's reaction in line 8 (The Farmer could not...with laughter) suggests that

A) the master was unaware of the Ass's cleverness before
B) the master thought the Ass was more talented than the lapdog
C) the master felt the Ass made him feel inadequate
D) the master felt the Ass was distressed by the unequal treatment
E) the master was angered

3

Read the statement from line 6 in the box below.

| The Ass, seeing this |

Based on the story, why did the Ass act in a way as it did?

A) the Ass was jealous
B) the Ass felt proud of itself
C) the Ass wanted to show it can do better
D) the Ass was extremely tired
E) the Ass practiced hard to imitate the lapdog

4

In line 6, "commenced" most nearly means

A) began
B) pretended
C) cried
D) worked
E) imitated

5

Which of the following proverbs best matches with the story?

A) Absence makes the heart grow fonder
B) Don't put all of your eggs in one basket
C) Hope for the best, prepare for the worst
D) Enough is better than too much
E) Laughter is the best medicine.

Questions 6-11 are based on the following passage.

Line   Chemistry is the science of chemical elements and compounds, and how these things work together. It is the study of the materials (things) that make up our bodies and everything in the world around us.

   Before 1600, people studied substances to figure out how to do things such as turning lead
5 into gold, but no one managed to do that. This was called alchemy.
   Alchemists (people that did alchemy) did discover some useful things, though. Sulphuric acid and nitric acid were two substances that they discovered. Only a few elements were known. Some of them are mercury, silver, gold, and carbon.

6

The first paragraph (lines 1-3) mainly describes
A) the history of chemistry
B) a well-known chemist
C) modern chemistry
D) chemical elements
E) what is chemistry?

7

Which of the following items should be included in the study of chemistry?
A) Human mind
B) Life and death
C) Turning lead into gold
D) Ingredients in lollipop
E) Animal habits

8

"substances" in line 4 and "substances" in line 7 can be represented respectively as
A) chemistry and chemical elements
B) art and science
C) materials and immaterial
D) alchemy and chemistry
E) lead and diamond

9

"gold" in line 5 and "gold" in line 8 can be represented respectively as
A) cheap and valuable
B) science and magic
C) new and old
D) impossibility and chemical element
E) wisdom and knowledge

10

The parenthesis in line 6 (people that did alchemy) is used to
A) reveal alchemist's ignorance
B) praise alchemist
C) praise chemist
D) define the meaning of a word
E) describe chemistry

11

The primary purpose of the passage is to
A) speculate the work of the great alchemist
B) find a way to turn lead into gold
C) introduce some great chemists in history
D) understand the brief history of science
E) show superiority of chemist to alchemist

*speculate = to think

Questions 12-17 are based on the following passage.

Line   There is in Shropshire a fine oak-tree which the country people there call the "Royal Oak". **They** say it is the great-grandson, or perhaps the great-great-grandson of another fine old oak, which more than two hundred years ago stood on the same spot, and served once as a shelter to an English king. This king was Charles II, the son of the unlucky Charles I who had his head cut
5 off by his subjects because he was a weak and selfish ruler.
   On the very day on which that unhappy king lost his head, the Parliament passed a law forbidding anyone to make his son, Prince Charles of Wales, or any other person, king of England. But the Scottish people did not obey this law. They persuaded the young prince to sign a paper, solemnly promising to rule the country as they wished; then they crowned him king.
10 As soon as the Parliament heard of this **they** sent Cromwell and his Ironsides against the newly-crowned king and his followers, and after several battles the Scottish army was at last broken up and scattered at Worcester.

12
According to the passage, the "Royal Oak" is in
A) Worcester
B) Scotland
C) in the country
D) in Wales
E) in Shropshire

13
Based on the story, which statement is true?
A) Scottish won the battle
B) There was a time when England had no king
C) Scottish people followed the parliament's law
D) King Charles I was widely respected
E) Charles II had his head cut off

14
Which of the following was the main cause of Charles I's death?
A) the King's greed
B) the poverty of the country
C) the legend of Royal Oak tree
D) the war against Cromwell
E) Scottish people's preference to Prince Charles of Wales.

15

"They" in line 2 and "they" in 10 can be best understood respectively as

A) the members of Parliament and common folks
B) the followers of Prince Charles and the Cromwell's army
C) the folks who know about the Royal Oak and the parliament
D) common folks and the Royal Oaks
E) the Ironsides army and the followers

16

It can be inferred that the "Parliament" in the second paragraph

A) was afraid of the Scottish people
B) supported king Charles I
C) killed Cromwell
D) invented the Royal Oak story
E) wanted to control the country

17

The passage implies that after the battles of Cromwell

A) the newly-crowned king secured England
B) Cromwell turned against the Parliament and became the king himself
C) the newly-crowned king stepped down from his position
D) the Royal Oak tree soon died
E) Scottish people built their own country

*secured = protected

Questions 18-22 are based on the following passage.

Line There are many mighty hunters, and most of them can tell of many very thrilling adventures personally undergone with wild beasts; but probably none of them ever went through an experience equaling that which Arthur Spencer, the famous trapper, suffered in the wilds of Africa.

5 As the right-hand man of Carl Hagenbach, the great Hamburg dealer in wild animals, for whom Spencer trapped some of the finest and rarest beasts ever seen in captivity, thrilling adventures were everyday occurrences to him. The trapper's life is infinitely more exciting and dangerous than the hunter's, inasmuch as the latter hunts to kill, while the trapper hunts to capture, and the relative risks are not, therefore, comparable; but Spencer's adventure with the
10 "scavenger of the wilds," as the spotted hyena is sometimes aptly called, was something so terrible that even he could not recollect it without shuddering.

18

Based on the story, Arthur Spencer is
A) a mighty hunter
B) a trapper
C) a dealer
D) an uninspired adventurer
E) an illegal poacher

19

"The right-hand man" in line 5 shows that Arthur Spencer was
A) known to use the right hand exceptionally well
B) the best man of Carl Hagenbach
C) the right-minded person
D) the hunter who lost his left hand
E) a very young righteous person

20

Compared to hunter, trapper's job is
A) less dangerous
B) similarly exciting to that of hunter
C) limited only in Africa
D) not allowed to kill animals
E) defined only to capture animals

21

The word "infinitely" in line 7 most nearly means
A) dangerously
B) very
C) automatically
D) unimaginably
E) extremely

22

In line 10 "scavenger of the wilds" emphasizes
A) Spencer's hunting skills
B) spencer's fame among hunters
C) fearful moment of trapping
D) pleasure of trapping
E) the official names for the spotted hyena

Questions 23-28 are based on the following passage.

Line
   Angry Birds is a video game franchise created by Finnish computer game developer Rovio Entertainment. Inspired primarily by a sketch of stylized wingless birds, the first game was first released for Apple's iOS. It has since expanded to video game consoles and for PCs.
   Angry Birds has been praised for its successful combination of addictive gameplay, comical
5 style, and low price. Its popularity led to versions of Angry Birds being created for personal computers and gaming consoles, a market for merchandise featuring its characters and even long-term plans for a feature film or **television series**. The game has been called "one of the most mainstream games out right now", "one of the great runaway hits of 2010", and "the largest mobile app success the world has seen so far".
10

23

In line 2, "inspired" most nearly means

A) instructed
B) encouraged
C) spied
D) purchased
E) rented

24

Read this statement from line 2

"Inspired primarily by a sketch of stylized wingless bird

The statement mainly refers to

A) through study of bird spices in wild
B) stylish birds in general
C) importance of bird in video games
D) the source of idea
E) sympathy for wingless bird

25

Read this statement from lines 4-5

> Angry Birds has been praised for its successful combination of addictive gameplay, comical style, and low price.

The above statement mainly describes

A) the users' loyalty
B) the comical style of birds
C) the reason birds are angry
D) how the game developer became rich
E) some essential ingredients for success

26

Which point led Angry Birds to television series?

A) A sudden popularity
B) A bird sketch
C) Apple's iOS
D) Rovio
E) Low price

27

The primary purpose of the passage is to

A) show how addictive Angry Birds game is
B) warn dangers of wild animals
C) compare Angry Birds with other bird games.
D) present a series of popular entertainment
E) introduce a brief story behind the successful video game.

*addictive means to become habit

28

Based on the passage, which of the following game developers is most likely to succeed?

A) A company that knows a lot about angry birds
B) A company that knows how to mix style, low price, and fun.
C) A company that sells its own video games
D) A company that knows well about handicap birds
E) A company develops dozens of different games every year

Verbal Test 3
20 MINUTES, 30 QUESTIONS

Directions: the synonym questions ask you to find the most appropriate synonym to the question.

The analogy questions ask you to find the most appropriate analogy to the question. Select the answer that best matches to the question.

Synonyms

Each of the following questions consists of one word followed by five words or phrases. You are to select the one word or phrase whose meaning is closest to the word in capital letters.

Sample Question:

ABILITY

A) mistake
B) **talent**
C) abandon
D) best student
E) late

1. ELEGANT

A) legs
B) length
C) graceful
D) between eleven and twelve
E) labor

2. LIBERTY

A) bookstore
B) small library
C) freedom
D) bear
E) virtue

3. ANCIENT

A) antique
B) cent
C) dime
D) antelope
E) ants

4. SUITABLE

A) clothing
B) jacket
C) table
D) desk
E) okay

5. ENABLE

A) endanger

B) nephew

C) bible

D) setup

E) start

6. PLUNGE

A) rise

B) lung

C) plus

D) fall

E) plural

7. CONVINCE

A) assure

B) convention

C) cooperation

D) vintage

E) vindicate

8. MURAL

A) mutation

B) rural

C) city

D) town

E) painting

9. TALENT

A) capacity

B) king

C) tyranny

D) entertainer

E) movie

10. WOE

A) animal

B) wolf

C) fox

D) woman

E) grief

11. DELICATE

A) delete

B) casket

C) delicious

D) soft

E) Hard

12. OUTCOME

A) strike

B) baseball

C) get in

D) result

E) leave

13. DECAY

A) corrosion

B) coffee

C) drink

D) café

E) cave

14. ORDEAL

A) order

B) affliction

C) lovely

D) dearly

E) arranged

15. TRIUMPH

A) trump

B) president

C) joy

D) trumpet

E) music

Analogies

The following questions ask you to find relationships between words. For each question, select the answer choice that best completes the meaning of the sentence.

SAMPLE QUESTION

Q: River is to Ocean as:

A) better is to good

B) rain is to cloud

C) father is to mother

D) city is to country

E) fork is to spoon

This question is Degree Analogy question (small to big movement).

Ⓓ is the correct answer. Just as river is smaller than Ocean, so is city to the country.

Ⓐ is incorrect because the order is flipped over.

Ⓑ is incorrect because this is 'Production Analogy—what-produce-what.'

Ⓒ and Ⓔ are incorrect because there are no big and small relations between mother and father, so does fork to spoon.

16. Fish is to water as bird is to

A) feather

B) wings

C) beak

D) tunnel

E) sky

17. Amphibian is to bear as

A) lion is to king

B) tiger is to lion

C) rat is insect

D) frog is to mammal

E) tadpole is to baby

18. Top is to bottom as

A) comics is to study

B) baby is to girl

C) head is to hat

D) close is to open

E) shut is to close

19. Quiet is to desert as ocean is to

A) sun

B) camel

C) wind

D) sand

E) loud

20. They're is to They are as he's is to

A) he had

B) his

C) he would

D) he was

E) he is

21. 'There is' is there's as 'she is' to

A) her

B) hers

C) she had

D) she was

E) she's

22. Ate is to eat as sleep is to

A) slept

B) slip

C) sleeps

D) dreaming

E) sleeping

23. Find is to found as

A) police is to report

B) lose is to lost

C) go is to goed

D) cheap is to cheaper

E) had is to has

24. Referee is to court as

A) judge is to football

B) minister is to church

C) mother is to home

D) banker is to bank

E) host is to show

25. Basketball is to rink as
A) MVP is to Most Valuable Player
B) stadium is to fan
C) soccer is to cheerleader
D) baseball is to catcher
E) ice hockey is to court

26. Pear is pair as close is to
A) shut
B) lock
C) clothes
D) open
E) shirts

27. Lack is to abundance as rich is to
A) happiness
B) luxury
C) short
D) power
E) enough

28. Clever is to carnivore as ignorant is to
A) herbivore
B) stupid
C) smart
D) I.Q.
E) aaverage

29. Prey is to Predator as
A) trap is to trapper
B) lion is to tiger
C) hunter is to poacher
D) jungle is to bait
E) give is to provide

30. Gentleman is to kind as
A) marvel is to wonder
B) lady is to first
C) police is to rude
D) comedian is to funny
E) beast is to wild

SSAT

Reading & Verbal Section

Test 3

Answer Explanations

The Pattern Analyses

If your Test 3 scores are unsatisfactory, Practice the answer Explanations and then solve the actual Test 3 again.

ALL THE LOGIC AND RULES BEHIND EVERY SINGLE SSAT QUESTION

TEST 3
READING SECTION

Please refer to the Reading Section AP Analyses

SYNONYM QUESTIONS
TEST 3 NO.1 ~ 15

ANALOGY QUESTIONS
TEST 3 NO. 16-30

Please refer to the analogy Section AP Analyses

1. C
2. C
3. A
4. E
5. D
6. D
7. A
8. E
9. A
10. E
11. D
12. D
13. A
14. B
15. C

ANSWER EXPLANATIONS FOR TEST 3

Test 3 Absolute Patterns for the Reading Section

Questions 1-5 are based on the following passage.

   A Farmer one day came to the stables to see to his beasts of burden: among them was his favorite Ass, that was always well fed and often carried his master. With the Farmer came his Lapdog, who danced about and licked his hand and frisked about as happy as could be.(Q3) **The Farmer felt in his pocket, gave the Lapdog some dainty food,** and sat down while he gave his orders to his servants. The Lapdog jumped into his master's lap, and lay there blinking while the Farmer stroked his ears. **The Ass, (Q4) seeing this**, broke loose from his halter and **commenced** prancing about in **imitation of the Lapdog**. The Farmer could not hold his sides with laughter, so the Ass went up to him, and putting his feet upon the Farmer's shoulder attempted to climb into his lap. (Q1 & Q2) **The Farmer's servants rushed up with sticks and pitchforks** and (Q5) **soon taught the Ass that clumsy jesting is no joke.**

Q1. Question Pattern: The **Ass's behavior** to his master is seen as
AP 8: Understanding Attitude (Tone) Find the tonality: positive vs. negative, mental vs. physical

■ **Question Keyword/Key phrase:** "Ass's behavior"
■ **Incorrect Pattern: A) foolish**   B) spontaneous—NI   C) witty—DC   D) sly—NI   E) sad——NI
■ **What Does The Question Really Ask?** The question asking for the character description—the Ass's behavior in this question—requires overall understanding of the character. If you are not so sure of it, you can always skip this type of question and come back later after all the remaining questions have been answered.

A is the best answer.   The servants in the last sentence rush up with sticks and pitchforks and taught the Ass that clumsy jesting is no joke. To the farmer and the servants, the Ass mimicking lapdog's behavior could be seen as a foolish because the Ass is too big for such a cute act.
Incorrect Answer Explanation
Choices B, D, E are irrelevant words. Choice C contradicts the Ass's foolish behavior.

Q2. Question Pattern: The master's reaction in line 8 (**The Farmer could not...with laughter**) suggests that
AP 8: Understanding Attitude (Tone) Find the tonality: positive vs. negative, mental vs. physical

■ **Question Keyword/Key phrase:** "The master's reaction"
■ **Incorrect Pattern:** A) the master was unaware of the Ass's cleverness before—NI
   B) the master thought the Ass was more talented than the lapdog—NI
   C) the master felt the Ass made him feel inadequate
   D) the master felt the Ass was distressed by the unequal treatment—IW   E) the master was angered—EX
■ **What Does The Question Really Ask?** The question asks how the master felt about the Ass, not how the Ass felt.
■ **Relevancy Check:** Choice D is incorrect because the phrase shows how the Ass, not the master, felt.

C is the best answer.   "The Farmer could not hold his sides with laughter"
The punishment from the servants in the last sentence indirectly reflects his master's feeling. That is, the punishment proves that the master must have felt inadequate for the Ass's action.
Not only are choices A and B unstated in the passage, they also contradict the overall mood in the story. The Ass was punished for imitating the lapdog. Choice E is extreme expression.

Q3. **Question Pattern:** Based on the story, why did the Ass act in a way as it did? **AP 8: Understanding Attitude (Tone)** Find the tonality: positive vs. negative, mental vs. physical

■ **Question Keyword/Key phrase:** "*The Ass, seeing this*" ■ **Incorrect Pattern: A) the Ass was jealous**   B) the Ass felt proud of itself—NI   C) the Ass wanted to show it can do better—NI   D) the Ass was extremely tired—NI   E) the Ass practiced hard to imitate the lapdog—NI ■ **We Already Found the answer:** It's A. The answer was found before reading the passage. ■ **What Does The Question Really Ask?** The question asks why the Ass imitated the lapdog.

A is the best answer. "The Farmer felt in his pocket, gave the Lapdog some dainty food"
The Ass, seeing the lapdog being well-treated from the master, was jealous. So it mimicked the lapdog and jumped into the master's lap. All the remaining choices are irrelevant not stated in the passage.

Q4. **Question Pattern:** In line 7, **"commenced"** most nearly means **AP 4: Word-In-Context Question**   Find the clue words and keywords from the sentence

■ **Question Keyword/Key phrase:** "commenced" ■ **Incorrect Pattern: A) began**   B) pretended—NI   C) cried—NI   D) worked—IS   E) imitated—IW ■ **What Does The Question Really Ask?** A word-in-context question with a difficult word asks the literal meaning.

A is the best answer. The Ass, seeing this, broke loose from his halter and <u>commenced</u> (began) prancing about in imitation of the Lapdog. The word "commence" means to "begin."
Incorrect Answer Explanation
Choices B and C are Irrelevant words. Choice D "worked" could have been right in other situation, but not for this sentence. For the word "worked" cannot be combined with the word "prancing."
Choice E is incorrect. The sentence already contains the word "imitation."

Q5. **Question Pattern:** Which of the following **proverbs** best **matches with the story**? **AP 7: Inference Question**   Find the indirect suggestion behind the sentence

■ **Question Keyword/Key phrase:** "**proverbs** best **matches**"
■ **Incorrect Pattern:** A) Absence makes the heart grow fonder—NI
   B) Don't put all of your eggs in one basket—NI   C) Hope for the best, prepare for the worst—NI
   D) Enough is better than too much   E) Laughter is the best medicine—NI
■ **We Already Found the answer:** It's D. The answer was found before reading the passage.
■ **What Does The Question Really Ask?** The word "proverbs" in the question definitely implies what lesson can be learned from the story. Just like any other passages, the narrator leaves the main theme or the evocative lesson at the conclusion.

D is the best answer. Choice D means that one should control one's attitude, which correctly points out the Ass's unruly behavior. The Ass should have known that "enough is better than too much."
Incorrect Answer Explanation
Choice A means that one feels more affection when parted away. Choice B means that one should set the good plan.

Choice C means that one should expect for the best and be prepared for the worst situation. Choice E means that healthy mind is always best way to live. As seen above, all other alternatives are unrelated to the main character Ass's negative behavior in the passage.

Questions 6-11 are based on the following passage.   (Q6 & Q11) **Chemistry is the science of chemical elements and compounds**, and how these things work together. It is the study of the (Q7.) **materials (things)** that make up our bodies and everything in the world around us. (Q8) **Before 1600, people studied** <u>substances</u> **to figure out how to do things such as** (Q9.D) **turning lead into gold** (Q10) Alchemists **(people that did alchemy)** did discover some useful things, though. **Sulphuric acid and nitric acid were two** <u>substances</u> that they discovered. Only a few elements were known. Some of them are mercury, silver**, gold,** and carbon.

Q6. **Question Pattern:** The **first paragraph** (lines 1-3) mainly describes **AP 1: Main Idea (Focus Shifts) Question** Find the main idea of the entire passage or the paragraph

■ **Question Keyword/Key phrase:** "first paragraph" ■ **Incorrect Pattern:** A) the history of chemistry—IW   B) a well-known chemist—NI   C) modern chemistry—NI   D) chemical elements—NI   **E) what is chemistry?** ■ **We Already Found the answer:** It's E. The answer was found before reading the passage. ■ **What Does The Question Really Ask?** The first paragraph normally introduces the main theme of the passage. ■ **Relevancy Check:** Choices B and D, compared to choice A, C, and E, deal with specific information, which are normally used as the examples in the body paragraph. Therefore they are rarely used in the first paragraph.

E is the best answer.   "Chemistry is the science of chemical elements and compounds" The first paragraph explains the basic principles of chemistry. Choice E expresses this in the form of rhetoric question "what is chemistry?" Choice A) the history, B) chemist, and C) modern chemistry are not even mentioned.

Q7. **Question Pattern:** Which of the following items should be included in the **study of chemistry**? **AP 7: Inference Question**   Find the indirect suggestion behind the sentence

■ **Question Keyword/Key phrase: "study of chemistry"** ■ **Incorrect Pattern:** A) Human mind—NI   B) Life and death—NI   C) Turning lead into gold—NI   **D) Ingredients in lollipop**   E) Animal habits—NI ■ **We Already Found the answer:** It's D. The answer was found before reading the passage. ■ **Reading Tip:** This is inference-type question and therefore the exact phrases used in the alternatives would not be found in the passage.

D is the best answer.   "It is the study of the materials (things)" As stated above, only "lollipop" is the material. Other alternatives are immaterial.

Q8. **Question Pattern: "substances"** in line 4 and **"substances"** in line 6 can be represented respectively as **AP 9: Relationship Question**   Find the relationship between cause and effect, between characters and between ideas

■ **Question Keyword/Key phrase:** "substance"
■ **Incorrect Pattern:** A) chemistry and chemical elements—IS   B) art and science—IS
   C) materials and immaterial—DC   **D) alchemy and chemistry**   E) lead and diamond—IS

D is the best answer. "Before 1600, people studied *substances* to figure out how to do things such as *turning lead into gold*... " *Sulphuric acid and nitric acid were two substances* that they discovered. mercury, silver, gold, and carbon. Stated above, the first "substance" is placed in the phrase "Before 1600," referring to the period of alchemy, not chemistry. For there was no science in 1600. The second paragraph accurately describes the actual chemical elements, referring to the chemistry. Overall, these two words represent two distinctively different eras.

Incorrect Answer Explanation

Choices A and E both are related to chemistry, referring only the second substances.
Choice B is incorrect because "art" belongs to nowhere.
Choice C is incorrect because the word-order is flipped. "Materials" must refer to chemistry—the "substances" in line 6; "immaterial" refers to alchemy—the "substances" in line 4.

Q9. Question Pattern: "gold" in line 5 and **"gold"** in line 7 can be represented as
AP 9: Relationship Question   Find the relationship between cause and effect, between characters and between ideas

■ **Question Keyword/Key phrase:** "gold"
■ **Incorrect Pattern:** A) cheap and valuable—NI   B) science and magic—DC   C) new and old—GE
   D) impossibility and chemical element   E) wisdom and knowledge—NI
■ **We Already Found the answer:** It's D. The answer was found before reading the passage.
■ **What Does The Question Really Ask?** This question applies the similar pattern used in Q8.

D is the best answer. 'such as turning lead into gold.'
The author emphasizes the alchemists' ignorance back then. In fact, trying to turn lead into "gold" is an act of "impossibility." The second "gold" refers to a mineral, the actual "chemical element."

Incorrect Answer Explanation

Choices A, C, and E are Irrelevant words to the questions. Choice B switched the word-order. It is more appropriate to call the first "gold" a magic and the second "gold" a science.

Q10. Question Pattern: The **parenthesis** in line 7 (people that did alchemy) is used to
AP 10: Structural Pattern of the Passage   Find the structural pattern of the paragraph or the passage

■ **Question Keyword/Key phrase:** "parenthesis"
■ **Incorrect Pattern:** A) reveal alchemist's ignorance—DC(TI)   B) praise alchemist—NI   C) praise chemist—NI
   D) define the meaning of a word   E) describe chemistry—DC
■ **We Already Found the answer:** It's D. The answer was found before reading the passage.
■ **What Does The Question Really Ask?** The question asks the basic functions of parenthesis, one of which is to define the term.
■ **Relevancy Check:** Unlike the correct answer D, other incorrect answers try to explain the content in the parenthesis, thereby not answering the question—"the purpose" of parenthesis.

D is the best answer. The parenthesis is used to define the term "Alchemists".

ANSWER EXPLANATIONS FOR TEST 3

Q11. **Question Pattern: The primary purpose** of the passage is to
AP 1: Main Idea (Focus Shifts) Question Find the main idea of the entire passage or the paragraph

■ **Question Keyword/Key phrase:** "purpose"
■ **Incorrect Pattern:** A) speculate the work of great alchemist—NI   B) find a way to turn lead into gold--IS
C) introduce some great chemists in history—NI   **D) understand a brief history of science**
E) show superiority of chemist to alchemist—NI

D is the best answer.   Chemistry is the science of chemical elements and compounds,...
The passage mainly describes the basic foundation (history) of chemistry (science) and how it developed from Alchemy.
Choices A,C and E are not stated in the passage. Choice B is incorrect because it was mentioned as an example for Alchemy, not as the primary purpose of the passage.

Questions 12-17 are based on the following passage.

There is (Q12) **in Shropshire** a fine oak-tree which the country people there call the "**Royal Oak**". **They** say it is the great-grandson, perhaps the great-great-grandson of another fine old oak, which more than two hundred years ago stood on the same spot and **served once as a shelter to an English king**. This king was Charles II, the son of the unlucky **Charles I** who had his head cut off by his subjects (Q14) **because he was a weak and selfish ruler.**

On the very day on which that unhappy king lost his head, (Q16) **the Parliament passed a law** (Q13) **forbidding anyone to make his son, Prince Charles of Wales, or any other person, king of England.** But the Scottish people did not obey this law. They persuaded the young prince to sign a paper, solemnly promising to rule the country as they wished; then they crowned him king. As soon as (Q15) **the Parliament heard of this, they** sent Cromwell and his Ironsides against the newly-crowned king and his followers, and after several battles (Q17) **the Scottish army was at last broken up and scattered at Worcester.**

Q12. **Question Pattern:** According to the passage, the "**Royal Oak**" is in
AP 2: Summary Question   Summarize the sentence or the entire paragraph

■ **Question Keyword/Key phrase:** "Royal Oak"
■ **Incorrect Pattern:** A) Worcester-IW   B) Scotland-IW   C) the country--IW   D) Wales--IW   **E) Shropshire**
■ **What Does The Question Really Ask?** The question asks where stands the royal oak tree. Because several names are scattered all over the passage, it would be time consuming to solve and would be better to deal with after all other questions have been solved.

C is the best answer. "There is in Shropshire a fine oak-tree which the country people call the "Royal Oak".
As stated above, "Royal Oak" is in Shropshire.
All the other alternatives are mentioned here and there in the passage for different purposes but not associated with the location of the tree.

Q13. **Question Pattern:** Based on the story, which **statement is true**?
AP 2: Summary Question   Summarize the sentence or the entire paragraph

■ **Question Keyword/Key phrase:** "true"
■ **Incorrect Pattern:** A) Scottish won the battle—DC   **B) There was a time when England had no king**
C) Scottish people followed the parliament law—DC   D) King Charles I was widely respected—DC
E) Charles II had his head cut off—DC

SSAT ABSOLUTE PATTERNS

B is the best answer. "Parliament passed a law forbidding anyone to make his son, Prince Charles of Wales, or any other person, king of England."
The above sentence proves that there was a time when England had no king.
Choices A, C, and D contradict the passage descriptions. Choice E is incorrect because it was Charles I who had his head cut off.

Q14. **Question Pattern:** Which of the following was the main cause of Charles I's death?
AP 2: Summary Question Summarize the sentence or the entire paragraph

- ■ **Question Keyword/Key phrase:** "cause of Charles I's death"
- ■ **Incorrect Pattern:** A) the King's greed   B) the poverty of the country—IS   C) the legend of Royal Oak tree—IS
  D) the war against Cromwell—IW   E) Scottish people's preference to Prince Charles of Wales—IW
- ■ **What Does The Question Really Ask?** The conjunction "because" in the passage is a strong indicator that leads to the answer.

A is the best answer. "Charles I had been his head cut off because he was a weak and selfish ruler."
As stated above, the passage explains that the king was selfish (greedy).

Incorrect Answer Explanation

All other alternatives are—whether the glimpse of information is mentioned in the passage—irrelevant issues to the death of Charles I.

Q15. **Question Pattern:** "They" in line 2 and "they" in line 11 can be best understood respectively as
AP 9: Relationship Question Find the relationship between cause and effect, between characters and between ideas

- ■ **Question Keyword/Key phrase:** "they"
- ■ **Incorrect Pattern:** A) the members of Parliament and common folks—DC   B) the followers of Prince Charles and Cromwell's army—IW   **C) the folks who know about the Royal Oak and the parliament**
  D) common folks and the Royal Oaks—IW   E) the Ironsides army and followers—IW
- ■ **What Does The Question Really Ask?** When the question asks about the compare-and-contrast statement, focus on the latter one—"they" in line 11 in this question. It's because the former—"they" in line 2 in this question—is usually true, while the second one usually more complicated and wrong. Also, remember that the proper antecedent (the answer) for the pronoun—"they" in this question—implies the closest noun nearby the pronoun.

C is the best answer. "As soon as the Parliament heard of this, they sent Cromwell and his Ironsides"
"they" in line 11, as stated above, refers to the closest preceding noun "the Parliament"

Incorrect Answer Explanation

Choice A is incorrect because the word-order is flipped over. Choices B and E describe neither of the pronoun "they."
Choice D is incorrect because "the royal Oaks" is an irrelevant word.

Q16. **Question Pattern:** Based on the story, the "**Parliament**" in the second paragraph
AP 7: Inference Question Find the indirect suggestion behind the sentence

ANSWER EXPLANATIONS FOR TEST 3

- ■ **Question Keyword/Key phrase:** "Parliament"
- ■ **Incorrect Pattern:** A) was afraid of Scottish people—IW   B) supported king Charles I—IW   C) killed Cromwell—IW   D) invented the Royal Oak story—IW   **E) wanted to control the country**.
- ■ **What Does The Question Really Ask?** This question is connected to Q13 and therefore can be solved without further information from the reading passage.

E is the best answer. "the Parliament passed a law forbidding anyone to make his son, Prince Charles of Wales, or any other person, king of England." The above sentence was used in Q13 wherein describes that the parliament wanted to control the country by not nominating their new king.

Incorrect Answer Explanation

Linked to Q13, this question focuses on the parliament.
All other alternatives are irrelevant information to the parliament.

Q17. Question Pattern: The passage implies that after the battles of Cromwell
AP 7: Inference Question   Find the indirect suggestion behind the sentence

- ■ **Question Keyword/Key phrase:** "after the battles"
- ■ **Incorrect Pattern:** A) The newly-crowned king secured England—DC
  B) Cromwell turned against the Parliament and became the king himself—NI
  C) The newly-crowned king stepped down from his position
  D) The Royal Oak tree soon died—NI   E) Scottish people built their own country—NI

C is the best answer. "the Scottish army was at last broken up and scattered at Worcester."
Because Cromwell defeated the Scottish army, it is obvious that the newly crowned king must have been forced to step down.

Incorrect Answer Explanation

Choice A contradicts the passage description and the probable ensuing incidents. Choice B is not stated in the passage. Choices D and E are fiction not stated in the passage.

Questions 18-22 are based on the following passage.
   There are many mighty hunters, and most of them can tell of many very thrilling adventures personally undergone with wild beasts; **but** probably none of them ever went through an experience equaling **which Arthur Spencer, the famous** (Q18) **trapper,** suffered in the wilds of Africa.
   (Q19) **As the right-hand man** of Carl Hagenbach, the great Hamburg dealer in wild animals, for whom Spencer trapped some of the finest and rarest beasts ever seen in captivity, thrilling adventures were everyday occurrences to him. The trapper's life is (Q21) **infinitely more exciting and dangerous than** the hunter's, inasmuch as the latter hunts to kill, (Q20) **while the trapper hunts to capture**, and the relative risks are not, therefore, comparable; but Spencer's adventure with the "**scavenger** of the wilds," as the spotted hyena is sometimes aptly called, was something so (Q22) **terrible that even he could not recollect it without shuddering.**

Q18. Question Pattern: Arthur Spencer is
AP 2: Summary Question   Summarize the sentence or the entire paragraph

- ■ **Question Keyword/Key phrase:** "Arthur Spencer"
- ■ **Incorrect Pattern:** A) a mighty hunter—IW **B) a trapper**
  C) a dealer—IW   D) an uninspired adventurer—DC(TI)   E) an illegal poacher—DC(TI)
- ■ **What Does The Question Really Ask?** The question asks who the main character Arther Spencer is and what he does
- ■ **Reading Tip:** The contradictory conjunction such as "But" in the passage plays a critical role for the answer.

B is the best answer. "Arthur Spencer, the famous **trapper**."
As stated above, Arthur Spencer is a trapper. The author, using the contradictory conjunction "but," distinguishes hunters from trappers.

Incorrect Answer Explanation

Choice A, as seen above, contradicts the passage description. Choice C is incorrect. It is Carl Hagenbach being described as a dealer. Choices D and E use the negative words and therefore incorrect because the passage describes him positively.

Q19. Question Pattern: The **right-hand man** in line 4. shows that Arthur Spencer was
AP 7: Inference Question   Find the indirect suggestion behind the sentence

- ■ **Question Keyword/Key phrase:** "right-hand man"
- ■ **Incorrect Pattern:** A) known to use the right hand exceptionally well—EX
  B) the best man of Carl Hagenbach   C) the right-minded person—IW
  D) the hunter who lost his left hand—IW   E) a very young righteous person—IW
- ■ **We Already Found the answer:** It's B. The answer was found before reading the passage.
- ■ **What Does The Question Really Ask?** The question asks about the proper idiom "right-hand man." Question such as this focuses on the direct meaning of the idiom. Therefore, it is not necessary to read the passage if you already know the meaning.
- ■ **Relevancy Check:** All the other choices are irrelevant information to the idiom.

B is the best answer. "The right-hand" in the sentence refers to the most valuable person.

Q20. Question Pattern: Compared to hunter, **trapper's job is**
AP 9: Relationships Question   Find the relationship between the cause and effect, characters, ideas

- ■ **Question Keyword/Key phrase:** "trapper's job"
- ■ **Incorrect Pattern:** A) less dangerous—DC   B) similarly exciting to that of hunter—DC
  C) limited only in Africa—IW   D) not allowed to kill animals—DC   **E) defined only to capture animals**

E is the best answer. "while the trapper hunts to capture, and the relative risks are not comparable"
The above sentence illustrates the trapper's job is to capture, not to hunt.

Incorrect Answer Explanation

Choices A and B contradict the passage. The author, as stated above, believes trappers are performing more dangerous and more exciting jobs than hunters. Choice C is not stated in the passage. Choice D is a distraction. The phrase "not allowed to" implies that trapper needs some sort of permission to kill animals. But the passage tells trappers' job is more dangerous. Therefore, it contradicts the passage.

ANSWER EXPLANATIONS FOR TEST 3

Q21. Question Pattern: The word, "**infinitely**" in line 6 most nearly means
AP 4: Word-In-Context Question   Find the clue words and keywords from the sentence

---

■ **Question Keyword/Key phrase:** "infinitely"
■ **Incorrect Pattern:** A) dangerously—IW   B) very—IS   C) automatically—IW   D) unimaginably—IW   **E) extremely**
■ **What Does The Question Really Ask?** This question asks the definition for the word 'infinitely'
■ **Relevancy Check:** Choice A and D are distraction. Choice A uses the same word in the same sentence instead of answering the question. Choice D uses a seemingly correct but irrelevant word.

E is the best answer.   "Trapper's life is infinitely more exciting and dangerous"
The word "infinitely" takes the tone to the "extreme" point.

Incorrect Answer Explanation

Choice A is a distraction. It simply repeats the word in the same phrase "dangerous." It is incorrect. For it does not make sense to say "dangerously dangerous."
Choice B is a weak implication for the word "infinitely." Choice C is a irrelevant word. Choice D, seemingly probable though, cannot be the answer because the word "infinitely" does not contain such a meaning.

Q22. Question Pattern: In line 8 "**scavenger of the wilds**" emphasizes
AP 5: Understanding the True Purpose   Find the explicitly stated true purpose of the sentence

---

■ **Question Keyword/Key phrase:** "scavenger of the wilds"
■ **Incorrect Pattern:** A) Spencer's hunting skills—DC   B) spencer's fame among hunters—DC
  C) fearful moment of trapping   D) pleasure of trapping—DC   E) the official names for the spotted hyena—NI

C is the best answer. The "scavenger of the wilds," ...was something so terrifying...it without shuddering."
The clue words in the above sentence "so terrifying" and "shuddering" convey the fearful moment of trapping.

Incorrect Answer Explanation

Choices A and B are incorrect because Spencer is a trapper, not a hunter. Choice D is incorrect because it is not a pleasurable moment. Choice E is incorrect. The term "scavenger of the wilds" visualizes the way hyena is seen in wild. It is not the official names.

Questions 23-28 are based on the following passage.
    Angry Birds is a video game franchise (Q23) **created by** Finnish computer game developer Rovio Entertainment. (Q24) **Inspired primarily by a sketch of stylized wingless birds, the first game was first** released for Apple's iOS in December 2009. Over 12 million copies of the game have been purchased from Apple's App Store, which has prompted the company to design versions for other touchscreen-based smartphones. It has since expanded to video game consoles and for PCs.
    Angry Birds has been praised for (Q25 &Q28) **its successful combination of addictive gameplay, comical style, and low price.** (Q26 & Q27) **Its popularity led to** versions of Angry Birds being created for personal computers and gaming consoles, a market for merchandise featuring its characters and even long-term plans for a feature film or television series. With a combined 1.7 billion downloads across all platforms and including both regular and special editions, the

---

SSAT ABSOLUTE PATTERNS

game has been called "one of the most mainstream games out right now", "one of the great runaway hits of 2010", and "the largest mobile app success the world has seen so far".

Q23. Question Pattern: In line 2, "**inspired**" most nearly means
AP 4: Word-In-Context Question   Finding clue words and keywords from the sentence in question

- **Question Keyword/Key phrase:** "inspired"
- **Incorrect Pattern:** A) instructed   **B) encouraged**   C) spied   D) purchased   E) rented
- **We Already Found the answer:** It's B. The answer was found before reading the passage.
- **What Does The Question Really Ask?** The word "inspired," in SSAT Elementary level, is considered difficult. Therefore, it is the question that asks for the literal meaning of the word.

B is the best answer.   "Inspired primarily by a sketch of stylized wingless birds"
The word "Inspired by" means creatively encouraged by.
Choice A is incorrect because the word "instructed" means being trained by someone, which is a passive act. Whereas "inspired" is a self-realization. Therefore, it is an active word.

Q24. Question Pattern: The statement below mainly refers **to**
AP 7: Inference Question   Find the indirect suggestion behind the sentence

- **Question Keyword/Key phrase:** *"Inspired primarily by a sketch of stylized wingless bird"*
- **Incorrect Pattern:** A) thorough study of bird spices in wild—EX   B) stylish birds in general—EX
  C) Importance of bird in video games—EX   **D) the source of idea**   E) sympathy for wingless bird—EX
- **Relevancy Check:** All other alternatives treating the "Angry bird" as if it were a real bird are incorrect.

D is the best answer.   *Inspired primarily by a sketch of stylized wingless bird*.
As stated above, the clue word "sketch" implies that the bird was a drawing, not the real one. In other words, it refers to the main source of idea before it was realized as the video game.
Choices A, B, and E are incorrect because the bird in the passage is not the real bird.   Choice C is extreme. It sounds as if "birds" are important characters in all video games. Remember, only one video game is discussed in this passage.

Q25. Question Pattern: The statement below mainly **describes**
AP 5: Understanding the True Purpose   Find the explicitly stated true purpose of the sentence

- **Question Keyword/Key phrase:** *"comical style, and low price."*
- **Incorrect Pattern:** A) the users' loyalty—IW   B) the comical style of birds—IS   C) why birds are angry—EX
  D) how the game developer became rich—NI   **E) some essential ingredients for the success of the game**
- **What Does The Question Really Ask?** Two keywords in the statement "praised" and "successful combination" provide sufficient evidence for the answer.
- **Relevancy Check:** Alternatives that do not directly mention about the video game such as choice A and D are bound to be incorrect.

E is the best answer.   "some essential ingredients" refers to "successful combination" in the passage.
Choices B and C are incorrect because both phrases focus only on the birds as if they are real birds.

ANSWER EXPLANATIONS FOR TEST 3

Q26. Question Pattern: Which point led Angry Birds to **television series**?
AP 2: Summary Question   Summarize the sentence or the entire paragraph

- **Question Keyword/Key phrase:** "television series"
- **Incorrect Pattern:** A) a sudden popularity   B) a bird sketch-IW   C) Apple's IOS-IW   D) Rovio-IW   E) low price-IW

A is the best answer.   The passage states "**Its popularity led to….**feature film or television series. "
As stated above, a sudden popularity led to the television series.
Choices B and E are the ingredients that made the successful video game. They, however, did not directly contribute to the production of the television series.
Choice C is the reward that came along with television series.   Choice D is the game developer's name.

Q27. Question Pattern: The **primary purpose** of the passage is to
AP 1: Main Idea (Focus Shifts) Question Find the main idea of the entire passage or the paragraph

- **Question Keyword/Key phrase:** "primary purpose"
- **Incorrect Pattern:** A) show how addictive Angry Birds game is—DC(TI)   B) warn dangers of wild animals—DC(TI)
   C) compare Angry Birds with other bird games—NI D) present a series of popular entertainment—NI
   E) summarize a brief story behind the successful video game.   *addictive = becoming habit
- **We Already Found the answer:** It's E. The answer was found before reading the passage.
- **Relevancy Check:** Choice A is incorrect because the statement is negative, while the passage is positive about the
   game. Choice B is incorrect because the bird in the passage is not real. Choices C and D are incorrect because the
   passage focus on one popular game called the "Angry bird." No other bird games are mentioned in the passage.

E is the best answer.   "one of the great runaway hits of 2010", and "the largest mobile app success"
As stated above, the primary purpose of the passage is to introduce a brief story behind the successful video game.

Q28. Question Pattern: Based on the passage, which of the following game developers is **most likely to** succeed?
AP 7: Inference Question   Find the indirect suggestion behind the sentence

- **Question Keyword/Key phrase:** "likely to succeed"
- **Incorrect Pattern:** A) A company that knows a lot about angry birds—EX
   B) A company that knows how to mix the style, low price, and fun   C) A company that sells its video game—IS
   D) A company that knows well about handicap birds—EX
   E) A company that develops dozens of different games every year—IS
- **We Already Found the answer:** It's B. The answer was found before reading the passage.
- **Relevancy Check:** Choices A and D are incorrect because "Angry bird" is not a real bird.   Choices C and E are
   incorrect because simply selling or developing video games does not guarantee success. Nor does the passage state
   that way.

B is the best answer.   "Angry Birds has been praised for its successful combination of addictive gameplay, comical style, and low price."
Thus, any company wishes to succeed should know how to mix all these ingredients.

SSAT ABSOLUTE PATTERNS

Test 3 Absolute Patterns for the analogy Section

AP1. Category Pattern   Find the Part and Whole Relation, the Same Type or Association

16. Fish is to water as bird is to   A) feather   B) wings   C) beak   D) tunnel   **E) sky**

E is the best answer.   This question asks to which environment (category) a certain animal lives. Fish live in the water; bird live in the sky. Choices A, B, and C are associated with "bird" but not with the entire question-stem.   Choice D is Irrelevant word.

AP1. Category Pattern   Find the Part and Whole Relation, the Same Type or Association

17. Amphibian is to bear as

A) lion is to king   B) tiger is to lion   C) rat is insect   **D) frog is to mammal**   E) tadpole is to baby

D is the best answer. Frog is amphibian as bear is mammal.   Choice A is Mental (Emotion) Pattern as "king" symbolizes lion—symbolically, not literally.   Choice B) is associated with "bear" but not with the entire question-stem. Choices C and E are very remotely related between the primary and secondary word.

AP2. Synonym/Antonym   Find the similar or opposite meaning between the words

18. Top is to bottom as

A) comics is to study   B) baby is to girl   C) head is to hat   **D) close is to open**   E) shut is to close

D is the best answer. Top is antonym to bottom as close is antonym to open.   Choice A is vague in relation between the primary and secondary word, if not unrelated.   Choice B is the Degree Pattern. Choice C is the Purpose (Tool) Pattern. Choice E is the Synonym Pattern

AP2. Synonym/Antonym   Find the similar or opposite meaning between the words

19. Quiet is to desert as ocean is to   A) sun   B) camel   C) wind   D) sand   **E) loud**

E is the best answer. Quiet is antonym to loud as desert is antonym to ocean.   Remember, how the question-stem and the answer are paired. First of all, keep an eye on "quiet"—the use of auditory sense in the question-stem. Therefore, the answer must contain the similar sensory word to meet the question-stem. Choice E can be relatively easily found. Choices A, B, C, D are associated with "desert" but not with the entire question-stem.

AP9. Syntax Pattern Find the Homophony, Contraction, Verb, Adjective, Tense, Confusing Words

20. They're is to They are as he's is to   A) he had   B) his   C) he would   D) he was   **E) he is**

E is the best answer. This question asks for the contraction (reduced form) of pronoun. "They're" is the contraction of "They are" as "he's" is the contraction of "he is".

AP9. Syntax Pattern Find the Homophony, Contraction, Verb, Adjective, Tense, Confusing Words

21. 'There is' is there's as 'she is' to   A) her   B) hers   C) she had   D) she was   **E) she's**

E is the best answer. "There's" is the contraction of "There is" as "she's" is the contraction of "she has" or "she is." Choice B is the possessive pronoun for "she." Choices C and D are the past tense of he's

ANSWER EXPLANATIONS FOR TEST 3

AP9. Syntax Pattern Find the Homophony, Contraction, Verb, Adjective, Tense, Confusing Words

22. Ate is to eat as sleep is to   **A) slept**   B) slip   C) sleeps   D) dreaming   E) sleeping

A is the best answer. 'Ate' is the past tense of 'eat' as 'slept' is the past tense of 'sleep.' This question asks the past tense of a certain verb. Choice B is homonym (the same sound) with the secondary word 'sleep.' Choice C is the singular verb for 'sleep'   Choice D is the Production Pattern for 'sleep'   Choice E is the progressive tense for 'sleep'

AP9. Syntax Pattern Find the Homophony, Contraction, Verb, Adjective, Tense, Confusing Words

23. Find is to found as A) police is to report   **B) lose is to lost**   C) go is to goed   D) cheap is to cheaper   E) had is to has

B is the best answer. 'Found' is the past tense of 'find' as 'lost' is the past tense of 'lose'
Choice A is the Production Pattern: police produce [investigation] report. Choice C is incorrect because there's no such a word as "goed"   Choice D is the Degree Pattern. Choice E has flipped the tense order. That is, "has," the present tense should be placed before "had," the past tense.

AP3. Purpose (Tool) Pattern Find the Purpose of Individual and the Goal, the Function of Tool

24. Referee is to court as

A) judge is to football   B) minister is to church   C) mother is to home   D) banker is to bank   E) host is to show

A is the best answer. Referee judges the football game as a judge judges in the court. Both "referee" and "judge" perform the similar functions. In that sense, they are conceptual synonyms. All the rest incorrect answers are vague in relation to the question-stem.

AP1. Category Pattern Find the Part and Whole Relation, the Same Type or Association

25. Basketball is to rink as   A) MVP is to Most Valuable Player   B) stadium is to fan
C) soccer is to cheerleader   D) baseball is to catcher   **E) ice hockey is to court**

E is the best answer. Basketball uses the court and ice hockey uses the rink to play games.
Choice A is acronym (an abbreviated form of word using the initials). Choices B, C, and D are, by and large, associated with "basketball" but not with the "rink," the secondary word in the question stem, therefore incorrect.

AP9. Syntax Pattern Find the Homophony, Contraction, Verb, Adjective, Tense, Confusing Words

26. Pear is pair as close is to   A) shut   B) lock   **C) clothes**   D) open   E) shirts

C is the best answer. Pear and pair make the same sound, and so do close and (C) clothes.
This question seeks neither function nor the meaning of the words in the question-stem. The question-stem is made of homophony. Choices A and B are Synonym Pattern to "close" but not related to the entire question-stem. Choice D is the antonym Pattern to 'close' but not related to the entire question-stem. Choice E is Irrelevant word.

AP2. Synonym/Antonym Find the similar or opposite meaning between the words

27. Lack is to abundance as rich is to   A) happiness   B) luxury   **C) short**   D) power   E) enough

C is the best answer. Lack is synonym to short as abundance is synonym to rich. Or, lack is antonym to abundance as rich is antonym to short.

Choices A and D are, in relation to the question-stem, not as clearly and closely defined as C, thereby becoming Irrelevant words to the question-stem. Choices B and E are synonym to "rich" or antonym to "lack" but not with the entire question-stem. To be the correct answer, like the question-stem, it must be applicable to both antonym and synonym.

AP2. Synonym/Antonym Find the similar or opposite meaning between the words

28. Clever is to carnivore as ignorant is to   **A) herbivore**   B) stupid   C) smart   D) I.Q.   E) average

A is the best answer. Clever is antonym to ignorant as carnivore is antonym to (A) herbivore.

Choices B, C, and D are either synonym or antonym to either 'ignorant' or "clever" but not associated with the entire question-stem. That is, the secondary word "carnivore" in the question stem should not be left out in finding the answer. Choice E is Irrelevant word to the question-stem.

AP2. Synonym/Antonym Find the similar or opposite meaning between the words

29. Prey is to Predator as

A) trap is to trapper   B) lion is to tiger   C) hunter is to poacher   D) jungle is to bait   E) give is to provide

A is the best answer. Prey is antonym to predator as trap is antonym to trapper. All four words belong to the same "hunting" category.

Choice B is the [animal] Category Pattern. Choices C and E are the Synonym Pattern. Choice D is associated with the question-stem but cannot be further subdivided into the antonym Pattern—the most fundamental pattern in the question-stem and choice A.

AP 4. The Characteristic Pattern Find the Characteristic of Person, Place, Object, or Idea

30. Gentleman is to kind as

A) marvel is to wonder   B) lady is to first   C) police is to rude   **D) comedian is to funny**   E) beast is to wild

D is the best answer. Gentleman is characteristically kind as (D) comedian is characteristically funny.

This question asks the unique characteristic of individual. Keep an eye on that the question-stem uses human. Having "gentleman" in the question-stem, choice A and E become disqualified. Choice B is incorrect because 'first' is not the defining characteristic of "lady." Choice C is, admittedly true statement, not an official definition for police.

SSAT ELEMENTARY LEVEL

Reading & Verbal Section

Test 4

Test 4 Reading Section
Time: 30 Minutes, 27 Questions

Directions: Each reading passage is followed by questions about it. Answer the questions that follow a passage on the basis of what is stated or implied in that passage.

Questions 1-5 are based on the following passage.

Line   Thirteen-year-old Chrissy had always known she could read people's minds. Oh, and she could do a few **neat** tricks such as floating small objects. But all of that seemed of very little importance as she found herself face to face with a huge, brown bear! A bear. Happily eating the purple berries from the branches with its huge mouth. She stood frozen for a moment, just
5 staring. The bear didn't seem to notice her as it continued its berry feast.
   She had heard that it was wise to leave what you carried behind to make good your escape…but these berries were for mother! They were going to have pie! Slowly, Chrissy backed her way round to the other side of the bush. She sprinted from the bush and up the steps of the small cottage. She threw open the door and then shoved it closed with both hands. Chrissy
10 turned to see the wide, startled blue eyes of her mother. "Mom!" she gasped. "A bear! Outside!" Inward laughter sprang up, replacing the building panic. Her mother smiled.

1

Read this statement from line 1

> Thirteen-year-old Chrissy had always known she could read people's minds.

The above statement chiefly suggests

A) a girl's naivety
B) Chrissy's humble nature
C) importance of reading
D) all young girls' dreams
E) superpower the girl possesses

*naivety means simple mindness

2

Read the sentence from line 2 in the box below.

> she could do a few neat tricks

Based on the sentence, what does the word "neat" mean?

A) smart
B) floating
C) near
D) reading minds
E) trick

3

When Chrissy escaped from the bear she was carrying

A) a bear
B) a sister
C) mother
D) berries
E) a few neat tricks

4

In lines 10-11 ("Mom! she gasped...smiled.), the mood of Chrissy changes from

A) horror to relief
B) happiness to sorrow
C) rest to concern
D) relief to thrill
E) ease to terror

* relief = ease

5

The description of Chrissy's mother suggests that

A) the relationship between mother and Chrissy is different from that of others
B) Chrissy is not the only one who was terrified
C) Chrissy's mother symbolizes the mysterious power
D) Chrissy finally understood the true meaning of motherhood
E) Chrissy's mother was more relaxed than Chrissy

Questions 6-11 are based on the following passage.

Line
"What we shall eat to-morrow, I haven't the slightest idea!" said Widow Wang to her eldest son, as he started out one morning in search of work.
"Oh, the gods will provide. I'll find a few **coppers** somewhere," replied the boy, trying to speak cheerfully, although in his heart he also had not the slightest idea in which direction to turn.
5 The winter had been a hard one: extreme cold, deep snow, and violent winds. A hurricane had blown a wall over, and Ming-li, the son, up all night and exposed to a bitter cold wind, had caught pneumonia. Long days of illness followed, with the spending of extra money for medicine. All their scant savings had soon melted away. When at last he arose from his sick-bed he was too weak for hard labor. Night after night he came home, trying not to be discouraged, but
10 in his heart feeling the deep pangs of sorrow that come to the good son who sees his mother suffering for want of food and clothing.

6
The primary purpose of the passage is to
A) illustrate peaceful days of life
B) encourage readers to help sick people
C) encourage children to study harder to avoid poverty
D) show sorrowful days of the characters
E) examine why the son got sick

7
Which of following is true to the son?
A) He is a copper builder
B) He is unwilling to search for work
C) He makes his mother suffer
D) He is jobless
E) He spends money unconsciously

8
Read the sentence from line 3 in the box below.

I'll find a few coppers somewhere

Based on the story, what does the phrase mean?
A) There should be some help somewhere
B) Only he knows where to get coppers
C) Copper has been known to cure illness
D) A few coppers worth a fortune
E) I will look for a job for money

9
In line 4 "although in his heart....to turn to" serves to
A) defend the son's faith
B) reveal son's interest
C) note another problem the son is facing
D) reject the view of other people
E) show the son's intelligence

10

The use of the phrase "Oh, the gods will provide." in line 3 best expresses the narrator's

A) disappointment
B) expectation
C) religious background
D) doubt
E) urgency

11

Read the sentence from line 8 in the box below.

| All their scant savings had soon melted away. |

The literary device used in the word "melted" is

A) Hyperbole
B) Metaphor
C) Personification
D) Onomatopoeia
E) Alliteration

Questions 12-16 are based on the following passage.

Line   Geography is the study of the Earth and its features, its inhabitants, and its phenomena. Its features are things like continents, seas, rivers and mountains. Its inhabitants are all the people and animals that live on it since they were born. Its phenomena are the things that happen like tides, winds, and earthquakes.
5   A person who is an expert in geography is a geographer. A geographer tries to understand the world and the things that are in it, how they started and how they have changed. Geography is divided into two main parts called physical geography and human geography. Physical geography studies the natural environment and human geography studies the human environment.

12

In lines 1-2, the author defines geography as the study of

A) our planet
B) human psychology
C) modern technology
D) ancient civilizations
E) the universe

13

The author mentions lines 5-6 "A person who is an expert...changed" mainly to

A) illustrate successful geographer's life
B) dramatize geographer's daily living
C) illustrate how difficult geographer's job is
D) give examples of the geographer's job
E) romanticizes geographer's job

14

This primary purpose of the passage is to

A) describe a particular natural phenomena
B) correct the false idea about geography
C) illustrate climate condition
D) describe some basics of geography
E) instruct how to become a geographer

15

Which of the following examples would be included as inhabitants in line 2?

A) an imported apple
B) a panda in a zoo originated from China
C) a rose bred with lily
D) a kangaroo living only in that region
E) a hybrid rice that resists better to bacteria

16

According to the passage, tides, winds, and earthquakes in line 4 would be studied in

A) physical geography
B) human geography
C) biology
D) astrology
E) history of geography

Questions 17-22 are based on the following passage.

Line   At the end of the fourth century, the gigantic Roman Empire was broken up into two, the Eastern, the capital of which was Constantinople, and the Western, the capital of which was Rome. It was to the former of these that Syria and Palestine were attached.

    Before the end of the fifth century the Western Empire had been destroyed by the eruption of
5 the German races, and the beginnings of a new European civilization were rising from its ruins.

    Meanwhile, the Eastern remained entire, till about the year 630, when the Arab nations, burning with the spirit of conquest infused into them by the religion of Mohammed, poured into its provinces.

17
Based on the story, Syria was once a part of
A) Italy
B) Germany
C) Eastern Roman Empire
D) Western Roman Empire
E) Palestine

18
According to the second paragraph (lines 4-5), the main cause for the destruction of Western Roman Empire was
A) the invasion of foreign country
B) the invasion of the Arab nations
C) the invasion of Eastern Roman Empire
D) the shortage of money and food
E) Syria revolution

19
The word "burning" in line 7 refers to a(an)
A) strong desire
B) heatwave
C) religious faith
D) big fire
E) imminent danger

20
In line 7, the phrase "infused...by the religion" indicates that the Arab nations
A) were ruthless to different religions
B) believed only Mohammed can save them
C) were jealous of Eastern Empire's richness
D) were deeply affected by moral obligations
E) were motivated by the religious belief

21
The author describes the Arab nations in line 6 as
A) ethical nations
B) religious nations
C) technologically advanced nations
D) weak nations
E) barbaric nations

22
The passage is primarily concerned with the
A) wars between the Eastern and the Western Roman empires
B) German invasion
C) Arab invasion
D) Syria and Palestine revolution
E) Chronicles of Ancient Roman Empire

Questions 23-27 are based on the following passage.

Line   Long ago, the mice had a general council to consider what measures they could take to outwit their common enemy, the Cat. Some said this, and some said that; but at last a young mouse got up and said he had a proposal to make, which he thought would meet the case. "You will all agree, if we could receive some signal of her approach, we could easily escape from her. I
5   propose that a small bell be procured and attached by a ribbon round the neck of the Cat. By this means we should always know when she was about, and could easily retire while she was in the neighborhood." This proposal met with general applause, until an old mouse got up and continued said: "That is all very well, but who is to bell the Cat?" The mice looked at one another and nobody spoke. Then the old mouse said: "It is easy to propose impossible to remedy"

23
Read this statement from lines 1

| what **measures** they could take. |

Which sentence has the same meaning as the word **"measures"** as in the box?
A) Mom measures out the ingredients for cake
B) Cindy measures her waistline
C) SSAT measures scholastic aptitudes
D) Capital punishment is an obsolete measure
E) When in Rome, measure up their standards.

24
The author would probably think that the proposal of the young mouse seems to be
A) easy
B) possible
C) worrisome
D) doubtful
E) brilliant

25
"a young mouse" in line 2 can be represented in human society as
A) a wise school teacher
B) a skillful scientist
C) an irritating grandma
D) a respectful church minister
E) an inexperienced bragger

26
Read this statement from lines 2

| Some said this, and some said that |

The above sentence suggests
A) many different opinions
B) the importance of having a general meeting
C) hatred among mice
D) diverse characteristics among mice
E) collective agreement

*diverse =various, a lot of difference
*characteristics = personality

27
Read the sentence from line 9 in the box below.

| It is easy to propose impossible to remedy |

Based on the story, the above sentence primarily illustrates
A) Great success requires great challenge
B) We should think outside of the box
C) There is nothing impossible
D) Things don't go as we plan
E) We can't avoid our fate

Verbal Test 3
20 MINUTES, 30 QUESTIONS

Directions: the synonym questions ask you to find the most appropriate synonym to the question.

The analogy questions ask you to find the most appropriate analogy to the question. Select the answer that best matches to the question.

Synonyms

Each of the following questions consists of one word followed by five words or phrases. You are to select the one word or phrase whose meaning is closest to the word in capital letters.

Sample Question:

ABILITY

A) mistake
B) **talent**
C) abandon
D) best student
E) late

1. CUSTOM
A) mistake
B) habit
C) client
D) shopper
E) owner

2. NECTAR
A) back
B) spine
C) drink
D) butterfly
E) jam

3. ADOPT
A) battery
B) depot
C) add
D) do
E) follow

4. PRIMARY
A) prince
B) king
C) first
D) marry
E) holy

5. FATAL
A) fate
B) destructive
C) fatty
D) fine
E) precious

6. PREVENT
A) venture
B) value
C) primary
D) inhibit
E) rule

7. FRAIL
A) train
B) fast
C) locomotive
D) slim
E) rich

8. PREDICT
A) dictionary
B) foresee
C) past
D) future
E) write

9. GASP
A) gasoline
B) spare
C) tire
D) exclamation
E) station

10. SCATTER
A) scooter
B) scissor
C) sprinkle
D) cast
E) scant

11. LAUNCH
A) meal
B) meal between breakfast and lunch
C) fire
D) crunch
E) stop

12. SPOIL
A) oil
B) petroleum
C) harm
D) recover
E) elasticity

13. FIERCE

A) angry

B) fire

C) brave

D) scary

E) cute

14. STEER

A) steel

B) iron

C) metal

D) drive

E) sister

15. SWIFT

A) rapid

B) honey

C) slow

D) wife

E) spouse

Analogies

The following questions ask you to find relationships between words. For each question, select the answer choice that best completes the meaning of the sentence.

SAMPLE QUESTION
Q: River is to Ocean as:

A) better is to good

B) rain is to cloud

C) father is to mother

D) city is to country

E) fork is to spoon

This question is Degree Analogy question (small to big movement).

Ⓓ is the correct answer. Just as river is smaller than Ocean, so is city to the country.

Ⓐ is incorrect because the order is flipped over.

Ⓑ is incorrect because this is 'Production Analogy—what-produce-what.'

Ⓒ and Ⓔ are incorrect because there are no big and small relations between mother and father, so does fork to spoon.

16. Zebra is to stripes as skunk is to

A) cat-size

B) odor

C) horse

D) wild

E) smart

17. Turtle is to swim as monkey is to

A) ape

B) jungle

C) funny

D) jump

E) banana

18. Baseball is to Ice Hockey as
A) sports is to play
B) MVP is to MVPs
C) final is to quarterfinal
D) glove is to stick
E) professional is to amateur

19. Canoe is to racket as tennis is to
A) ball
B) pole
C) sports
D) sudden-death
E) court

20. Honest is to dishonest as real is to
A) deception
B) imagination
C) truth
D) seriousness
E) unreal

21. Cheerleader is to encourage as trainer is to
A) coach
B) trainee
C) study
D) football
E) train

22. Eat is to eating as study is to
A) knowledge
B) studied
C) learning
D) studying
E) has studied

23. Textbook is to magazine as tree is to
A) flower
B) newspaper
C) computer
D) ocean
E) money

24. Grandma is to old as cub is to
A) older
B) grandpa
C) young
D) bear
E) honey

25. Playground is to play as
A) police is to catch
B) teacher is to learn
C) baby is to boy
D) singer is to dance
E) robber is to donate

26. Woman is to human as
A) teacher is to adult
B) book is to magazine
C) fish is to bird
D) color is to black-and-white
E) study is to play

27. Convenient store is to supermarket as
A) chocolate is to milk
B) orange juice is to yellow
C) summer is to hot
D) now is to past
E) thin is to long

28. Queen is to elegance as bat is to
A) fish
B) movie
C) man
D) fun
E) fear

29. North Pole is to cold as
A) singer is to hot
B) country is to state
C) desert is to oasis
D) sauna is to hot
E) fat is to slow

30. Flute is to oboe as
A) saxophone is to trumpet
B) piano is to violin
C) drum club is to clarinet
D) guitar is to cello
E) castanets is to accordion

SSAT ELEMENTARY LEVEL

Reading & Verbal Section

Test 4

Answer Explanations

The Pattern Analyses

ALL THE LOGIC AND RULES BEHIND EVERY SINGLE SSAT QUESTION

TEST 4
READING SECTION

Please refer to the Reading Section AP Analyses

| SYNONYM QUESTIONS | ANALOGY QUESTIONS |
| TEST 4 NO.1 ~ 15 | TEST 4 NO. 16-30 |

Please refer to the analogy Section AP Analyses

1 B
2 C
3 E
4 C
5 B
6 D
7 D
8 B
9 D
10 C
11 C
12 C
13 A
14 D
15 A

Test 4 Absolute Patterns for the Reading Section

Questions 1-5 are based on the following passage.

Thirteen-year-old Chrissy had always known she could read people's minds. Oh, and she could do a few (Q2) **neat** tricks such as (Q1) **floating small objects**. But all of that seemed of very little importance as she found herself face to face with a huge, brown bear! Happily eating the purple berries from the branches with its huge mouth. She stood frozen for a moment, just staring. The bear didn't seem to notice her as it continued its berry feast.

She had heard that it was wise to leave what you carried behind to make good your escape (Q3) **but these berries were for mother**! They were going to have pie! Slowly, Chrissy backed her way round to the other side of the bush. Then, despite her mother's repeated warnings about not running from wild animals, she sprinted from the bush and up the steps of the small cottage. She threw open the door and then shoved it closed with both hands. Chrissy turned to see the wide, startled blue eyes of her mother. (Q4 & Q5) **"Mom!" she gasped. "A bear! Outside!"** Inward laughter sprang up, replacing the building panic. Her mother smiled.

Q1. Question Pattern: The statement below chiefly **suggests**
AP 8: Understanding Attitude (Tone) Find the tonality: positive vs. negative, mental vs. physical

---

- **Question Keyword/Key phrase** *"Thirteen-year-old Chrissy had always known she could read people's minds"*
- **Incorrect Pattern: A) a girl's naivety**   B) Chrissy's humble nature—DC   C) the importance of reading—NI
  D) all young girls' dreams—EX   E) superpower the girl possesses—DC
- **We Already Found the answer:** It's A. The answer was found before reading the passage.
- **What Does The Question Really Ask?** The question basically asks how to understand the character's speech.
- **Reading Tip:** Many questions such as this one can be solved through common sense and reading the passage is not necessary to find the answer. From the clue word "Thirteen-year-old," we can sense that Chrissy's claim "she could read people's minds" is her naïve imagination rather than her true capability.
- **Relevancy Check:** Choice B contradicts the passage that reveals Chrissy's bragging. Choice C misinterprets the phrase "reading minds" too literally. Choice D "all young girls" is not mentioned and extreme expression.

A is the best answer. The author is merely telling us what the little girl believes of herself. This naive belief, however, vaporizes as soon as she discovers a huge, brown bear. Remember, the contradictory conjunction "But" always provides an important clue for the answer.
Choice B "humble" contradicts the Chrissy's showy nature. Choice E is Chrissy's imagination, therefore, incorrect.

Q2. Question Pattern: Based on the sentence, what does the word **"neat"** mean?
AP 4: Word-In-Context Question   Find the clue words and keywords from the sentence

---

- **Question Keyword/Key phrase:** "she could do a few neat tricks"
- **Incorrect Pattern: A) smart**   B) floating—IW   C) near—NI   D) reading minds—IW   E) trick—IW
- **We Already Found the answer:** It's A. The answer was found before reading the passage.
- **What Does The Question Really Ask?** Some word-in-context questions uses a trick, wherein students tend to find and choose apparently more important word than the correct answer for the question.
- **Relevancy Check:** Choice E is incorrect because it eventually becomes "trick tricks." The question asks the meaning of the word "neat," not the "neat trick."

A is the best answer. "neat" means smart that describes the following word "trick."

Choices B and D are two of the tricks that Chrissy claims she possesses. The word "neat" does not contain such definitions.

Q3. Question Pattern: When Chrissy escaped from the bear **she was carrying**

AP 2: Summary Question   Summarize the sentence or the entire paragraph

- ■ **Question Keyword/Key phrase:** "she was carrying"
- ■ **Incorrect Pattern:** A) a bear—IW   B) a sister—IW   C) mother—IW   **D) berries**   E) a few neat tricks—IW
- ■ **We Already Found the answer:** It's D. The answer was found before reading the passage.
- ■ **Relevancy Check:** Choices A, B and C are all incorrect because the question asks what Chrissy was actually carrying. These are not the ones that a 13-year-old girl could carry. Choice E is not even a thing that can be physically carried.

D is the best answer. "but these berries were for mother" Chrissy is determined to escape while carrying berries.

Q4. Question Pattern: In lines 16-17 ("Mom! she gasped...smiled.), the **mood of Chrissy changes** from

AP 8: Understanding Attitude (Tone) Find the tonality: positive vs. negative, mental vs. physical

- ■ **Question Keyword/Key phrase:** "mood of Chrissy changes"
- ■ **Incorrect Pattern: A) horror to relief**   B) happiness to sorrow—DC   C) rest to concern—DC
  D) relief to thrill—EX   E) ease to terror—DC
- ■ **What Does The Question Really Ask?** The question asks the tonality shift, a changing mood from negative to positive.

A is the best answer. "Mom!" she gasped (horror, the negative mood)... Her mother smiled (relief, the positive mood)
As shown above, Chrissy's emotion has changed from the negative to positive.
It is evident that she felt horror when she saw the bear. On the other hand, mother's smile should have given Chrissy a relief, a positive emotion. Mother doesn't seem to be bothered too much for the bear due to its habitual appearance. Choices C and E have switched the mood from positive to negative. Choice D "thrill" is extreme expression.

Q5. Question Pattern: The description of **Chrissy's mother** suggests that

AP 8: Understanding Attitude (Tone) Find the tonality: positive vs. negative, mental vs. physical

- ■ **Question Keyword/Key phrase:** "Chrissy's mother"
- ■ **Incorrect Pattern:** A) the relationship between mother and Chrissy is different from that of others—NI
  B) Chrissy is not the only one who was terrified—DC   C) Chrissy's mother symbolizes the mysterious power— NI
  D) Chrissy finally understood the true meaning of motherhood-NI **E) Chrissy's mother was more relaxed than Chrissy**
- ■ **What Does The Question Really Ask?** The question asks basically the same thing as Q4.
- ■ **Relevancy Check:** Choice B contradicts the passage.

E is the best answer.   "Inward laughter sprang up, Her mother smiled."
The above phrase implies that the mother doesn't seem to be bothered too much to the bear due to its habitual appearance. So, she must have been more relaxed.
All the remaining alternatives are irrelevant information not specified in the passage.

Questions 6-11 are based on the following passage.

(Q6) "**What we shall eat to-morrow,** I haven't the slightest idea!" said Widow Wang to her eldest son, as he started out one morning in search of work. "Oh, the gods will provide. (Q7 & Q8 & Q10) **I'll find a few coppers somewhere,**" replied the boy, trying to speak cheerfully, although in his heart he also had not the slightest idea in which direction to turn. The winter had been a hard one: extreme cold, deep snow, and violent winds. A hurricane had blown a wall over, and (Q9) **Ming-li, the son, up all night and exposed to a bitter cold wind, had caught pneumonia**. Long days of illness followed, with the spending of extra money for medicine. (Q11) **All their scant savings had soon melted away. When at last he arose from his sick-bed he was too weak for hard labor**. Night after night he came home, trying not to be discouraged, but in his heart feeling the deep pangs of sorrow that come to the good son who sees his mother suffering for want of food and clothing.

Q6. Question Pattern: The primary purpose of this passage is to
AP 1: Main Idea (Focus Shifts) Question Find the main idea of the entire passage or the paragraph

---

- **Question Keyword/Key phrase:** "The primary purpose"
- **Incorrect Pattern:** A) illustrate peaceful days of life—DC   B) encourage readers to help sick people—NI
  C) encourage children to study harder to avoid poverty—NI   **D) show sorrowful days of the characters**
  E) examine why the son got sick—IS
- **Reading Tip:** The answer to the primary purpose type of question can normally be found at the topic or at the concluding sentence of the passage.
- **Relevancy Check:** Choice B and C rely on a general statements not stated in the passage.

D is the best answer. "What we shall eat to-morrow,...."
As stated above, the primary purpose of this passage is to show sorrowful days of the characters.
Incorrect Answer Explanation
Choice A contradicts the negative mood of the passage. Choice E is incorrect because it is a minor Issue, not the Primary, therefore, Insufficient to be the answer.

Q7. Question Pattern: Which of following is true to the son?
AP 2: Summary Question   Summarize the sentence or the entire paragraph

---

- **Question Keyword/Key phrase:** "son is currently"
- **Incorrect Pattern:** A) He is a copper builder—NI   B) He is unwilling to search for work—DC
  C) He makes his mother suffer—DC   **D) He is jobless**   E) He spends money unconsciously—DC
- **What Does The Question Really Ask?** The phrase "which of the following is true" is a typical summary question that requires overall understanding of the entire passage. It may take some time to identify all the alternatives from the passage. Therefore, if you are not so sure of the passage, you can skip the question and come back later.

D is the best answer. In line 3 the son says "I will find a few coppers," which implies that the son is looking for a job (money). Therefore, he is currently jobless.
Incorrect Answer Explanation
Choice A took the word "copper" too literally. Choice B, C, and E are direct contradiction.

ANSWER EXPLANATIONS FOR TEST 4

Q8. Question Pattern: Based on the story, what does **the phrase mean**?
Absolute Pattern 7: Inference Question Find the indirect suggestion behind the sentence

- ■ **Question Keyword/Key phrase:** "I'll find a few coppers somewhere"
- ■ **Incorrect Pattern:** A) There should be some help somewhere—NI   B) Only he knows where to get coppers—EX
  C) Copper has been known to cure illness—IW   D) a few coppers worth a fortune—IW
  E) I will look for a job for money
- ■ **What Does The Question Really Ask?** The question is basically the same thing as Q7. It asks to identify the figurative meaning for the word "copper."
- ■ **Relevancy Check:** Choices B, C, and D take the word "coppers" too literally as if the son is seeking a metal.

E is the best answer.   When the son says "copper" he meant to say money in a figurative term.
Choice A is incorrect because the phrase is ambiguous without mentioning "earning money."

Q9. Question Pattern: In line 4 "**although in his heart....to turn to**" serves to
AP 5: Understanding the True Purpose   Find the explicitly stated true purpose of the sentence

- ■ **Question Keyword/Key phrase:** "although in his heart....to turn to"
- ■ **Incorrect Pattern:** A) defend the son's faith—DC   B) reveal son's interest—NI
  C) note another problem the son is facing   D) reject the view of other people-NI   E) show the son's intelligence-NI
- ■ **What Does The Question Really Ask?** This question asks about the function of concession statement. The word 'concession" means an acknowledgment that there is other opinion other than the main issue. Here for the son, finding a few coppers (or money) is the main issue. Yet, he does not know where to get one—another problem.

C is the best answer. "although in his heart he also had not the slightest idea in which direction to turn"
The phrase starting with "although" is called a concession statement, in which the son reveals that he had no idea where to find a job. Thus, it serves to express another problem other than finding coppers.

Incorrect Answer Explanation
Choice A contradicts the concession statement in the passage. For the son shows no faith. Choices B, D, and E are irrelevant information that simply adopted some meaningful words in the passage.

Q10. Question Pattern: The use of the phrase "Oh, the gods will provide." in line 3 best expresses the narrator's
AP 8: Understanding Attitude (Tone)   Find the tonality: positive vs. negative, mental vs. physical

- ■ **Question Keyword/Key phrase:** "Oh, the gods will provide"
- ■ **Incorrect Pattern:** A) disappointment—DC(TI)   **B) expectation**   C) religious background—NI
  D) doubt—DC(TI)   E) urgency—NI
- ■ **We Already Found the answer:** It's B. The answer was found before reading the passage.
- ■ **What Does The Question Really Ask?** The question asks to identify the narrator's mood when he says a certain words.
- ■ **Relevancy Check:** Choices A and D are negative while the statement in the passage is clearly positive, therefore contradict the tone. Choice C takes the word "gods" too literally. The passage didn't say that the son is religious person. Choice E uses an Irrelevant word.

B is the best answer. "Oh, the gods will provide" The phrase contains, though glimmering, a positive expectation.

Q11. **Question Pattern:** The literary device used in the word "melted" is
AP 7: Inference Question   Find the indirect suggestion behind the sentence

- ■ **Question Keyword/Key phrase:** "All their scant savings had soon melted away"
- ■ **Incorrect Pattern:** A) Hyperbole-NI   **B) Metaphor**   C) Personification-Ni   D) Onomatopoeia-NI   E) Alliteration-NI
- ■ **We Already Found the answer:** It's B. The answer was found before reading the passage.
- ■ **Relevancy Check:** Choices A, C, D, and E are irrelevant words.

C is the best answer. A metaphor is an imaginative way of describing something. Here the narrator describes the situation by using the word "melted" as if "their savings are snow under the sun.
Hyperbole is a literary term that refers to an exaggeration.
Personification is a literary term for giving human attributes to animals.
Onomatopoeia is a literary term used when a word imitates the sound.
Alliteration is a literary term that means two or more words in a row start with the same consonant sounds.

Questions 12-16 are based on the following passage.

(Q12 & Q14) **Geography is the study of the Earth** and its features, its inhabitants, and its phenomena. Its features are things like continents, seas, rivers and mountains. Its **inhabitants (Q15) are all the people and animals** that originally live on it. Its phenomena are the things that happen like **tides, winds, and earthquakes. (Q13) A person who is an expert in geography is a geographer.** A geographer tries to understand the world and the things that are in it, how they started and how they have changed. Geography is divided into two main parts called physical geography and human geography. (Q16) **Physical geography studies the natural environment** and human geography studies the human environment.

Q12. **Question Pattern:** In lines 1-2, the author defines **geography as the study of**
AP 2: Summary Question   Summarize the sentence or the entire paragraph

- ■ **Question Keyword/Key phrase:** "that geography is the study about "
- ■ **Incorrect Pattern: A) our planet**   B) human psychology—NI   C) modern technology—NI
  D) the Ancient civilizations—NI   E) the universe—NI
- ■ **Relevancy Check:** In common sense, the definition of geography contains anything but choices B, C, D and E. Geography is the study of countries and within it the climates, lands, and environments.

A is the best answer. "Geography is the study of the Earth and its features, its inhabitants, and its..."
As stated above, the passage defines geography as the study of our planet (the earth).
All the remainings are neither mentioned in the passage nor true to the definition of geography.

ANSWER EXPLANATIONS FOR TEST 4

Q13. The author mentions "A person who is an expert ...how they have changed" (lines 4-5) mainly to
AP 10: Structural Pattern of the Passage Find the structural pattern of the paragraph or the passage

- ■ **Question Keyword/Key phrase:** "A person who is an expert ...how they have changed"
- ■ **Incorrect Pattern:** A) illustrate successful geographer's life—NI   B) dramatize geographer's daily living—NI
  C) illustrate how difficult geographer's job is—EX   D) give examples of the geographer's job
  E) romanticizes geographer's job—EX
- ■ **What Does The Question Really Ask?** Identify the passage genre. This passage is science genre using the objective tone.
- ■ **Relevancy Check:** Choices such as B) "daily living," C) "difficult," E) "romanticizes" are all subjective words inappropriate for the scientific passage.

D is the best answer. "A person who is an expert in geography is a geographer."
The phrase describes the job of geographer in objective tone.

Incorrect Answer Explanation

Choice A is incorrect. When the author In lines 4-5 expresses the geographer's job, he did not say a "successful geographer's life."

Q14. Question Pattern: This primary purpose of the passage is to
AP 1: Main Idea (Focus Shifts) Question Find the main idea of the entire passage or the paragraph

- ■ **Question Keyword/Key phrase:** "primary purpose "
- ■ **Incorrect Pattern:** A) describe a particular natural phenomena—IS   B) correct a false idea about geography—DC
  C) illustrate climate condition-IS   **D) describe some basics of geography**   E) instruct how to become a geographer-NI
- ■ **What Does The Question Really Ask?** The answer for the primary purpose question must embrace broad issues discussed in the passage. Specific information such as choice A or C, on the other hand, cannot be the answer for the primary purpose question. Anything specific becomes minor information. The answer should also be held in neutral tone—neither too positive nor too negative, nor subjective. In science passage, the author maintains a neutral tone.
- ■ **Relevancy Check:** Choice B is incorrect for using the negative tone. The author does not correct a false idea.

D is the best answer.   The passage describes the basic concepts of geography and geographer.
Choice E is not stated in the passage.

Q15. Question Pattern: Which of the following examples would be included as **inhabitants** in line 2?
AP 7: Inference Question Find the indirect suggestion behind the sentence

- ■ **Question Keyword/Key phrase:** "inhabitants"
- ■ **Incorrect Pattern:** A) an imported apple—DC   B) a panda in a zoo originated from China—DC
  C) a rose bred with lily—DC   **D) a kangaroo living only in that region**
  E) a hybrid rice that resists better to bacteria—DC
- ■ **What Does The Question Really Ask?** The question asks the definition of "inhabitants"

SSAT ABSOLUTE PATTERNS

D is the best answer. "Its *inhabitants* are all the people and animals that live on it since they were born"
As stated above, only choice D belongs to the definition of the inhabitants.

Incorrect Answer Explanation

Choices A, B, C, and E are incorrect because the definition for "inhabitants" is limited to the people and animals only. Choice A describes a foreign fruit. Choice B is incorrect because "a panda in a zoo" cannot be called the inhabitant. Choices C and E are manufactured items.

Q16. Question Pattern: According to the passage, **tides, winds, and earthquakes** would be studied in

AP 2: Summary Question   Summarize the sentence or the entire paragraph

---

- **Question Keyword/Key phrase:** "tides, winds, and earthquakes"
- **Incorrect Pattern:** A) **physical geography**   B) human geography—DC   C) biology—NI
  D) astrology—NI   E) history of geography—IW
- **We Already Found the answer:** It's A. The answer was found before reading the passage.
- **What Does The Question Really Ask?** The question asks to which study subject the examples belongs.
- **Relevancy Check:** Choice B is incorrect because "tides, winds, and earthquakes" cannot possibly become the study subjects for human society. Choices C and D are Irrelevant words to geography.

A is the best answer.   In lines 7-8, the author describes Physical geography in which the natural events are studied. "Tides, winds, and earthquakes are all natural events.

Incorrect Answer Explanation

Choice E is incorrect because "history of geography" is not mentioned in the passage.

Questions 17-22 are based on the following passage.

At the end of the fourth century, the gigantic Roman Empire was broken up into two, the Eastern, the capital of which was Constantinople, and the Western, the capital of which was Rome. It was to (Q17) **the former** of these that **Syria** and Palestine were attached.

Before the end of the fifth century (Q18) **the Western Empire had been destroyed by the eruption of the German races,** and the beginnings of a new European civilization were (Q21) **rising from its ruins.**   Meanwhile, the Eastern remained entire, till about the year 630, when (Q19 & Q20 & Q22) **the Arab nations, burning with the spirit of conquest infused into them by the religion of Mohammed,** poured into its provinces.

Q17. Question Pattern: Based on the story, **Syria was a part of**

AP 2: Summary Question   Summarize the sentence or the entire paragraph

---

- **Question Keyword/Key phrase:** "Syria was a part of"
- **Incorrect Pattern:** A) Italy—NI   B) Germany—IW   **C) Eastern Roman Empire**
  D) Western Roman Empire—IW   E) Palestine—IW
- **What Does The Question Really Ask?** The "former" refers to the first one of two, and the "latter" refers to the second one of two.

ANSWER EXPLANATIONS FOR TEST 4

C is the best answer. "the Eastern, and the Western. It was to the former of these that Syria attached"
"The former of these" refers to the Eastern Roman. "The Western," meantime, is called the latter.

Incorrect Answer Explanation

Choices A and B are unrelated countries to the question. Choice D, as stated above, refers to "the latter"
Choice E is stated in line 3 right next to "Syria" as another country attached to the Eastern Roman empire.

Q18. According to the second paragraph (lines 5-7), the main **cause for the destruction of Western Roman** Empire was
AP 2: Summary Question   Summarize the sentence or the entire paragraph

■ Question Keyword/Key phrase: "the destruction of Western "
■ Incorrect Pattern: A) the invasion of foreign country   B) the invasion of the Arab nations—DC
   C) the invasion of Eastern Roman Empire—IW   D) the shortage of money and food—NI   E) Syria revolution—NI
■ What Does The Question Really Ask? In most cases the correct answers do not use the exact words from the
   passage. Rather, they use synonyms.

A is the best answer. "the Western Empire had been destroyed by the eruption of the German races,"
"eruption" in this sentence can be understood as an "invasion." "foreign country" refers to the German races.
Choice B is incorrect. The Arab nations (line 6) invaded Eastern, not the Western empire. Choice C is incorrect because
the passage does not mention about the invasion of Eastern empire. Choice D is not stated in the passage. Choice E
"Syria" is stated in line 3 as the attached country to the Eastern empire, not as the invader.

Q19. **Question Pattern:** The word "**burning**" in line 10 refers to a (an)
AP 4: Word-In-Context Question   Find the clue words and keywords from the sentence

■ Question Keyword/Key phrase: "burning"
■ Incorrect Pattern: A) strong desire   B) heatwave-NI   C) religious faith-IW   D) big fire-NI   E) imminent danger-DC
■ We Already Found the answer: It's A. The answer was found before reading the passage.
■ What Does The Question Really Ask? As seen here, the easy word in the Word-in-Context question is never meant
   to ask its literal meaning. Instead, it always asks the figurative meaning.
■ Relevancy Check: Choices B and D are incorrect because they interpret the word "burning" too literally without
   considering the figurative meaning for word in the passage.

A is the best answer. "Burning with Spirit of conquest" implies a strong desire of invasion.

Incorrect Answer Explanation

Choice C is incorrect because the word "burning" itself does not contain "religious faith." There's no way to relate
these two words. Choice E is incorrect. As described above, "strong desire" and "danger" show stark contrast in
tonality. The phrase where "burning" belongs to contains a positive tone. "Imminent danger" is negative.

Q20. **Question Pattern:** In line 7, the phrase "infused...by the religion" indicates that the Arab nations
AP 2: Summary Question Summarize the sentence or the entire paragraph

- ■ **Question Keyword/Key phrase:** "Arab nations"
- ■ **Incorrect Pattern:** A) were ruthless to different religions—NI B) believed only Mohammed can save them—NI(GE)

    C) were jealous of Eastern Empire's richness—NI   D) were deeply affected by moral obligations—NI

    E) were motivated by the religious belief

E is the best answer. "the Arab nations, burning with infused into them by the religion of Mohammed"
Thus, beneath the invasion, believe the Arab nations, lay their religious belief.

Incorrect Answer Explanation

Choices A, B, and C are, although probable historical fact, not stated in the passage. Choice D "moral obligation" is not the same thing as religious belief, therefore incorrect.

Q21. **Question Pattern:** The author describes the **Arab nations in line 6 as**
AP 2: Summary Question Summarize the sentence or the entire paragraph

- ■ **Question Keyword/Key phrase:** "Arab nations"
- ■ **Incorrect Pattern:** A) ethical nations—NI   **B) religious nations**

    C) technologically advanced nations—NI   D) weak nations—NI   E) barbaric nations—NI
- ■ **Relevancy Check:** Choice A "ethical" applies the generalization. Being religious does not mean being ethical. Moreover, the passage describes Arab nations as invaders. Choice D contradicts the passage. It invaded other country by force.

B is the best answer. The passage describes the Arab as the invader vested with the religion of Mohammed. Choice C is incorrect because there was no technology in the sixth century. Choice E "barbaric" is not stated in the passage.

Q22. **Question Pattern:** The passage is primarily concerned with the
AP 5: Understanding the True Purpose Find the explicitly stated true purpose of the sentence

- ■ **Question Keyword/Key phrase:** "primarily"
- ■ **Incorrect Pattern:** A) wars between the Eastern and the Western Roman empires—NI B) German invasion—IS

    C) Arab invasion—IS   D) Syria and Palestine revolution—NI   E) Chronicles of Ancient Roman Empire
- ■ **We Already Found the answer:** It's E. The answer was found before reading the passage.
- ■ **What Does The Question Really Ask?** Having gone through several questions, we can assume that this is the history of the Ancient Roman empire.

B is the best answer. Starting with the phrase "At the end of the fourth century" to the last sentence ending with the phrase "till about the year 630," this passage briefly introduces the chronicle of the Ancient Roman empire. Choice A and D are incorrect because they were not mentioned in the passage. Choice B and C are incorrect because they were mentioned only briefly.

ANSWER EXPLANATIONS FOR TEST 4

Questions 23-27 are based on the following passage.
   Long ago, the mice had a general council to consider (Q23) **what measures they could take** to outwit their common enemy, the Cat. (Q26) **Some said this, and some said that**; but at last **a young mouse** got up and said he had a proposal to make, which he thought would meet the case. "You will all agree," said he, "that our chief danger consists in the sly and treacherous manner in which the enemy approaches us. Now, if we could receive some signal of her approach, we could easily escape from her. I venture, therefore, to propose that a small bell be procured and attached by a ribbon round the neck of the Cat. By this means we should always know when she was about, and could easily retire while she was in the neighborhood." This proposal met with general applause, (Q24)**until an old mouse got up** and continued said: "That is all very well, but who is to bell the Cat?" The mice looked at one another and nobody spoke. Then the old mouse said: (Q25 &Q27) "**It is easy to propose impossible to remedy**"

Q23. Question Pattern: Which sentence has the **same meaning as "measures"** in the sentence below?
AP 4: Word-In-Context Question Find the clue words and keywords from the sentence

- ■ **Question Keyword/Key phrase:** "what measures they could take."
- ■ **Incorrect Pattern:** A) Mom measures out the ingredients—verb   B) Cindy measures her waistline—verb
  C) SSAT measures scholastic aptitudes—verb   **D) Capital punishment is an obsolete measure**
  E) When in Rome, measure up their standards—verb
- ■ **We Already Found the answer:** It's D. The answer was found before reading the passage.
- ■ **What Does The Question Really Ask?** The word "Measure" in the passage is a noun, meaning a method. Focus on how the same word changes its meaning depending on the phrases.
- ■ **Relevancy Check**: Choices A, B, and C are verbs meaning "to check." Choice E means "to follow"

D is the best answer.   "what measures (methods) they could take."
In other words, the mice were debating over what methods they could use to get rid of the cat.
Choice D) Capital punishment is an obsolete measure also means "methods."

Q24. Question Pattern: The author would probably think that **proposal of the young mouse** may be
AP 8: Understanding Attitude (Tone) Find the tonality: positive vs. negative, mental vs. physical

- ■ **Question Keyword/Key phrase:** "proposal of a young mouse"
- ■ **Incorrect Pattern:** A) easy—DC   B) possible—DC   C) complex—IS   **D) doubtful**   E) brilliant—DC
- ■ **Reading Tip:** The basic step to find the answer is to find the tone. When in doubt about tone, read the conclusion.

D is the best answer.   "It is easy to propose impossible to remedy"   As shown in the concluding sentence, the author believes that the young mouse's proposal is, however appealing it may seem, impossible, or doubtful.
Incorrect Answer Explanation
Choices A, B, and E are all positive, therefore, contradict the passage.
Choice C is incorrect because "complexity" is laid in possibility that contradicts the word "impossible."

SSAT ABSOLUTE PATTERNS   210

SSAT 8 Reading & Verbal Elementary Level

Q25. Question Pattern: "a young mouse" in line 2 can be represented in human society as
AP 6: Analogy Question   Find the logically-supported similar situation

- **Question Keyword/Key phrase:** "a young mouse"
- **Incorrect Pattern:** A) a wise school teacher—DC   B) a skillful scientist—DC   C) an irritating grandma—DC
  D) a respectful church minister—DC   **E) an inexperienced bragger**
- **What Does The Question Really Ask?** The previous question indicates the young mouse's plan as a doubtful attempt. Based on this fact, we can assume that the "young mouse" alludes an inexperienced bragger.
- **Relevancy Check:** Known that the young mouse depicted as a negative character, choices with a positive tone such as A, B, and D become incorrect answers. Choice C "grandma" directly contradicts the word "young."

E is the best answer. "Then the old mouse said: "It is easy to propose impossible to remedy""
The old mouse here chastises the young mouse. Thus, the old mouse's comment at the end of the passage indirectly suggests that the young mouse is an inexperienced bragger.

Q26. Question Pattern: The phrase "**Some said this, and some said that**" (line 2) suggests
AP 5: Understanding the True Purpose   Find the explicitly stated true purpose of the sentence

- **Question Keyword/Key phrase:** "Some said this, and some said that"
- **Incorrect Pattern: A) many different opinions**   B) the importance of having a general meeting—IW
  C) hatred among mice—EX   D) diverse characteristics among mice—EX   E) collective agreement—DC
- **We Already Found the answer:** It's A. The answer was found before reading the passage.

A is the best answer. "Some said this, and some said that" hints that many mice had different proposals without an agreement. Choice B is incorrect because the phrase "Some said this, and some said that" does not show "the importance of meeting." Instead, it reveals many different opinions among the mice.
Choices C and D are extreme expressions. Having no collective agreement does not mean they hate each other or their having diverse characteristics. Choice E "collective" contradicts the word "many different opinions."

Q27: Based on the story, the **sentence below primarily illustrates**
AP 5: Understanding the True Purpose   Find the explicitly stated true purpose of the sentence

- **Question Keyword/Key phrase:** "It is easy to propose impossible to remedy"
- **Incorrect Pattern:** A) Great success requires great challenge—EX   B) We should think outside of the box—NI
  C) There is nothing impossible—DC   **D) Things don't go as planned**   E) We can't avoid our fate—EX
- **We Already Found the answer:** It's D. The answer was found before reading the passage.
- **What Does The Question Really Ask?** The question asks what conclusion can be made and how it can be interpreted in a proverb.
- **Relevancy Check:** Choice B uses Irrelevant Information. Choice C contradicts the passage. Choice E is extreme.

D is the best answer.   "It is easy to propose impossible to remedy"
The statement illustrates that there are things that don't go as planned.
Choice A is incorrect because the statement is not focusing on "great" success. It rather focuses on difficulties of achieving goal. These are two different concepts. For example, doing a difficult homework requires a lot of effort; it doesn't mean, however, that he or she, once completed, would be called great achievers.

ANSWER EXPLANATIONS FOR TEST 4

Test 4 Absolute Patterns for the analogy Section

AP4. Characteristic Pattern Find the Characteristic of Person, Place, Object, or Idea

16. Zebra is to stripes as skunk is to   A) cat-size   **B) odor**   C) horse   D) wild   E) smart

B is the best answer. Zebra uses stripes to camouflage as skunk uses (B) odor to protect itself. This question asks animals' self-defense mechanism (characteristics). Choices A and E are Irrelevant words to the question-stem. Choice C is associated with "zebra," the primary word in the question stem but not with the entire question-stem. Choice D is associated with 'zebra' and 'skunk' but not with "stripes," or with the entire question-stem.

AP4. Characteristic Pattern Find the Characteristic of Person, Place, Object, or Idea

17. Turtle is to swim as monkey is to   A) ape   B) jungle   C) funny   **D) jump**   E) banana

D is the best answer. Turtle swims; Monkey jumps.
Choices A, B, and E are associated with "monkey" but not with the entire question-stem. Choice C is Irrelevant word.

AP3. Purpose (Tool) Pattern Find the Purpose of Individual and the Goal, the Function of Tool

18. Baseball is to Ice Hockey as

A) sports is to play   B) MVP is to MVPs   C) final is to quarterfinal   **D) glove is to stick**   E) professional is to amateur

D is the best answer. This question asks about the sport gear. Baseball uses gloves as ice hockey uses stick.
Choice A is vague in relation between the primary and secondary word. Choice B uses the Syntax Pattern indicating the singular and plural form. Choices C and E can be applicable to the question-stem. The problem is that the question-stem does not use the Degree pattern. Therefore, the possible answer cannot use the degree pattern.

AP3. Purpose (Tool) Pattern Find the Purpose of Individual and the Goal, the Function of Tool

19. Canoe is to racket as tennis is to   A) ball   **B) pole**   C) sports   D) sudden-death   E) court

B is the best answer. Canoe uses the pole as tennis uses (B) racket.
Choices A, D, and E are associated with "tennis" but not with "canoe" or with the entire question-stem. Choice C is incorrect because there is no "racket" in sport category.

AP2. Synonym/Antonym Find the similar or opposite meaning between the words

20. Honest is to dishonest as real is to   A) deception   B) imagination   C) truth   D) seriousness   **E) unreal**

E is the best answer. Honest is antonym to dishonest as real is antonym to (E) unreal.
Choices A and B are incorrect because, although "deception" and "imagination" can be the conceptual antonym to "real," the relations between "honest" and "dishonest" are a direct antonym that requires the same degree of direct antonymic words like "real" and "unreal." Choice C is synonym to "real." Choice D is Irrelevant to the question-stem.

SSAT ABSOLUTE PATTERNS

AP3. Purpose (Tool) Pattern Find the Purpose of Individual and the Goal, the Function of Tool

21. Cheerleader is to encourage as trainer is to   A) coach   B) trainee   C) study   D) football   **E) train**

E is the best answer. This question asks about the people's roles in the same sport category
The purpose of cheerleader is to cheer (encourage) crowd as the purpose of trainer is to train the team. Choices A, B, and D are associated with "trainer" but not with "cheerleader" or with the entire question-stem. Choice C is Irrelevant word.

AP9. Syntax Pattern Find the Homophony, Contraction, Verb, Adjective, Tense, Confusing Words

22. Eat is to eating as study is to   A) knowledge   B) studied   C) learning   **D) studying**   E) has studied

D is the best answer. This question asks for the progressive form of verb (~ing).
The primary word in the question stem "Eat" becomes eating as "study" becomes (D) studying. All the rest are associated with the word "study" but not with the entire question-stem.

AP1. Category Pattern Find the Part and Whole Relation, the Same Type or Association

23. Textbook is to magazine as tree is to   **A) flower**   B) newspaper   C) computer   D) ocean   E) money

A is the best answer. This question finds the bigger category that can embrace the question-stem. That is, Textbook and magazine belong to the bigger category—"book."
Similarly, tree and (A) flower belong to the bigger category "plant." Choice B is associated with textbook and magazine but not with tree. Therefore, it is not answer. All the rest are Irrelevant words to the question-stem.

AP1. Category Pattern Find the Part and Whole Relation, the Same Type or Association

24. Grandma is to old as cub is to   A) older   B) grandpa   **C) young**   D) bear   E) honey

C is the best answer. Grandma is old as a cub is young.
Choices A and B are incorrect because they are the characteristics of "Grandma," not the characteristics of "cub." Choice D is incorrect for the same reasoning as A and B. Choice E is associated with "cub" but not with the entire question-stem.

AP3. Purpose (Tool) Pattern Find the Purpose of Individual and the Goal, the Function of Tool

25. Playground is to play as

A) police is to catch   B) teacher is to learn   C) baby is to boy   D) singer is to dance   E) robber is to donate

A is the best answer.
The purpose of the playground is to play as A) the purpose of the police is to catch. Choice D is incorrect because the purpose of 'singer' is to sing, not to 'dance.'

ANSWER EXPLANATIONS FOR TEST 4

AP1. Category Pattern Find the Part and Whole Relation, the Same Type or Association

26. Woman is to human as

A) teacher is to adult   B) book is to magazine   C) fish is to bird   D) color is to black-and-white   E) study is to play

A is the best answer.

Woman belongs to human as (A) teacher belongs to adult. All four words belong to human category.

Choices B and C do not use human. Therefore, they do not follow the question-stem. Choices D and E use the antonym Pattern.

AP1. Category Pattern Find the Part and Whole Relation, the Same Type or Association

27. Convenient store is to supermarket as

A) chocolate is to milk   B) orange juice is to yellow   C) summer is to hot   D) now is to past   E) thin is to long

A is the best answer. Both chocolate and milk can be purchased at either convenient store or supermarket.

Choice B is the Characteristic Pattern specifying color. Choice C is the characteristic pattern. Choice D is Antonym Pattern. Choice E is Irrelevant to the question-stem.

AP7. Mental (Emotion) Pattern Find the Human Emotion or the Word related to Mentality

28. Queen is to elegance as bat is to   A) fish   B) movie   C) man   D) fun   **E) fear**

E is the best answer. Queen displays elegance as bat causes fear. Both the word 'elegance' and "fear" refer to our emotion, the way we perceive and feel about something or someone. Through this approach, we can eliminate choices A, B, and C. Choice D is incorrect because bat is not perceived as 'funny' animal.

AP4. Characteristic Pattern Find the Characteristic of Person, Place, Object, or Idea

29. North Pole is to cold as

A) singer is to hot   B) country is to state   C) desert is to oasis   **D) sauna is to hot**   E) fat is to slow

D is the best answer.   North pole is cold as (D) sauna is to hot.

Both the question-stem and choice D use the same temperature category.

Choice A is Irrelevant word to the question-stem. Choices B and C use the part-whole in Category Pattern and do not contain temperature. Choice E is the Subjective-Objective Pattern

AP1. Category Pattern Find the Part and Whole Relation, the Same Type or Association

30. Flute is to oboe as   **A) saxophone is to trumpet**   B) piano is to violin   C) drum club is to clarinet

   D) guitar is to cello   E) castanets is to accordion

A is the best answer. Both the question-stem and choice A indicate the wind instruments.

All the rest are musical instrument but not the wind instruments.

SSAT
Reading & Verbal Section
Test 5

Test 5 Reading Section
Time: 30 Minutes, 28 Questions

Directions: Each reading passage is followed by questions about it. Answer the questions that follow a passage on the basis of what is stated or implied in that passage.

Questions 1-5 are based on the following passage.

Line   The piglet did not get paid for her job, which was very unfair considering how dangerous it was. She did get a certain satisfaction from carrying out her duties, but this was not the main reason that she never once complained about her lack of pay. The fact was that she had no idea about money. You might say that a more intelligent piglet would have figured it out by her age.
5   Thinking about it afterwards, with the benefit of old age and wisdom, the piglet concluded that she had just not needed to know about money at that stage in her life. She was fed daily. She had clean straw to sleep on. She had plenty of free time to play with the circus children. In return, she allowed herself to be fired from a cannon three times daily.

1

What might the author say to the statement in line 1 ("The piglet did not get paid for her job")

A) The piglet is having a unique experience
B) The piglet knows the job is not that dangerous
C) The piglet seems happy in spite of situation
D) The piglet should work harder to get paid
E) The piglet experiences unjust treatment

2

In line 2, "duties" most nearly means

A) dangerous circumstances
B) job
C) play
D) satisfaction
E) pay

3

Why did the piglet not get paid?
A) The piglet met such a poor boss
B) The piglet concerned circus more than money
C) The piglet didn't ask for money
D) The piglet was confused money with foods
E) The piglet did not know the existence of money

4

Read this statement from line 4

> You might say that a more intelligent piglet would have figured it out by her age.

The above statement primarily tells us that
A) readers are familiar with money
B) piglets live under harsh working conditions
C) the piglet is not too young to understand money
D) there are other piglets more intelligent
E) the piglet knows what is money.

5

The comparison between "straw" in line 7 and "cannon" in line 8 can be best described respectively as
A) unhappiness and happiness
B) sadness and enjoyment
C) comfort and responsibility
D) death and life
E) soft and heavy

Questions 6-11 are based on the following passage.

Line   Hu-lin was a little slave girl. She had been sold by her father when she was scarcely more than a baby, and had lived for five years with a number of other children in a wretched houseboat. Her cruel master treated her very badly. He made her go out upon the street, with the other girls he had bought, to beg for a living. This kind of life was especially hard for Hu-lin. She longed to
5 play in the fields, above which the huge kites were sailing in the air like giant birds. But if her master ever caught her idling her time away in this manner he beat her most cruelly and gave her nothing to eat for a whole day. In fact, he was so wicked and cruel that all the children called him Black Heart.

6

The passage describes Hu-lin's father as

A) financially affluent person
B) sympathetic person
C) highly ethical person
D) condemnable person
E) lazy person

7

Which word best represents Hu-lin's life?

A) fortunate
B) difficult
C) uninteresting
D) comfortable
E) regretful

8

The "kites" (line 5) most likely represents

A) wisdom
B) master
C) flying object
D) home
E) freedom

9

The word "idling" in line 6 indicates

A) master's belief about Hu-lin
B) carefree nature of Hu-lin's father
C) Hu-lin's true character
D) master's difficult life
E) Hu-lin's comfortable life

10

The primary purpose of the passage is to

A) show a poor girl's excruciating life
B) introduce the general poor condition of slavery
C) criticize a wicked man
D) highlight intense relation with father and child
E) describe a miserable living of one family

*excruciating means extremely painful

11

The use of the phrase "Black Heart" (line 8) conveys

A) the cruelty of the master
B) colorful description of the master's heart
C) the real name of the master
D) friendly relationship between Hu-lin and the master
E) the unknown nature of the master

SSAT ABSOLUTE PATTERNS

Questions 12-17 are based on the following passage.

Line   India, the great peninsula stretching from the Himalayas to Cape Comorin, is nearly half as large as Europe, and contains a population of 150,000,000. Myth and tradition claim for this people a very great antiquity, and there are many evidences that in arts, government, and literature, India is at least coeval with China and Egypt, the three constituting the most ancient
5 civilizations of the world. While Western Europe was still the bode of barbarians, and while even Greece had scarcely felt the impulse which aroused her to intellectual life, the fabrics of India had reached a marvelous degree of fineness and beauty; and the monarchs of the West counted it a great privilege to be clothed in the "purple and fine linen" of the Orient.

12

The passage supports which of the following about China and Egypt in line 4?
A) They had more populations than that of Europe
B) They were bigger than India
C) They had no civilization
D) They were as competitive nations as India
E) They were less advanced than Western Europe

13

Which aspect made the Ancient India great?
A) Myth
B) Advanced science
C) Art
D) Food
E) Dancing

14

Line 7 "the monarchs of the West...to be clothed" suggests that the monarchs of the West
A) was protected by India
B) loved clothing from India
C) enjoyed the strong relationship with India
D) effectively banned imported linen from India
E) wore clothing only imports from India

15

The author's tone of the Ancient India is one of
A) celebratory
B) doubtful
C) mythic
D) cheerful
E) denial

16

The passage mainly discusses about
A) the Ancient India
B) the Ancient China
C) Western Europe
D) modern India
E) the Ancient Egypt

17

Which of the following statements is true about ancient Western Europe?
A) Its military attacked the barbaric India
B) It was less developed than India
C) The monarchs of the West was afraid of India
D) It was more advanced than India
E) It preferred China and Egypt to India

Questions 18-23 are based on the following passage.

Line   It happened that a Fox caught its tail in a trap, and in struggling to release himself lost all of it but the stump. At first he was ashamed to show himself among his fellow foxes. But at last he determined to put a bolder face upon his misfortune, and summoned all the foxes to a general meeting to consider a proposal which he had to place before them.

5   When they had assembled together the Fox proposed that they should all do away with their tails. He pointed out how inconvenient a tail was when they were pursued by their enemies, the dogs; how much it was in the way when they desired to sit down and hold a friendly conversation with one another. He failed to see any advantage in carrying about such a useless encumbrance. "That is all very well," said one of the older foxes; "but I do not think you

10   would have asked us to dispense with our chief ornament if you had not lost yours."

18

The Fox that lost its tail changed its mood from
A) puzzlement to enthusiasm
B) anger to concernment
C) violence to sadness
D) hostility to friendliness
E) concernment to daring

19

Why did the Fox tell other foxes to cut loose their tails?
A) He wanted to hide his lost tail
B) He wanted them to be convenient too
C) He wanted them to outsmart dogs
D) He wanted them to avoid traps
E) He truly loved his fellow foxes

20

The old fox's attitude towards the Fox that lost its tail is one of
A) regret
B) envy
C) appreciation
D) suspicion
E) trust

21

What is the ultimate goal of the Fox that lost its tail ?
A) removing inconvenience
B) hiding his own defect
C) taking revenge on dog
D) cutting loose all the others' tails

22

"release" in line 1 most nearly means?
A) cut
B) free
C) lace
D) reduce
E) revenge

23

The old fox believes the tail is a(an)
A) legacy
B) decoration
C) timeworn tradition
D) essential part of body
E) unnecessary unit

Legacy = a thing handed down by ancestors

Questions 24-28 are based on the following passage.

Line   Physical fitness refers to good body health, and is the result of regular exercise, proper diet and nutrition, and proper rest for **its** recovery. A person who is physically fit will be able to walk or run without getting breathless and they will be able to carry out the activities of everyday living and not need help. How much each person can do will depend on their age and
5   whether they are a man or woman. A physically fit person usually has a normal weight for their height. The relation between their height and weight is called their Body Mass Index. A taller person can be heavier and still be fit. If a person is too heavy or too thin for their height it may affect their health

24
In line 2 "**its**" refers to
A) physical
B) physical fitness
C) health
D) exercise
E) proper diet

25
All of the following refer to the "Physical fitness" (line 1) EXCEPT
A) good diet
B) good mentality
C) measured exercise
D) good health
E) enough rest

26
The passage was probably taken from the
A) world history book
B) children's dietary guidelines
C) fashion magazine
D) child psychology textbook
E) new clinical research

27
A girl whose Body Mass Index is subject to improve may have a problem with
A) age
B) school work
C) gender
D) weight
E) race

28
Which of the following child best fits for Body Mass Index (line 6)?
A) A boy with an honored degree at school
B) The tallest girl in the class
C) A girl wanting to have a pretty body
D) A boy with kind personality
E) A boy with the average height and normal weight

Verbal Test 5
20 MINUTES, 30 QUESTIONS

Directions: the synonym questions ask you to find the most appropriate synonym to the question.

The analogy questions ask you to find the most appropriate analogy to the question. Select the answer that best matches to the question.

Synonyms

Each of the following questions consists of one word followed by five words or phrases. You are to select the one word or phrase whose meaning is closest to the word in capital letters.

Sample Question:

ABILITY

A) mistake
B) **talent**
C) abandon
D) best student
E) late

1. INTERMEDIATE

A) internet
B) online
C) game
D) medium
E) larger

2. GALE

A) girlish
B) gallon
C) windstorm
D) strong
E) bad

3. GIGANTIC

A) elegant
B) sweet
C) mammoth
D) trouble
E) lovely

4. STATIONARY

A) motionless
B) office depot
C) school
D) supply
E) knife

5. OUTSTANDING

A) unfinished

B) superior

C) strike

D) baseball

E) standing alone

6. UNION

A) conciliation

B) onion

C) vegetable

D) sour

E) sweet

7. FUME

A) fuel

B) name

C) smoke

D) gasoline

E) fire

8. INTACT

A) flawless

B) stick

C) indoor

D) outdoor

E) tacit

9. CONFLICT

A) fight

B) discussion

C) togetherness

D) flight

E) air

10. BOAST

A) ship

B) boat

C) sail

D) exaggeration

E) luxury

11. IDENTICAL

A) equal

B) denture

C) dentistry

D) identification card

E) idea

12. AWKWARD

A) awesome

B) unrefined

C) kiwi

D) fruit

E) advice

13. REVOLT

A) chicken

B) thunderbolt

C) car

D) fast

E) mutiny

14. CEASE

A) scissor

B) quit

C) cheese

D) sweet

E) soda

15. IMPEACH

A) fruit

B) stop

C) criticize

D) share

E) president

Analogies
The following questions ask you to find relationships between words. For each question, select the answer choice that best completes the meaning of the sentence.

SAMPLE QUESTION
Q: River is to Ocean as:

A) better is to good

B) rain is to cloud

C) father is to mother

D) city is to country

E) fork is to spoon

This question is Degree Analogy question (small to big movement).

Ⓓ is the correct answer. Just as river is smaller than Ocean, so is city to the country.

Ⓐ is incorrect because the order is flipped over.

Ⓑ is incorrect because this is 'Production Analogy—what-produce-what.'

Ⓒ and Ⓔ are incorrect because there are no big and small relations between mother and father, so does fork to spoon.

16. Time is to money as golden is to

A) silence

B) stopwatch

C) ring

D) pretty

E) underground

17. 100 is complete as 10 is

A) misleading

B) bad

C) imperfect

D) disqualified

E) Immoral

SSAT ABSOLUTE PATTERNS

18. Art is to creativity as
A) Biology is to high school
B) Math is to logic
C) English is to second language
D) Science is to Physics
E) Music is to boring

19. Garage is to baby as car is to
A) cute
B) noise
C) mother
D) cradle
E) diapers

20. Car is to pollution as to friend is to
A) human being
B) school
C) classmate
D) love
E) friendship

21. Lion is to zebra as
A) strong is to ox
B) cow is to hay
C) eagle is to brave
D) stripe is to coward
E) grass is to weed

22. Exercise is to knowledge as
A) reading is to gym
B) gym is to sweat
C) power is to young
D) practice is to success
E) death is to live

23. Weather is to steak as mild is to
A) expensive
B) restaurant
C) medium
D) well done
E) meal

24. Africa is to North Pole as hot is to
A) cold
B) Ice
C) Igloo
D) far away
E) Santa Clause

25. Arrival is to departure as
A) dessert is to appetizer
B) fire is to firefighter
C) garbage is to can
D) plane is to airport
E) ticket is to access

26. Rose is to socks as
A) fragrance is to smell
B) pretty is to ugly
C) flower is to plastic
D) plant is to leather
E) fragrance is to dirty

27. Eyeglass is to bicycle tire as
A) dog is to legs
B) lamp is to light
C) cat is to seven
D) sandwich is to subway
E) T.V. monitor and cell phone

28. Laundry room is to washing machine as
A) attic is to old photo album
B) oasis is to desert
C) pig is to bacon
D) bank is to robber
E) university is to high school

29. Ship is to submarine as
A) nephew is to annoying
B) pet is to cute
C) failure is disappointment
D) grade 10 is to grade 11
E) bird is to airplane

30. Zoo is to hospital as
A) animal is to patient
B) circus is to ticket
C) lion is to rabbit
D) sack is to heavy
E) song is to mellow

SSAT ELEMENTARY LEVEL

Reading & Verbal Section

Test 5

Answer Explanations

The Pattern Analyses

ALL THE LOGIC AND RULES BEHIND
EVERY SINGLE SSAT QUESTION

TEST 5
READING SECTION

Please refer to the Reading Section AP Analyses

SYNONYM QUESTIONS
TEST 5 NO.1 ~ 15

1	D
2	C
3	C
4	A
5	B
6	A
7	C
8	A
9	A
10	D
11	A
12	B
13	E
14	B
15	C

ANALOGY QUESTIONS
TEST 5 NO. 16-30

Please refer to the analogy AP Analyses

Test 5 Absolute Patterns for the Reading Section

Questions 1-5 are based on the following passage.
The piglet did not get paid for her job, **(Q1) which was very unfair** considering how dangerous it was. She did get a certain satisfaction from carrying out her **duties,** but this was not the main reason that she never once complained about her lack of pay. The fact was that she had no idea about money. **(Q4) You might say that a more intelligent piglet would have figured it out by her age.** Thinking about it afterwards, with the benefit of old age and wisdom, **(Q3) the piglet concluded that she had just not needed to know about money at that stage in her life**. She was fed daily. She had clean **straw** to sleep on. She had plenty of free time to play with the circus children. **(Q2 & Q5) In return, she allowed herself to be fired from a cannon three times daily.**

Q1. Question Pattern: What might the author say to the statement in line 1
AP 5: Understanding the True Purpose   Find the explicitly stated true purpose of the sentence

---

■ **Question Keyword/Key phrase:** "The piglet did not get paid for her job"
■ **Incorrect Pattern:** A) The piglet is having a unique experience—IS
   B) The piglet knows the job is not that dangerous—DC   C) The piglet seems happy in spite of situation—DC
   D) The piglet should work harder to get paid—DC   **E) The piglet experiences unjust treatment**
■ **We Already Found the answer:** It's E. In the process of finding the correct answer one must inevitably eliminate the incorrect answers not supported by evidence from the passage. Take this simple question.
Passage: This pen is made of plastic.
What does the word "pen" suggest?
A) it is yellow   B) it is cheap   C) it is disposable   D) it would not last very long   E) it used a synthetic material.
Choice E is the correct answer. Although probable, all the other alternatives are not stated in the passage. Whereas choice E is based on the fact that the pen is plastic or synthetic material.

E is the best answer.   Choice E is stated in the first sentence.
Incorrect Answer Explanation
All the alternatives are incorrect because those statements came from our imagination, not from the evidence in the passage. Choice A is a weak implication. Calling "a unique experience" for the job that didn't pay is understatement.

Q2. Question Pattern: line 2, "**duties**" most nearly means
AP 4: Word-In-Context Question   Find the clue words and keywords from the sentence

---

■ **Question Keyword/Key phrase:** "duties"
■ **Incorrect Pattern:** A) dangerous circumstances—EX   **B) job**   C) play—EX   D) satisfaction—IW   E) pay—IW
■ **We Already Found the answer:** It's B. The answer was found before reading the passage.
■ **Relevancy Check:** Choices A and E cannot be the definition for the word "duties." Choice C "play" is antonym to a duty or job.

B is the best answer. The word "duties" means job.
This is the type of question that measures one's vocabulary skill and thus requires no passage reading.

ANSWER EXPLANATIONS FOR TEST 5

Q3. Question Pattern: Why did the piglet **not get paid**?
AP 7: Inference Question   Find the indirect suggestion behind the sentence

- ■ **Question Keyword/Key phrase:** "not get paid"
- ■ **Incorrect Pattern:** A) The piglet met such a poor boss—NI   B) The piglet concerned circus more than money—IW
  C) The piglet didn't ask for money   D) The piglet was confused money with foods—IW
  E) The piglet did not know the existence of money—DC
- ■ **What Does The Question Really Ask?** The question asks a subtle inference beneath what is actually written in the passage.

C is the best answer. "the piglet concluded that *she had just not needed to know* about money at that stage in her life." The above statement does not mean the piglet did not know the existence of money. It implies that money, at her stage in life, is not necessary.

Incorrect Answer Explanation

Choices A and D are—although plausible—not stated in the passage. Choice B is incorrect because the phrase sounds as if the piglet likes circus job. The piglet is depicted in the story as a performer who has to continue the circus to be provided with food and bed. Choice E is incorrect. It knew the existence of money.

Q4. Question Pattern: The **statement below primarily** tells us that
AP 5: Understanding the True Purpose   Find the explicitly stated true purpose of the sentence

- ■ **Question Keyword/Key phrase:** "You might say a more intelligent piglet should figure it out by her age."
- ■ **Incorrect Pattern:** A) readers are familiar with money—NI   B) piglets live under harsh working conditions—IW
  C) the piglet is not too young to understand money
  D) there are other piglets more intelligent—IW   E) the piglet knows what is money—IW.
- ■ **What Does The Question Really Ask?** When you read the statement, read from the author's point of view. That is, here in this phrase, the author speaks as if he is the parent of the piglet, saying " you are (the piglet is) not too young to understand money."
- ■ **Relevancy Check:** Choice A uses a general statement. The "reader" is not the main point of the phrase, but the piglet is. Choice B and E are irrelevant issues to this question—although mentioned in the passage. Choice D took the phrase too literally. The author's main point is not comparing the intelligence among piglets, therefore incorrect.

C is the best answer. *"You might say a more intelligent piglet should figure it out by her age"*
The clue word "by her age" implies that the author thinks the piglet is not too young to understand money at her age.

Q5. The comparison between **"straw" in line 8 and "cannon" in line 10** can be best described respectively as
AP 9: Relationships Question   Find the relationship between the cause and effect, characters, ideas

- ■ **Question Keyword/Key phrase:** "straw" and "cannon"
- ■ **Incorrect Pattern:** A) unhappiness and happiness—DC   B) sadness and enjoyment—DC
  C) comfort and responsibility   D) death and life—EX   E) soft and heavy—IS
- ■ **We Already Found the answer:** It's C. The answer was found before reading the passage.
- ■ **What Does The Question Really Ask?** The question asks the tone lay under the words "straw" and "cannon"

SSAT ABSOLUTE PATTERNS

C is the best answer.   Straw describes the comfort and cannon describes her work with responsibility.

Incorrect Answer Explanation

The word-orders in choices A, B, and D are, by and large, flipped over. Choice D is extreme expression as well. Choice E is Insufficient Information. The author finds dangers from the word "cannon," not the actual weight of it. Thus choice E becomes too literal implication to the words.

Questions 6-11 are based on the following passage.

   Hu-lin was a little slave girl. (Q6) **She had been sold by her father when she was scarcely more than a baby**, and had lived for five years with a number of other children in a wretched houseboat. (Q7 & Q10) **This kind of life was especially hard for Hu-lin.** She longed to play in the fields, above which the huge **kites** were (Q8) **sailing in the air like giant birds.** (Q9) **But if her master ever caught her idling her time away in this manner he beat her most cruelly** and gave her nothing to eat for a whole day. In fact, (Q11) **he was so wicked and cruel that all the children called him Black Heart**.

Q6. Question Pattern: The passage describes **Hu-lin's father** as

AP 8: Understanding Attitude (Tone) Find the tonality: positive vs. negative, mental vs. physical

- ■ **Question Keyword/Key phrase:** "Hu-lin's father"
- ■ **Incorrect Pattern:** A) financially affluent person—DC   B) sympathetic person—DC
   C) highly ethical person—DC **D) condemnable person**   E) lazy person—NI
- ■ **What Does The Question Really Ask?** The narrator's observation towards Hu-lin's father is definitely negative. Once tonality is known, it will be very straightforward to find the answer.

D is the best answer.   The narrator disapproves Hu-lin's father of his malicious act. For he sold his daughter when she was a baby.

Incorrect Answer Explanation

Choices A, B, and C are incorrect because they are all positive words. Choice E is incorrect because there's no indication that he is lazy person.

Q7. Question Pattern: Which word best represents **Hu-lin's life**?

AP 8: Understanding Attitude (Tone) Find the tonality: positive vs. negative, mental vs. physical

- ■ **Question Keyword/Key phrase:** "Hu-lin's life"
- ■ **Incorrect Pattern:** A) fortunate—DC   **B) difficult**   C) uninteresting—NI   D) comfortable—DC   E) regretful—NI
- ■ **We Already Found the answer:** It's B. The answer was found before reading the passage.
- ■ **What Does The Question Really Ask?** Found from the previous question, the overall mood of Hu-line's life is sad.
- ■ **Relevancy Check:** Choices A and D are positive, while the story is pervasively negative, therefore incorrect. Choices C and E are irrelevant words to describe Hu-lin's excruciating life.

B is the best answer.   The passage mainly describes Hu-lin's difficult life as a slave girl.

Q8. Question Pattern: The **"kites"** (line 4) most likely represents

AP 4: Word-In-Context Question   Find the clue words and keywords from the sentence

ANSWER EXPLANATIONS FOR TEST 5

- ■ **Question Keyword/Key phrase:** "kites"
- ■ **Incorrect Pattern:** A) wisdom—NI   B) master—IW   C) flying object—EX   D) home—Ni   **E) freedom**
- ■ **We Already Found the answer:** It's E. The answer was found before reading the passage.
- ■ **What Does The Question Really Ask?** Imagine, contrary to Hu-lin's toiling life, kites freely sailing in the sky.
- ■ **Relevancy Check:** All the rest incorrect answers are irrelevant to the image of kites that represents freedom. Choice C applies the word 'kite' too literally.

E is the best answer. "Sailing kites in the air like giant birds" implies freedom.

Q9. Question Pattern: The word "**idling**" in line 4 indicates
AP 8: Understanding Attitude (Tone) Find the tonality: positive vs. negative, mental vs. physical

- ■ **Question Keyword/Key phrase:** "idling"
- ■ **Incorrect Pattern:** A) master's belief about Hu-lin   B) carefree nature of Hu-lin's father—IW
  C) Hu-lin's true character—DC   D) master's difficult life—DC   E) Hu-lin's comfortable life—DC
- ■ **What Does The Question Really Ask?** If you do not know the exact meaning for the word "idling," find the clue words (meaningful words) in the same sentence and then identify whether the clue word is positive or negative.
- ■ **Relevancy Check:** The word "idling" is a negative word, meaning not working. With such an apparently negative meaning, choice C, D, and E, based on information from the previous questions, contradict the true description about Hulin and the master.

A is the best answer. "But if her master ever caught her idling her time"
As stated above, the word "idling" comes from the master's unjust belief about Hulin.
Choice B is incorrect because the word "idling" reflects the relation between the master and Hulin, not Hulin's father.

Q10. Question Pattern: The **primary purpose** of the passage is to
AP 1: Main Idea (Focus Shifts) Question Find the main idea of the entire passage or the paragraph

- ■ **Question Keyword/Key phrase:** "primary purpose"
- ■ **Incorrect Pattern:** A) show a poor girl's excruciating life   B) introduce the general poor condition of slavery—EX
  C) criticize a wicked man—IS   D) highlight an intense relation with father and child—IS
  E) describe a miserable living of one family—NI
- ■ **We Already Found the answer:** It's A. The answer was found before reading the passage.
- ■ **Relevancy Check:** Choice B "general poor condition of slavery" uses a general statement. The passage is based on the fictional story about a slave girl.

A is the best answer. Throughout the passage, the narrator describes a slave girl name Hu-lin experiencing a painful life.

Incorrect Answer Explanation

Choice C "wicked man" refers to the master, who is not the main character, therefore incorrect.
Choice D is, as choice C, only minor information. Choice E "one family" is never mentioned.

Q11. Question Pattern: The use of the phrase "**Black Heart**" (line 8) conveys
AP 5: Understanding the True Purpose   Find the explicitly stated true purpose of the sentence

- **Question Keyword/Key phrase:** "Black Heart"
- **Incorrect Pattern:** A) the cruelty of the master   B) colorful description of the master's heart—NI
  C) the real name of the master—NI   D) friendly relationship between Hu-lin and the master—DC
  E) the unknown nature of the master—DC
- **We Already Found the answer:** It's A. The answer was found before reading the passage.
- **What Does The Question Really Ask?** The word "Black" is used figuratively implying the master's cruelty.
- **Relevancy Check:** Choice B uses the word "black" too literally. Choice C is not stated in the passage. Choice D and E contradict the passage. For instance, E should change to "known nature" instead of "unknown nature."

A is the best answer. "he was so wicked and cruel that all the children called him Black Heart."
The phrase shows how cruel the master is.

Questions 12-17 are based on the following passage.

India, the great peninsula stretching from the Himalayas to Cape Comorin, is nearly half as large as Europe, and contains a population of 150,000,000. **(Q16) Myth and tradition claim for this people a very great** antiquity, and there are many evidences that **(Q13)** in arts, government, and literature, **(Q12) India is at least coeval** with **China and Egypt**, the three constituting **(Q16) the most ancient civilizations** of the world. **(Q17) While Western Europe was still the bode of barbarians,** and while even Greece had scarcely felt the impulse which aroused her to intellectual life, **(Q14) the fabrics of India had reached a marvelous degree of fineness and beauty; and the monarchs of the West counted it a great privilege to be clothed in** the "purple and fine linen" of the Orient.

Q12. Question Pattern: The passage supports which of the following about **China and Egypt** in line 4?
AP 9: Relationships Question Find the relationship between the cause and effect, characters, ideas

- **Question Keyword/Key phrase:** "China and Egypt"
- **Incorrect Pattern:** A) They had more populations than that of Europe—NI   B) They were bigger than India—NI
  C) They had no civilization—DC   **D) They were as competitive nations as India**
  E) They advanced less than Western Europe—DC
- **What Does The Question Really Ask?** The relationship question is confusing. The first step is by finding a meaningful transitional word within the sentence in question.
- **Reading Tip:** Limit your reading scope to the words "China and Egypt" in line 4.

D is the best answer. "India is at least coeval with China and Egypt"
The transitional words "at least" along with the keyword 'coeval' imply that India was as equal a rival as these two countries. In other words, China and Egypt were as competitive nations as India.
                              Incorrect Answer Explanation
India is the main focus of the sentence in question. The answer choice should therefore focus on India, which makes choice A and E incorrect. Choice A and B are incorrect because the landmass or population of these nations was not mentioned. Choices C and E contradict the passage.

Q13. Question Pattern: Which aspect made the Ancient **India great**?
AP 2: Summary Question   Summarize the sentence or the entire paragraph

ANSWER EXPLANATIONS FOR TEST 5

- **Question Keyword/Key phrase:** "India great"
- **Incorrect Pattern:** A) Myth—IW   B) Advanced science—NI   **C) Art**   D) Food—NI   E) Dancing—NI
- **Relevancy Check:** B) is incorrect because "advanced science" refers to the modern invention.

C is the best answer. "many evidences that in arts, government, and literature, **India is at least coeval**".
As stated above, "art" is one of the aspects that made India great. Choice A is incorrect because "myth" is where the author lays the source of his belief about the superior Ancient India. Choices D and E are not stated in the passage.

Q14. Question Pattern: The clause below tells that the **monarchs of the West**
AP 2: Summary Question   Summarize the sentence or the entire paragraph

- **Question Keyword/Key phrase:** "the monarchs of the West counted it a great privilege to be clothed in"
- **Incorrect Pattern:** A) was protected by India—EX   **B) loved clothing from India**
  C) enjoyed the strong relationship with India—EX   D) effectively banned imported linen from India—DC
  E) wore clothing only imported from India—EX
- **Relevancy Check:** E) is incorrect because the phrase is extreme.

B is the best answer. "*the fabrics of India; and the monarchs of the West ...privilege to be clothed*"
"Fabric" means clothes. The sentence describes that the Western kings loved fabrics from India.

Incorrect Answer Explanation

Choices A and C are extreme expressions and irrelevant to the question. Choice D contradicts the passage.

Q15. Question Pattern: The **author's tone** of the Ancient India is one of
AP 8: Understanding Attitude (Tone) Find the tonality: positive vs. negative, mental vs. physical

- **Question Keyword/Key phrase:** "author's tone"
- **Incorrect Pattern: A) celebratory**   B) doubtful—DC   C) mythic—IW   D) cheerful—NI   E) denial—DC
- **We Already Found the answer:** It's A. The answer was found before reading the passage.
- **What Does The Question Really Ask?** It is important to identify—always—the genre of the passage. This passage describes the Ancient India, and therefore it is the history genre that mainly conveys historical facts. History or science genre uses a neutral tone. In that respect, choice D is highly likely to be incorrect because the word "cheerful" is not a neutral tone, but considered the subjective tone unfit for the history passage.
- **Relevancy Check:** Choice B and E are negative words, while the passage is supportive about the Ancient India. Choice C is not the author's tone. It is a distraction taking the meaningful word "myth" from the passage.

A is the best answer. "celebratory" means officially acknowledging the accomplishment.
The overall passage is written to celebrate the Ancient India.

SSAT ABSOLUTE PATTERNS

SSAT 8 Reading & Verbal Elementary Level

Q16. Question Pattern: The passage **mainly discusses about**
AP 1: Main Idea (Focus Shifts) Question Find the main idea of the entire passage or the paragraph

- **Question Keyword/Key phrase:** "mainly discusses"
- **Incorrect Pattern: A) the Ancient India** B) the Ancient China—IS   C) Western Europe—IS
   D) modern India—NI   E) the Ancient Egypt—IS
- **We Already Found the answer:** It's A. The answer was found before reading the passage.
- **What Does The Question Really Ask?** Seen in Chapter 2, the keyword most frequently appeared in the passage tends to be the answer for the primary purpose question. Throughout the passage, the word "India" appeared most frequently than any other words.
- **Relevancy Check:** Choice D is incorrect because modern India is not mentioned.

A is the best answer. The passage starts with "India," and it ends with "India."
Other nations are only briefly mentioned to support the main theme "Ancient India." Therefore, they cannot be the answer for the main idea question.

Q17. Question Pattern: Which of the following statements is **true about Ancient Western Europe**?
AP 9: Relationships Question Find the relationship between the cause and effect, characters, ideas

- **Question Keyword/Key phrase:** "true about ancient Western Europe"
- **Incorrect Pattern:** A) Its military attacked the barbaric India—DC   **B) It was less developed than India**
   C) The monarchs of the West was afraid of India—NI   D) It was more advanced than India—DC
   E) It preferred China and Egypt to India—NI

B is the best answer. "While Western Europe was still the bode of barbarians,...." tells that Western Europe was less developed than India back then.

Incorrect Answer Explanation

Choices A and D contradict the passage. It describes Western Europe as "barbaric nations" Choices C and E are not stated in the passage.

Questions 18-23 are based on the following passage.
   It happened that a Fox (Q22) **caught its tail in a trap**, and in struggling to **release** himself lost all of it but the stump. (Q18) **At first he was ashamed to show himself among his fellow foxes.**
But at last he determined to put a bolder face upon his misfortune, and summoned all the foxes to a
general meeting to consider a proposal which he had to place before them. When they had assembled
together the Fox proposed that they should all do away with their tails. He pointed out how inconvenient a tail was
when they were pursued by their enemies, the dogs; how much it was in the way when they desired to sit down and
hold a friendly conversation with one another. He failed to see any advantage in carrying about such a useless encumbrance. "That is all very well," said one of **the older foxes**; (Q19 & Q20 & Q21) **"but I do not think you would have
asked us to dispense with our chief** (Q23) **ornament if you had not lost yours."**

ANSWER EXPLANATIONS FOR TEST 5

Q18. Question Pattern: The Fox that lost its tail **changed its mood from**
AP 8: Understanding Attitude (Tone) Find the tonality: positive vs. negative, mental vs. physical

- **Question Keyword/Key phrase:** "changed its mood from"
- **Incorrect Pattern:** A) puzzlement to enthusiasm—NI   B) anger to concernment—IS
  C) violence to sadness—IS   D) hostility to friendliness—NI   **E) concernment to daring**
- **We Already Found the answer:** It's E. The answer was found before reading the passage.
- **What Does The Question Really Ask?** In case of comparison: when two words, two characters, two events are being compared, focus on the latter one; the former (first) one is frequently correct and easier to identify; the second one requires more thinking, however. Test creators know very well that students focus on the former word and lose attention on the latter.
- **Reading Tip:** Test creators focus on contradictory conjunction such as "but" wherein many arguments arise.

E is the best answer. *At first he was ashamed* (CONCERNMENT) of himself showing among his fellow foxes his tail cutoff. But at last he *determined to put a bolder face* (DARING) upon his misfortune,

Incorrect Answer Explanation

Choice A is incorrect for the fox felt neither "puzzled" nor "enthused." Choice B is incorrect. Both "anger" and "concernment" reflect only the moment when he lost his tail, not the feeling afterwards. Choice C "violence" is irrelevant word while "sadness" reflects only the moment when he lost his tail. Choice D is incorrect. The fox felt neither "hostility" nor "friendliness."

Q19. Question Pattern: Why did the Fox tell other foxes to **cut loose their tails**?
AP 5: Understanding the True Purpose   Find the explicitly stated true purpose of the sentence

- **Question Keyword/Key phrase:** "cut loose their tails"
- **Incorrect Pattern: A) He wanted to hide his lost tail**   B) He wanted them to be convenient too—DC
  C) He wanted them to outsmart dogs—DC   D) He wanted them to avoid traps—DC
  E) He truly loved his fellow foxes—DC
- **Reading Tip:** Always focus on "but"—the contradictory conjunction. It is the linchpin of logic that connects between the question and the answer.

A is the best answer.   "but...have asked us to dispense with our chief ornament if you had not lost yours."
In the last sentence he suggests others, too, cut loose their tails wherein he finds a way to hide his lost tail.

Incorrect Answer Explanation

All the remaining incorrect answers are mere excuses of the fox.

Q20 Question Pattern: The old fox's attitude towards the Fox that lost its tail is one of
AP 8: Understanding Attitude (Tone) Find the tonality: positive vs. negative, mental vs. physical

SSAT ABSOLUTE PATTERNS

- **Question Keyword/Key phrase:** "the old fox's attitude"
- **Incorrect Pattern:** A) regret—NI   B) envy—DC   C) appreciation—DC   **D) suspicion**   E) trust—DC
- **We Already Found the answer:** It's D. The answer was found before reading the passage.
- **What Does The Question Really Ask?** This question basically asks about the same thing with the previous question.
- **Reading Tip:** Whenever unclear, read the conclusion.
- **Relevancy Check:** Choice A is irrelevant word to describe the passage. Choices B, C and E contradict the old fox's attitude.

D is the best answer. but I don't think...have asked us to dispense with our chief ornament if you had not lost yours." As stated above, the old fox already knew why he persuades other fellow foxes to cut loose their tails. Thus, the old fox's attitude can be seen as suspicion.

Q21. **Question Pattern:** What is the ultimate goal of the Fox that lost its tail ?

AP 5: Understanding the True Purpose   Find the explicitly stated true purpose of the sentence

- **Question Keyword/Key phrase:** "ultimate goal"
- **Incorrect Pattern:** A) removing inconvenience—DC   **B) hiding his own defect**   C) take revenge on dog—DC   D) cutting loose all the others' tails—IS   E) sitting better—IS
- **We Already Found the answer:** It's B. The answer was found before reading the passage.
- **Relevancy Check:** As same as the last two questions, this question focuses on one thing: the ultimate goal of the fox that lost its tail. Seen from the previous questions, the fox wanted to hides that he had lost his tail.

B is the best answer. "but I do not think you would have asked us to dispense with our chief ornament..."
The old fox reveals the ultimate goal of the fox that lost its tail.

Incorrect Answer Explanation

Choices A, C, and E are all fake excuses to encourage other foxes' participations.
Choice D is incorrect. Cutting loose all the others' tails is only a means to achieve his ultimate goal.

Q22. **Question Pattern:** "release" in line 1 most nearly means?

AP 4: Word-In-Context Question   Find the clue words and keywords from the sentence

- **Question Keyword/Key phrase:** "release"
- **Incorrect Pattern:** A) cut—NI   **B) free**   C) lace—NI   D) reduce—NI   E) revenge—NI
- **We Already Found the answer:** It's B. The answer was found before reading the passage.
- **What Does The Question Really Ask?** Fox caught its tail in a trap. Therefore, the word "release" means to set free.
- **Relevancy Check:** All the other choices are irrelevant information.

B is the best answer. "a Fox caught its tail in a trap, and in struggling to release himself"
The clue word "release" is the synonym to 'free.' The clue word "caught" also helps find the answer "to set free."

ANSWER EXPLANATIONS FOR TEST 5

Q23. **Question Pattern:** The **old fox believes** the tail is a(an)
AP 2: Summary Question   Summarize the sentence or the entire paragraph

- **Question Keyword/Key phrase:** "old fox believes"
- **Incorrect Pattern:** A) legacy—NI   **B) decoration**   C) timeworn tradition—NI
  D) essential part of body—DC   E) unnecessary unit—DC
- **Reading Tip:** Focus on sentence where the old fox speaks.
- **Relevancy Check:** Choice E is incorrect. Throughout the passage and through the previous questions, the main issue was the anxiety of the fox that lost its tail. It is therefore obvious that the tail must be the necessary unit for fox.

B is the best answer.   "but I do not think you would have asked us to dispense with **our chief <u>ornament</u>**"
ornament means decoration.

Incorrect Answer Explanation

Choices A and C are not stated in the passage. Choices D and E contradict the passage. The old fox defines the tail as "ornament." Ornament is, in fact, something not essential, yet it does not mean unnecessary. (imagine woman's makeup) Having a tail may not be essential for survival. However, it is not unnecessary either for "decoration." The old fox believes that it is a decoration.

Questions 24-28 are based on the following passage.

   (Q25) **Physical fitness refers to good body health, and is the result of regular exercise**, (Q28) **proper diet and nutrition, and proper rest** for (Q24) **its recovery.** A person who is physically fit will be able to walk or run without getting breathless and they will be able to carry out the activities of everyday living and not need help. How much each person can do will depend on their age and whether they are a man or woman. (Q26) **A physically fit person usually has a normal weight for their height**. The relation between their height and weight is called their **Body Mass Index**. A taller person can be heavier and still be fit. (Q27) **If a person is too heavy or too thin for their height it may affect their health.**

Q24. **Question Pattern:** In line 2 **"its"** refers to
AP 4: Word-In-Context Question   Find the clue words and keywords from the sentence

- **Question Keyword/Key phrase:** "its"
- **Incorrect Pattern: A) physical**   B) physical fitness—IS   C) health—IW   D) exercise—IW   E) proper diet—IW
- **What Does The Question Really Ask?** "Its" in the question phrase is called the pronoun. The author sometimes emphasizes the main idea through the following sentence by using the pronoun. It is called the "amplifier."
  The amplifier technique is described in chapter 2.

A is the best answer. "physical fitness refers...rest for **its** recovery."
The pronoun—"its" in this question—is used to emphasize the preceding portion of the sentence.
The clue word "recovery" clearly indicates that the pronoun "its" refers to "physical."

Incorrect Answer Explanation

Choice B overshot the description because "fitness recovery" doesn't make sense. The word "fitness" in choice B should be removed. All the rest incorrect answers do not fit the following word "recovery"

Q25. Question Pattern: All of the following refer to the "Physical fitness" (lines 1-2) EXCEPT
AP 2: Summary Question   Summarize the sentence or the entire paragraph

- ■ **Question Keyword/Key phrase:** "Physical fitness EXCEPT "
- ■ **Incorrect Pattern:** A) good diet—IW   **B) good mentality**   C) measured exercise—IW
  D) good health—IW   E) enough rest—IW
- ■ **We Already Found the answer:** It's B. The answer was found before reading the passage.
- ■ **What Does The Question Really Ask?** Pay attention to the word "EXCEPT." it is called the negative-type of question. The negative-type of question is difficult and time consuming because four out of five alternatives are true. One remaining untrue statement becomes the correct answer. To get clearer idea about the question, you can skip such a negative-type question and come back later.
- ■ **Relevancy Check:** The answer for this question can be solved through a common sense. "mentality" has no direct connection to physical fitness, although it may indirectly help maintain physicality.

B is the best answer. "mentality" is not related to "physicality." Physical fitness refers to (D) good body health, which is the result of (C) regular exercise. Choice (A) good diet and (E) enough rest are also good for the physical fitness and recovery. Thus, they are connected to physical fitness and therefore incorrect.

Q26. Question Pattern: The **passage** was probably **taken from the**
AP 7: Inference Question   Find the indirect suggestion behind the sentence

- ■ **Question Keyword/Key phrase:** "passage taken from "
- ■ **Incorrect Pattern:** A) world history book—NI   **B) children's dietary guidelines**
  C) fashion magazine—NI   D) child psychology textbook—NI   E) new clinical research—NI
- ■ **We Already Found the answer:** It's B. The answer was found before reading the passage.
- ■ **Relevancy Check:** This is inference question. The answer will not be directly stated in the passage. It requires a guessing skill vested with logical understanding of the passage.

B is the best answer. The author's main focus was on body mass index, a measurement associated with proper body height and weight. It is reasonable to assume that, to maintain proper physical fitness, a proper diet (food) is needed. When these two factors are combined, it generates Choice B "children's dietary guidelines."
Incorrect Answer Explanation
Choice A and C are Irrelevant information to the passage. Choice D is incorrect because "psychology" Is about human mentality, not physicality. Choice E is incorrect because "physical fitness" is nothing new a research.

ANSWER EXPLANATIONS FOR TEST 5

Q27. Question Pattern: A girl whose **Body Mass Index** is subject to improve may have **a problem** with
AP 7: Inference Question Find the indirect suggestion behind the sentence

- ■ **Question Keyword/Key phrase:** "a problem"
- ■ **Incorrect Pattern:** A) age—NI B) school work—NI C) gender—NI **D) weight** E) race—NI
- ■ **We Already Found the answer:** It's D. The answer was found before reading the passage.
- ■ **What Does The Question Really Ask?** Body Mass Index measures the normal body with average height and weight.
- ■ **Relevancy Check:** All the other incorrect answers are irrelevant information to the "body mass index."

D is the best answer.   A girl who has a problem with body mass index has a problem with weight.

Q28. Question Pattern: Which of the following child best **fits for Body Mass Index (line 6)?**
AP 7: Inference Question Find the indirect suggestion behind the sentence

- ■ **Question Keyword/Key phrase:** "fits for Body Mass Index"
- ■ **Incorrect Pattern:** A) A boy with an honored degree at school—NI   B) The tallest girl in the class—DC
  C) A girl who wants to have a pretty body—NI   D) A boy with kind personality—NI
  E) A boy who is about the average height and normal weight
- ■ **We Already Found the answer:** It's E. The answer was found before reading the passage.
- ■ **What Does The Question Really Ask?** The term "body mass index" indicates that the measurements should be based on the normal body mass.
- ■ **Relevancy Check:** Choice A, C, and D are not related to body mass.

E is the best answer.   "The relation between height and weight is called their Body Mass Index"
Body Mass Index refers to a *normal (average) height and weight.*
Choice B is incorrect because "the tallest" does not best fits for the average body mass index.

SSAT ABSOLUTE PATTERNS

Test 5 Absolute Patterns for the analogy Section

AP1. Category Pattern   Find the Part and Whole Relation, the Same Type or Association

16. Time is to money as golden is to   **A) silence**   B) stopwatch   C) ring   D) pretty   E) underground

A is the best answer.
This question is based on proverbs. Time is money as (A) silence is golden. Choice B is associated with 'time' but not with the entire question-stem. Choice C is associated with 'golden' but not with the entire question-stem. Choices D and E are Irrelevant words to the question-stem

AP5. Degree Pattern   Find the Degree (Increase or Decrease), Find the Shape of place or thing

17. 100 is complete as 10 is   A) misleading   B) bad   **C) imperfect**   D) disqualified   E) Immoral

C is the best answer.   This question asks whether the degree between the primary and the secondary word increases or decreases in value, size, color, quantity, quality, emotion, etc.
If 100 is complete, 10 should be (C) imperfect or incomplete. The rest are Irrelevant words to the question-stem

AP4. Characteristic Pattern   Find the Characteristic of Person, Place, Object, or Idea

18. Art is to creativity as   A) Biology is to high school   **B) Math is to logic**   C) English is to second language
    D) Science is to Physics   E) Music is to boring

B is the best answer.   Art applies creativity as math applies logic.
Choices A, C, and D are associated with the school subject but not with "creativity," the secondary word in the question stem.   Choice E is incorrect because "boring" is not the characteristics of music.

AP3. Purpose (Tool) Pattern   Find the Purpose of Individual and the Goal, the Function of Tool

19. Garage is to baby as car is to   A) cute   B) noise   C) mother   **D) cradle**   E) diapers

D is the best answer. Garage is used to store car as cradle is used to sleep baby. All the rest are associated with "baby," the secondary word in the question stem but not with the entire question-stem.

AP8. Production Pattern   Find What Produces What and the Cause and Effect Relation

20. Car is to pollution as to friend is to   A) human being   B) school   C) classmate   D) love   **E) friendship**

E is the best answer. Car produces pollution as friend produces friendship.
Choices A, B, and C are associated with "friend," but not with the car; therefore, do not work with the entire question-stem.   Choice D does not work with "Car is to pollution."

ANSWER EXPLANATIONS FOR TEST 5

AP1. Category Pattern Find the Part and Whole Relation, the Same Type or Association

21. Lion is to zebra as

A) strong is to ox   **B) cow is to hay**   C) eagle is to brave   D) stripe is to coward   E) grass is to weed

B is the best answer. Lion eats zebra as cow eats hay. Choices A and C are the Mental or Definition Pattern that figuratively symbolize ox as a strong animal and eagle as a brave animal. Choice D uses Irrelevant words to the question-stem. Choice E uses "zebra" in the question-stem but not the animals.

AP3. Purpose (Tool) Pattern Find the Purpose of Individual and the Goal, the Function of Tool

22. Exercise is to knowledge as

A) reading is to gym   B) gym is to sweat   C) power is to young   D) practice is to success   E) death is to live

A is the best answer. The purpose of gym is to exercise as the purpose of reading is to gain knowledge. Choice B is associated with "exercise," the primary word in the question stem but not with "knowledge," the entire question-stem. Choices C, D, and E are almost Irrelevant words to the question-stem.

AP4. Characteristic Pattern Find the Characteristic of Person, Place, Object, or Idea

23. Weather is to steak as mild is to   A) expensive B) restaurant **C) medium** D) well done E) meal

C is the best answer. Mild weather and a medium steak are similar in their temperature-related state. The rest are associated with "steak," the secondary word in the question stem but not with the "weather," the entire question-stem.

AP4. Characteristic Pattern Find the Characteristic of Person, Place, Object, or Idea

24. Africa is to North Pole as hot is to   **A) cold**   B) Ice   C) Igloo   D) far away   E) Santa Clause

A is the best answer. This question asks the temperature in certain region.
Africa is hot as North Pole is (A) cold. The rest are associated with "North Pole," the secondary word in the question stem but not with entire the question-stem.

AP2. Synonym/Antonym Find the similar or opposite meaning between the words

25. Arrival is to departure as

A) dessert is to appetizer   B) fire is to firefighter   C) garbage is to can   D) plane is to airport   E) ticket is to access

A is the best answer. Arrival is an antonym to departure as (A) dessert is a conceptual antonym to appetizer.
Choices B, C, D, and E are, by and large, the Purpose (Tool) Pattern.

SSAT ABSOLUTE PATTERNS

AP 8. The Production Pattern Find What Produces What and the Cause and Effect Relation

26. Rose is to socks as

A) fragrance is to smell   B) pretty is to ugly   C) flower is to plastic   D) plant is to leather   E) fragrance is to dirty

A is the best answer. Rose produces fragrance as socks produce [bad] smell. Choice B is the Mental (Emotion) Pattern. Choice C and D is Irrelevant to the question-stem. Choice E "dirty" is not linked to "fragrance" nor to "Rose."

AP5. Degree Pattern Find the Degree (Increase or Decrease), Find the Shape of place or thing

27. Eyeglass is to bicycle tire as

A) dog is to legs   B) lamp is to light   C) cat is to seven   D) sandwich is to subway   **E) T.V. monitor and cell phone**

E is the best answer. Both eyeglass and bicycle tire are round shape as (E) T.V. monitor and cell phone are rectangular shape. Choice A is the part-whole in Category Pattern. Choice B is the Purpose (Tool) Pattern.
Choices C and D use largely Irrelevant words between their primary-and-secondary-word combinations.

AP1. Category Pattern Find the Part and Whole Relation, the Same Type or Association

28. Laundry room is to washing machine as   **A) attic is to old photo album**   B) oasis is to desert
    C) pig is to bacon   D) bank is to robber   E) university is to high school

A is the best answer. Laundry room keeps washing machine as (A) attic keeps old photo album.
Choice B is the Category Pattern but the words order is flipped. Choice C is the Production Pattern. Choice E is the Degree Pattern.

AP1. Category Pattern Find the Part and Whole Relation, the Same Type or Association

29. Ship is to submarine as   A) nephew is to annoying   B) pet is to cute   C) failure is disappointment
    D) grade 10 is to grade 11   **E) bird is to airplane**

E is the best answer. Both ship and submarine are operated on/under the sea as (E) both bird and airplane are flown in the sky. Choices A and B are irrelevant words to the question-stem.
Choice C is the Mental Pattern. Choice D is the Degree Pattern. None of them are related to the question-stem.

AP4. Characteristic Pattern Find the Characteristic of Person, Place, Object, or Idea

30. Zoo is to hospital as

A) animal is to patient   B) circus is to ticket   C) lion is to rabbit   D) sack is to heavy   E) song is to mellow

A is the best answer. This question asks to find a certain place for something or someone.
Zoo is paired with animals as (A) hospital is paired with patients.
Choice B is the Purpose (Tool) Pattern related to "Zoo" but not the entire question-stem. Choice C is the Category Pattern related to "Zoo" but not the entire question-stem.
Choices D and E are Subjective-Objective Pattern unrelated to the question-stem.

SSAT

Reading & Verbal Section

Test 6

Test 6 Reading Section
Time: 30 Minutes, 28 Questions

Directions: Each reading passage is followed by questions about it. Answer the questions that follow a passage on the basis of what is stated or implied in that passage.

Questions 1-6 are based on the following passage.

Line Cave paintings are paintings on cave walls and ceilings. Usually these paintings were made in prehistoric times. The oldest are from about 32,000 years ago, but scientists still disagree if this dating is correct. It is not known why these paintings were made.
  Most Scientists think they may have had a function for rituals. They may also have been a way
5 to transit information; to tell other people about something. Most paintings are in caves that are difficult to access. These caves usually also do not show signs that people lived there all year round.
  Today, there are about 350 caves known which have paintings in them. Fewer of those have survived though, because of erosion. One such example are the rock paintings in Astuvs.

1

Which of the following choice is true with the Cave paintings?

A) They are drawn in ancient people's house
B) Scientists agree with the date they were painted
C) The oldest one is less than 30,000 years old
D) Cave painting may have had some functions
E) Most cave paintings are easy to access

2

In line 2, "prehistoric" most nearly means

A) ancient
B) modern
C) past
D) historically unknown time in the past
E) since the beginning of civilization

3

Read the sentence from line 4 in the box below.

| they may have had a function for rituals |

The tone of the statement tells that
A) there's a lack of confidence among scientists
B) some scientists have unreasonable expectation
C) scientists have strong belief about their findings
D) scientists are deeply religious people
E) scientists are naturally humble people

4

Based on paragraph 2 (lines 4-7), scientists are primarily concerned with?
A) the comparison to modern paintings
B) the purpose of the painting
C) the way people lived in the cave
D) the painting skills
E) the monetary value of paintings
*the word "monetary" means related to money

5

The author mentions "erosion" in line 9 in order to
A) explain the reasons many paintings did not survive
B) point out a possible location of the undiscovered cave paintings
C) show the genuine values of the remaining paintings
D) show respect to the painters
E) tell many paintings are still well-preserved

6

In line 9, "**Astuvs**" mainly suggests that some paintings
A) can be found in museums
B) are extremely well preserved
C) are harder to understand the meanings of the paintings
D) were drawn by well-known artists
E) experienced a great deal of spoilage

Questions 7-11 are based on the following passage.

Line   A Countryman's son by accident trod upon a Serpent's tail, which turned and bit him so that he died. The father in a rage got his axe, and pursuing the Serpent, cut off part of its tail. So the Serpent in revenge began stinging several of the Farmer's cattle and caused him severe loss. Well, the Farmer thought it best to make it up with the Serpent, and brought food and honey to
5   the mouth of its lair, and said to it: 'Let's forget and forgive; perhaps you were right to punish my son, and take vengeance on my cattle, but surely I was right in trying to revenge him; now that we are both satisfied why should not we be friends again?' 'No, no,' said the Serpent; 'take away your gifts; you can never forget the death of your son, nor I the loss of my tail.' Injuries may be forgiven, but not forgotten.

7

What could be the best lesson from the passage?

A) Human's greatest enemy: Serpent
B) A farmer's sorrow
C) Revenge can't be forgotten
D) A true companionship
E) An inescapable fate of the farmer

8

In line 6 "vengeance" most nearly means?

A) revenge
B) enemy
C) kill
D) take care of
E) veneration

9

The farmer's mood shifts from anger to

A) courage
B) forgiveness
C) uncertainty
D) hostility
E) indifference

10

The word "gifts" in line 8 can be best understood as

A) revenge
B) peace
C) old story
D) the future
E) lost tail

11

In line 8 ("take away...my tail"), the serpent is being characterized as

A) easy-going
B) humorous
C) sly
D) resentful
E) ineffective

Questions 12-17 are based on the following passage.

Line   The climate on earth has not stayed the same through human history. There are long periods of time where it is generally warmer, and there are those where it is generally colder. When it is generally colder, there is more ice on the poles of the planet. That is why such a period is called an Ice Age.

5   Two have **affected** humans.   From 70,000 to around 10,000 years ago there was a big ice age which affected humans and the way that they lived. Between 1600 AD to around 1900 AD there was a period called the Little Ice Age when the climate was colder than usual.

   Climate has an effect on the types of food that can be found in different parts of the world. Everywhere that humans live, there is a unique staple food

12
The climate on earth through human history can be seen as
A) unchanging
B) extremely irregular
C) generally colder
D) generally warmer
E) periodic

13
Read this statement from lines 5

Two have **affected** humans.

In which sentence below does the word **affected** mean the same as in the sentence above?
A) Tom was affected deeply by the sad movie
B) Cindy affected she didn't eat the pizza
C) David's foot injury affected his limbs
D) The impact of climate change is great
E) The ill-effect of air pollution changes our lives

14
The discussion of the Little Ice Age in line 7 primarily suggests that
A) the Little Ice Age is approaching near future
B) the animation "Ice Age" is based on the Little Ice Age
C) the Little Ice Age is a historical fact
D) scientists know very little about the Little Ice Age
E) the Little Ice Age was warmer than commonly supposed

15
The primary tone of the passage is
A) informative
B) celebratory
C) anecdotal
D) argumentative
E) mythic

16

The literary device used in lines 5-7 (From 70,000 to around 10,000 years ...colder than usual.) is

A) metaphor
B) oxymoron
C) flashback
D) comparison
E) personification

17

Which of the following choices belongs to the **staple food** category (line 9)?

A) Imported pineapple
B) Maize in Mexico
C) Organic vegetable
D) Cereal and milk
E) Bread and beans at a restaurant

Questions 18-22 are based on the following passage.

Line   Babette and Antone were the children of a very poor woodcutter. Now though their father toiled in this forest from dawn until dark, he could earn but little. Their mother made fine laces which Antone carried to the market to sell; but in spite of all their efforts, the poor parents seldom could give their children more than bread and broth to eat. But it worried the woodcutter that Antone
5   was ten years old and had not yet gone to school. Antone's mother taught him to read and write. Often as he sat doing his sums on the hearthstone, with a bit of charcoal for a pencil, his mother would sigh sadly. Antone did not like his mother to be sad, and so he always laughed to cheer her.

18
The children helped their parents by
A) hunting
B) cutting woods
C) selling on the market
D) setting traps in the woods
E) star working at dawn until dark

19
"**toiled**" in line 1 most nearly means
A) worked in a bathroom
B) worked extremely hard
C) prepared
D) looked for
E) escaped

20
As Antone was getting older, the parents' main concern was
A) introducing him his bride
B) teaching him how to make money
C) training him woodcutting
D) providing him education
E) helping him to be excel at school

21
Who acted as a teacher for Antone?
A) Babette
B) father
C) mother
D) other woodcutters
E) Antone himself

22
Which of the following best reflects Antone as a poor kid?
A) Babette
B) forest
C) fine laces
D) mother
E) charcoal

Questions 23-28 are based on the following passage.

Line   In some societies, people think that art belongs to the person who made it, such as Indigenous Aboriginal Australian Art. They think that the artist put his or her "talent" into the art. In this view, the art is the property of the artist. In other societies, people think that art belongs to no one They think that society has put its social capital into the artist and the artist's work. In this
5 view, society made the art, through the artist.
   An artwork is normally judged and valued by how much impact it has on people, the mount of people who can relate to it, and how much people appreciate it.

23
"Indigenous Aboriginal Australian Art" describes that some societies
A) do not appreciate beautiful art
B) think art belongs to its creator
C) have no talented artists
D) think art doesn't exist
E) believe Aboriginal Australian Art is the best art

*Indigenous = native. Aboriginal = original

24
What does the word **property** in line 3 mean
A) quality
B) characteristic
C) stuff
D) possession
E) effort

25
Read the clause from line 3 in the box below.

> In other societies, people think that art belongs to no one.

Which choice correctly describes the above sentence?
A) True artists do not exist
B) Society concerns less on art
C) Society concerns less on artist
D) Society made the art
E) Art actually made society

26
According to the last sentence (lines 6-7), an artwork is valued by
A) the market price
B) arts that have impacted on people
C) artist's skill
D) governmental support
E) the age and reputation of artists

27
The main purpose of the passage is to
A) praise great artists
B) discuss the value of art
C) explain the importance of art education
D) compare art and science
E) celebrate indigenous aboriginal art

28
Read the clause from line 7 in the box below.

> how much **people** appreciate it.

Based on the passage, which person belongs to the people in the above statement?
A) artist
B) art historian
C) Aboriginal Australians
D) pianist
E) audience

Verbal Test 6
20 MINUTES, 30 QUESTIONS

Directions: the synonym questions ask you to find the most appropriate synonym to the question.

The analogy questions ask you to find the most appropriate analogy to the question. Select the answer that best matches to the question.

Synonyms

Each of the following questions consists of one word followed by five words or phrases. You are to select the one word or phrase whose meaning is closest to the word in capital letters.

Sample Question:

ABILITY

A) mistake
B) **talent**
C) abandon
D) best student
E) late

1. FADE
A) fashion
B) age
C) add
D) dim
E) bright

2. DOSE
A) measurement
B) does
C) did
D) allowance
E) freedom

3. RENDEZVOUS
A) encounter
B) labor
C) rocket
D) stars
E) bulldozer

4. INHALE
A) cyclone
B) draw in
C) extract
D) shock
E) breath

5. GLARE
A) flare
B) look
C) shy
D) gladiator
E) movie

6. MISTY
A) soft
B) comfortable
C) wild
D) murky
E) swamp

7. NOOK
A) alcove
B) annoyance
C) okay
D) disapprove
E) noon

8. HOIST
A) host
B) guest
C) heave
D) respect
E) disdain

9. BOYCOTT
A) body
B) boy
C) adolescent
D) refuse
E) boy scout

10. JUMBLE
A) patchwork
B) bee
C) honey
D) togetherness
E) stick

11. ARCH
A) tail
B) head
C) mother
D) father
E) house

12. PERK
A) hockey
B) ball
C) extra
D) play
E) icy

13. CIRCUMSTANCE

A) round

B) circus

C) play

D) situation

E) standing

14. UNREST

A) disquiet

B) rest

C) dreamless

D) sleepless

E) sound

15. DEMAND

A) jewelry

B) diamond

C) valuable

D) plea

E) accept

Analogies

The following questions ask you to find relationships between words. For each question, select the answer choice that best completes the meaning of the sentence.

SAMPLE QUESTION

Q: River is to Ocean as:

A) better is to good

B) rain is to cloud

C) father is to mother

D) city is to country

E) fork is to spoon

This question is Degree Analogy question (small to big movement).

Ⓓ is the correct answer. Just as river is smaller than Ocean, so is city to the country.

Ⓐ is incorrect because the order is flipped over.

Ⓑ is incorrect because this is 'Production Analogy—what-produce-what.'

Ⓒ and Ⓔ are incorrect because there are no big and small relations between mother and father, so does fork to spoon.

16. Production is to make as

A) arrival is to come

B) factory is worker

C) cost is to price

D) shop is to retailer

E) discount is premium

17. Music is to Yoga as ear is to

A) exercise

B) body

C) gym

D) earphone

E) relax

18. Panda is to coyote as
A) video game is to online
B) bamboo is to tree
C) cute is to ugly
D) bear is to hibernation
E) eye is to black

19. Gang is to teach as rob is to
A) bank
B) teacher
C) school
D) student
E) money

20. Speed limit is 50 miles as
A) success is to failure
B) knife is to gun
C) 20 Celsius is to 48 Fahrenheit
D) boiling point is 100 degree
E) grace is to ugly

21. Food is to energy as
A) mountain is to vantage point
B) cup is to coffee
C) sleep is to rest
D) exam is to cheat
E) factory is to machine

22. Swamp is to water as cola is to
A) pumpkin
B) bakery
C) bread
D) cake
E) oil

23. Mosquito is to bee as
A) cat is to butterfly
B) insect is to animal
C) pretty is to ugly
D) disease is to pollination
E) hot is to cold

24. White House is to president as
A) zoo is to zoologist
B) teacher is to school
C) house is to door
D) mother is to cook
E) office is to father

25. Penguin is to camel as
A) cactus is to hot
B) tattoo is to skin
C) bird is to warm
D) flu is to cough
E) cold is to hot

26. Ant is to bird as eagle is to
A) sky
B) king
C) insect
D) beak
E) brave

27. Surgery is to wilderness as
A) hunting is to hospital
B) medicine is to pill
C) nurse is to help
D) doctor is to kind
E) patient is to cure

28. Receipt is to shop as
A) ticket is to airplane
B) tip is to restaurant
C) sales tax is to expire
D) retail is to wholesale
E) good to goods

29. Police is to badge as
A) kindergarten boy is to name tag
B) car is to plate
C) tire is to flat
D) dish is to restaurant
E) jail is to bar

30. Rain is to cane as
A) grandma is to snow
B) old is to umbrella
C) young is to computer
D) father is to mother
E) sunglass is to dark

SSAT ELEMENTARY LEVEL

Reading & Verbal Section

Test 6

Answer Explanations

TEST 6
READING SECTION

Please refer to the Reading Section AP Analyses

SYNONYM QUESTIONS
TEST 6 NO.1 ~ 35

ANALOGY QUESTIONS
TEST 6 NO. 16-30

Please refer to the Reading Section AP Analyses

1 D
2 A
3 A
4 E
5 B
6 D
7 A
8 C
9 D
10 D
11 B
12 C
13 D
14 A
15 D

ANSWER EXPLANATIONS FOR TEST 6

Test 6 Absolute Patterns for the Reading Section

Questions 1-6 are based on the following passage.
   Cave paintings are paintings on cave walls and ceilings. Usually these paintings were made in (Q2) **prehistoric** times. The oldest are from about 32,000 years ago, but scientists still disagree if this dating is correct. It is not known why these paintings were made.

   Most Scientists think (Q1 & Q3 Q4) **they may have had a function for rituals**. They may also have been a way to transit information; to tell other people about something. Most paintings are in caves that are difficult to access. These caves usually also do not show signs that people lived there all year round.

   Today, there are about 350 caves known which have paintings in them. **Fewer of those have survived** (Q5 & Q6) **because of erosion. One such example are the rock paintings in Astuvs.**

Q1. **AP Question Pattern:** Which of the following choice is **true with the Cave paintings**?
AP 2: Summary Question   Summarize the sentence or the entire paragraph

---

■ **Question Keyword/Key phrase:** "true about Cave paintings"
■ **Incorrect Pattern:** A) They are drawn in ancient people's house-DC
   B) Scientists agree about the date they were made-DC   C) The oldest one is less than 30,000 years old—DC
   D) Cave painting may have had some functions   E) Most cave paintings are easy to access—DC
■ **What Does The Question Really Ask?** "true with Cave painting" implies overall understanding of the passage. This sort of questions can always be dealt with later and skip it for now.

D is the best answer. "Most Scientists think they may have had a function for rituals."
All the other incorrect answers contradict the passage descriptions.

Q2: **Question Pattern:** In line 2, **"prehistoric"** most nearly means
AP 4: Word-In-Context Question   Find the clue words and keywords from the sentence

---

■ **Question Keyword/Key phrase:** "prehistoric"
■ **Incorrect Pattern: A) ancient**   B) modern—DC   C) past—IW   D) historically unknown time in the past—EX
   E) since the beginning of civilization—EX
■ **We Already Found the answer:** It's A. The answer was found before reading the passage.
■ **What Does The Question Really Ask?** The question asking for the literal definition—"Pre/historic"—does not require passage reading.
■ **Relevancy Check:** Choice B is a direct contradiction. Choice C is a weak implication. 'prehistoric" does not simply refer to the "past."

A is the best answer. "Prehistoric" means ancient.
Choice D is incorrect because the phrase emphasizes "unknown." "prehistoric" does not mean "unknown."
Choice E is unclear with its definition.

Q3. **Question Pattern: The tone** of the statement tells that
AP 8: Understanding Attitude (Tone) Find the tonality: positive vs. negative, mental vs. physical

SSAT ABSOLUTE PATTERNS

■ **Question Keyword/Key phrase:** "they may have had a function for rituals"
■ **Incorrect Pattern:** A) there's a lack of confidence among scientists
B) some scientists have unreasonable expectation—EX C) scientists have strong belief about their findings—DC
D) scientists are deeply religious people—NI   E) scientists are naturally humble people—NI
■ **We Already Found the answer:** It's A. The answer was found before reading the passage.
■ **What Does The Question Really Ask?** The keyword "tone" in the question phrase is seeking the author's tone. In other words, the question does not look for the content meaning in the phrase.
■ **Relevancy Check:** B) "unreasonable expectation" implies that the scientists demand too much, an extreme phrase. Choice C is a direct contradiction in tonality.

A is the best answer. "Most Scientists think they **may have had** a function for rituals."
'may have had,' reveals lacks of confidence among scientists.
Choices D and E are not stated in the passage.

Q4. Question Pattern: Based on paragraph 2 (lines 5-8), scientists are primarily concerned with?
AP 2: Summary Question   Summarize the sentence or the entire paragraph

■ **Question Keyword/Key phrase:** "scientists are concerned with"
■ **Incorrect Pattern:** A) the comparison between modern paintings—NI **B) the purpose of the painting**
C) the way people lived in the cave—NI D) the painting skills—NI E) the monetary value of paintings—NI

B is the best answer. The second paragraph describes many different opinions about the purpose of paintings drawn in the caves. All the other alternatives are not mentioned in the second paragraph.

Q5. Question Pattern: The author mentions "**erosion**" in line 11 in order to
AP 5: Understanding the True Purpose   Find the explicitly stated true purpose of the sentence

■ **Question Keyword/Key phrase:** "erosion"
■ **Incorrect Pattern: A) explain the reasons many paintings did not survive** B) point out a possible location of the undiscovered cave paintings—NI C) show the genuine values of the remaining paintings—NI
D) show respect to the painters NI E) tell many paintings are still well-preserved DC
■ **We Already Found the answer:** It's A. The answer was found before reading the passage.
■ **Reading Tip:** It is important to focus on and understand what is being said between the conjunction "because" in the sentence in the passage.

A is the best answer. "Fewer of those have survived though, because of erosion."
As stated above, the author mentions "erosion" to tell many paintings did not survive.
The conjunction "because" in sentence is very important to understand the cause-effect relation. The cause (because in the passage) and the "effect" (the correct answer) work as a pair.
<div align="center">**Incorrect Answer Explanation**</div>
Choices B, C, and D are irrelevant information not stated in the passage. Choice E contradicts the passage because "Erosion" means spoilage, the antonym of "preserved."

ANSWER EXPLANATIONS FOR TEST 6

Q6. **Question Pattern:** In line 11, "**Astuv**s" mainly suggests that some paintings
AP 3: Example Question Find the primary reason for using the example sentence

---

- **Question Keyword/Key phrase:** "**Astuv**s"
- **Incorrect Pattern:** A) can be found in museums—NI   B) are extremely well preserved —DC
  C) are harder to understand the meanings of the paintings—NI   D) were drawn by well-known artists—NI
  E) experienced a great deal of spoilage
- **What Does The Question Really Ask?** Guess immediately that this question is using the specific name "Astuvs." Since "Astuvs" is not the main idea of the passage, it must be an example. The example type of question provides the answer right below or above the example sentence. For the author states his main argument right before or after the example sentence.
- **Relevancy Check:** Choices A and D are incorrect. We now know the passage is about cava paintings in prehistoric time, during which neither well-known artists nor museum could possibly exist.

E is the best answer.   Fewer of those have survived though, because of erosion.   One such example is the rock paintings of Astuv.
As stated above, "One such example" shows paintings that experienced a great deal of spoilage to survive.

The Relevancy Check

Choice B contradicts the passage . Choice C is irrelevant information not stated in the passage.

Questions 7-11 are based on the following passage.
   A Countryman's son by accident trod upon a Serpent's tail, which turned and bit him so that he died. The father in a rage got his axe, and pursuing the Serpent, cut off part of its tail. So the Serpent in revenge began (Q11) **stinging** several of the Farmer's cattle and caused him severe loss.
   Well, the Farmer thought it best to make it up with the Serpent, and brought food and honey to the mouth of its lair, and said to it: (Q9 & Q10) **'Let's forget and forgive**; perhaps you were right to punish my son, and take vengeance on my cattle, but surely I was right in trying to (Q8) **revenge** him; now that we are both satisfied why should not we be friends again?' 'No, no,' said the Serpent; 'take away your **gifts;** you can never forget the death of your son, nor I the loss of my tail.' (Q7) **Injuries may be forgiven, but not Forgotten.**

Q7. **Question Pattern:** What could be the best **lesson from the passage**?
AP 1: Main Idea (Focus Shifts) Question Find the main idea of the entire passage or the paragraph

---

- **Question Keyword/Key phrase:** "lesson"
- **Incorrect Pattern:** A) Human's greatest enemy: Serpent—NI(GE)   B) A farmer's sorrow—IS
  C) Revenge can't be forgotten   D) A true companionship—DC   E) An inescapable fate of the farmer—IS
- **Reading Tip:** When in doubt, read the conclusion. The conclusion—in almost all cases—provides the most clear idea about the passage. It provides the author's primary tonality and the main theme wherein lies "the best lesson."
- **Relevancy Check:** Choice A is irrelevant information that merely used generalization.

C is the best answer. "Injuries may be forgiven, but not forgotten."
The last sentence clearly summarizes the passage wherein provides the "lesson": "Injuries may be forgiven, but not forgotten. In other words, revenge can't be forgotten.

SSAT ABSOLUTE PATTERNS

Incorrect Answer Explanation
Choices B and E are Insufficient Information. They are elements of the story but cannot be the lesson of the passage. Choice D contradicts the original story.

Q8. Question Pattern: In line 6 **"vengeance"** most nearly means? **AP 4: Word-In-Context Question** Find the clue words and keywords from the sentence

■ **Question Keyword/Key phrase:** "vengeance" ■ **Incorrect Pattern:** A) revenge   B) enemy—NI   C) kill—EX   D) take care of—IS   E) veneration—DC ■ **We Already Found the answer:** It's A. The answer was found before reading the passage. ■ **What Does The Question Really Ask?** For the Word-in-Context question, read the passage and find the clue words ■ **Relevancy Check:** Choice B is related with the word "vengeance, " yet still, not the synonym.   Choice C is extreme expression. Choice D is a weak implication. Choice E is the antonym to vengeance.

A is the best answer. "you were right to **punish** my son, and take <u>vengeance</u> on my cattle, but surely I was right in trying to **revenge** him." Focus on the above bold-faced clue words. We can see that 'Vengeance' means revenge.

Q9. Question Pattern: Throughout the story, the farmer's **mood shifts from anger to** **AP 8: Understanding Attitude (Tone)** Find the tonality: positive vs. negative, mental vs. physical

■ **Question Keyword/Key phrase:** "mood shifts from anger to " ■ **Incorrect Pattern:** A) courage—NI   **B) forgiveness**   C) uncertainty—NI   D) hostility—DC   E) indifference—NI ■ **What Does The Question Really Ask?** The question asks how farmer's mood (tone) has shifted. ■ **Relevancy Check:** Choice C is incorrect because the word "uncertainty" has no clearly defined tonality. The correct answer usually contain either positive or negative tone. In almost all questions, no tone means no answer.

B is the best answer. "The father in a rage got his axe, and pursuing the Serpent, cut off part of its tail." The phrase shows the Farmer's "ANGER." "The Farmer thought it best to make it up with the Serpent." The above phrase shows the Farmer's "FORGIVENESS." Choices A and E are irrelevant words to the passage. Choice D contradicts the passage .

Q10. Question Pattern: The word **"gifts"** in line 10 can be best understood as **AP 5: Understanding the True Purpose**   Find the explicitly stated true purpose of the sentence

■ **Question Keyword/Key phrase:** "gifts" ■ **Incorrect Pattern:** A) revenge—DC   **B) peace**   C) death—DC   D) the future—NI   E) lost tail—DC ■ **We Already Found the answer:** It's B. The answer was found before reading the passage. ■ **What Does The Question Really Ask?** The word "gifts" is positive. It is therefore obvious to choose the positive words. ■ **Relevancy Check:** Choices A, C and E are negative words. Therefore, they contradict the word "gift." Choice D is irrelevant word.

ANSWER EXPLANATIONS FOR TEST 6

B is the best answer. "take away your gifts; you can never forget the death of your son"
The gift alludes peace or forgiveness.

Q11. Question Pattern: In line 9 ("take away...my tail"), the serpent is being characterized as
AP 8: Understanding Attitude (Tone) Find the tonality: positive vs. negative, mental vs. physical

- ■ **Question Keyword/Key phrase:** "serpent as being"
- ■ **Incorrect Pattern:** A) easy-going—DC   B) humorous—DC   C) sly—Ni   **D) resentful**   E) ineffective—NI
- ■ **We Already Found the answer:** It's D. The answer was found before reading the passage.
- ■ **What Does The Question Really Ask?** The author characterizes the serpent as a resentful animal because it refused to accept the "gift" stated in the question phrase.
- ■ **Reading Tip:** This question can be solved through information in the previous question.
- ■ **Relevancy Check:** Choices A and B contradict the passage description about the serpent. Choices C and E are irrelevant words.

C is the best answer.   "no,' take away your gifts; you can never forget the death of your son I"
The farmer's apology and peaceful gesture was denied by the resentful serpent.

Questions 12-17 are based on the following passage.
   (Q15) **The climate on earth** (Q12) **has not stayed the same through human history**. There are long periods of time where it is generally warmer, and there are those where it is generally colder. When it is generally colder, there is more ice (Q14) **on the poles of the planet.** That is why such a period is called an ice age. Two have (Q13) **affected** humans.
From 70,000 to around 10,000 years ago there was (Q16) **a big ice age** which affected humans and the way that they lived. Between 1600 AD to around 1900 AD there was a period called (Q16) **the Little Ice Age** when the climate was colder than usual. Climate has an effect on the types of food that can be found in
different parts of the world. Everywhere that humans live, there is a (Q17) **unique** staple food.

Q12. Question Pattern: The climate on earth through human history can be seen as
AP 2: Summary Question   Summarize the sentence or the entire paragraph

- ■ **Question Keyword/Key phrase:** "The climate on earth "
- ■ **Incorrect Pattern:** A) unchanging—DC   B) extremely irregular—EX   C) generally colder—IS
  D) generally warmer—IS   **E) periodic**

E is the best answer. "The climate on earth has not stayed the same through human history."
In other words, it has been periodic.

Incorrect Answer Explanation

Choice A contradicts the passage. Choice B is extreme expression. Choices C and D are incorrect. To be the correct answer, they both should be combined. They are thus Insufficient Information.

Q13. Question Pattern: In which sentence below does the word **affected** mean the same as in the sentence?
AP 4: Word-In-Context Question   Find the clue words and keywords from the sentence

- ■ **Question Keyword/Key phrase:** "Two have affected humans."
- ■ **Incorrect Pattern:** A) Tom was <u>affected</u> deeply by the sad movie—NI   B) Cindy <u>affected</u> she didn't eat the pizza—NI
  C) David's foot injury <u>affected</u> his limbs
  D) The <u>impact</u> of Climate change is great—NI   E) The ill-<u>effect</u> of air pollution changes our lives—NI

C is the best answer. Two have **affected** humans.

"Two" refers to the Ice ages. "affected" in the sentence means "to have an effect on." The answer is C that describes physical impact on human.

Incorrect Answer Explanation

Choice A is incorrect because the word "affected" in this sentence describes emotional impact, not the physical impact. Choice B) "affected" means to have pretended.   Choice D) "impact" is used as a noun describing a collision. Choice E) "ill-effect" is used as a noun and is different meaning.

Q14. Question Pattern: The discussion of **the Little Ice Age** in line 7 primarily suggests that
AP 3: Example Question   Find the primary reason for using the example sentence

---

- ■ **Question Keyword/Key phrase:** "the Little Ice Age"
- ■ **Incorrect Pattern:** A) the Little Ice Age is approaching near future—NI
   B) the animation "Ice Age" is based on the Little Ice Age—NI
   C) the Little Ice Age is a historical fact   D) scientists know very little about the Little Ice Age—NI
   E) the Little Ice Age was warmer than commonly supposed—DC
- ■ **What Does The Question Really Ask?** The answer should be based on the evidence found in the passage.
- ■ **Relevancy Check:** Choice B, D, and E apply the generalization: Choice B is true but not stated in the passage. Choice D and E can be solved with common sense. They are convincingly opposite statements.

C is the best answer. "1600 AD to around 1900 AD there was a period called the Little Ice Age"

As stated above, the passage discusses the Little Ice Age as the historical fact.

Incorrect Answer Explanation

Choices A and D are not stated in the passage. Choice E contradicts the passage. For the passage describes it "colder."

Q15. Question Pattern: The primary **tone** of the passage is
AP 8: Understanding Attitude (Tone) Find the tonality: positive vs. negative, mental vs. physical

---

- ■ **Question Keyword/Key phrase:** "tone"
- ■ **Incorrect Pattern: A) informative**   B) celebratory—NI   C) anecdotal—NI   D) argumentative—NI   E) mythic—NI
- ■ **We Already Found the answer:** It's A. The answer was found before reading the passage.
- ■ **What Does The Question Really Ask?** This passage provides scientific information based on the historical fact. Therefore, it is informative.
- ■ **Relevancy Check:** B) "celebratory" means expressing happiness; C) "anecdotal" refers to a personal short story;
   E) "mythic" is related to myth, none of which properly represents the scientific tone.
   D) "argumentative" is a negative word. The passage is informative and is not negative about the issue.

ANSWER EXPLANATIONS FOR TEST 6

A is the best answer.   The passage "informs" "the climate on earth" and then focuses on the Ice Age.

Q16. Question Pattern: The **literary device** used in lines 5-7 (From 70,000 to around 10,000 years ...colder) is
AP 4: Word-In-Context Question   Find the clue words and keywords from the sentence

- **Question Keyword/Key phrase:** "literary device"
- **Incorrect Pattern:** A) metaphor—NI   B) simile—NI   C) flashback —NI   **D) comparison**   E) personification—NI

D is the best answer.   Lines 5-7 compares Big Ice Age and the Little Ice Age. Therefore, it uses the comparison.

Incorrect Answer Explanation

A) "metaphor" is a figure of speech applied to an object or action Ex) Her dance is a great poem.
B) "oxymoron" is a figure of speech with contradictory terms. Ex) this is a jumbo shrimp.
C) "flashback" is set in a time earlier than the main story. Example can be found in a *Christmas Carol* by Charles Dickens
E) "personification" gives human characteristics to something nonhuman Ex) The wind whispered through dry grass.

Q17. Question Pattern: Which of the following choices belongs to the **staple food category** (lines 8)?
AP 7: Inference Question   Find the indirect suggestion behind the sentence

- **Question Keyword/Key phrase:** "staple food category "
- **Incorrect Pattern:** A) Imported pineapple—DC   **B) Maize in Mexico**   C) Organic vegetable—DC
  D) Cereal and milk—DC   E) Bread and beans at a restaurant—DC

B) is the Best Choice.   "Everywhere that humans live, there is a unique staple food"
"unique" in the passage is the keyword.   As stated above, only Maize in Mexico can be properly categorized as a staple food because it grows only in Mexico. Other foods are not unique, therefore, cannot be classified as a unique food.

Questions 18-22 are based on the following passage.
   Babette and Antone were the children of a very poor woodcutter.
Now though their father **toiled** in this forest (Q19) **from dawn until dark**, he could earn but little. Their mother made fine laces which (Q18) **Antone carried to the market to sell**; but in spite of all their efforts, the poor parents seldom could give their children more than bread and broth to eat. (Q20) **But it worried the woodcutter that Antone was ten years old and had not yet gone to school.** (Q21) **Antone's mother taught him to read and write**. Often as he sat doing his sums on the hearthstone, with a bit of (Q22) **charcoal for a pencil,** his mother would sigh sadly. Antone did not like his mother to be sad, and so he always laughed to cheer her.

Q18. Question Pattern: The **children helped** their parents by
AP 2: Summary Question   Summarize the sentence or the entire paragraph

- **Question Keyword/Key phrase:** "children helped "
- **Incorrect Pattern:** A) hunting—IW   B) cutting woods—IW   **C) selling on the market**
  D) setting traps in the woods—IW   E) start working at dawn until dark——IW
- **Relevancy Check:** In commonsense, some alternatives, when considering "the children" in the question phrase, are apparently wrong.

SSAT ABSOLUTE PATTERNS

C is the best answer. "Their mother made fine laces which Antone carried to the market to sell"
As stated above, "Antone" as a child helped the parents by selling on the market. The other alternatives are what Antone's father did and could do. And they are the work descriptions beyond what the child can do.

Q19. Question Pattern: "toiled" in line 2 most nearly means
AP 4: Word-In-Context Question Find the clue words and keywords from the sentence

■ **Question Keyword/Key phrase:** "toiled"
■ **Incorrect Pattern:** A) worked in a bathroom—NI   B) **worked extremely hard**   C) prepared—NI
   D) looked for—NI   E) escaped—NI
■ **What Does The Question Really Ask?** The question asks about the literal definition for the word "toiled"

B is the best answer. Now though their father <u>toiled</u> in this forest from dawn until dark,
As the clue words "from dawn until dark" suggest, "toiled" means worked extremely hard.
The other alternatives do not make sense in the phrase.

Q20. Question Pattern: As Antone was getting older, the **parents' main concern** was
AP 2: Summary Question Summarize the sentence or the entire paragraph

■ **Question Keyword/Key phrase:** "parents' main concern"
■ **Incorrect Pattern:** A) introducing his bride—NI   B) teaching how to make money—NI
   C) training woodcutting—IW   **D) providing education**   E) helping him to be excel at school—DC
■ **Reading Tip:** Conjunction "But" in the passage is a very important source to find the answer.

D is the best answer. "But it worried the woodcutter that Antone was ten years old and had not yet gone to school"
As stated above, as Antone was getting older, the parents' main concern was to provide him a proper education.

Incorrect Answer Explanation

Choices A, B and C are not stated in the passage. Choice E contradicts the passage because Antone did not attend school.

Q21. Question Pattern: Who acted as a **teacher for Antone**?
AP 2: Summary Question Summarize the sentence or the entire paragraph

■ **Question Keyword/Key phrase:** "teacher for Antone"
■ **Incorrect Pattern:** A) Babette—IW   B) father—IW   **C) mother**   D) other woodcutters—IW   E) Antone himself—IW

C is the best answer. "Antone's mother taught him to read and write."
As stated above, Antone's mother acted as a teacher for Antone.
Other choices are irrelevant information not stated in the passage.

ANSWER EXPLANATIONS FOR TEST 6

Q22. Question Pattern: Which of the following best reflects **Antone as a poor kid?**
AP 2: Summary Question   Summarize the sentence or the entire paragraph

- **Question Keyword/Key phrase:** "Antone as a poor kid"
- **Incorrect Pattern:** A) Babette—IW   B) forest—IW   C) fine laces—IW   D) mother—IW   **E) charcoal**
- **What Does The Question Really Ask?** The question focuses on "Antone," not on Antone's mother or father. It is important to check on whom the question is focusing. Be careful, incorrect answers often provide the true statement taken from the passage but use different characters' references.

E is the best answer. "he sat doing his sums on the hearthstone, with a bit of charcoal for a pencil,"
The passage describes Anton of his using a charcoal for a pencil, implying he is so poor kid that couldn't afford pencil.

Incorrect Answer Explanation

Choices A and D are family members irrelevant to the question. Choices B and C are related to the works of Antone's parents, unrelated to the question.

Questions 23-28 are based on the following passage.
   In some societies, (Q23 & Q27) **people think that art belongs to the person who made it, such as Indigenous Aboriginal Australian Art**. They think that the artist put his or her "talent" into the art. In this view, the art is the (Q24) **property** of the artist. In other societies, people think (Q25) **that art belongs to no one. They think that society has put its social capital** into the artist and the artist's work. In this view, (Q25) **society made the art,** through the artist. An artwork is normally (Q26) **judged and valued by how much impact** it has on people, the mount of people who can relate to it, and how much (Q28) **people appreciate** it.

Q23. Question Pattern: "Indigenous Aboriginal Australian Art" in line 2 describes that some societies
AP 5: Understanding the True Purpose   Find the explicitly stated true purpose of the sentence

- **Question Keyword/Key phrase:** "Indigenous Aboriginal Australian Art"
- **Incorrect Pattern:** A) do not appreciate beautiful art—EX   **B) think art belongs to its creator**   C) have no talented artists—EX   D) think art doesn't exist—EX   E) believe Aboriginal Australian Art is the best art—EX
- **What Does The Question Really Ask?** The question asks the reason for stating an example.

B is the best answer. "In some societies,...art belongs to the person who made it, such as Indigenous aboriginal..."
As stated above, indigenous aboriginals think that arts belong to the artists who created them.
Choices A, C, D, and E are not stated and also extreme expressions.

Q24. Question Pattern: What does the word **property** in line 3 mean
AP 4: Word-In-Context Question   Find the clue words and keywords from the sentence

SSAT ABSOLUTE PATTERNS

SSAT 8 Reading & Verbal Elementary Level

| ■ **Question Keyword/Key phrase:** "property" |
| ■ **Incorrect Pattern:** A) quality—NI   B) characteristic—NI   C) stuff—IS   **D) possession**   E) effort—IS |
| ■ **What Does The Question Really Ask?** It is important to find the clue word from the same sentence. |

D is the best answer. "the art is the property of the artist. ...people think that art belongs to no one"
The clue word "belong to" suggests that "possession" is the closest meaning for the word "property."

Incorrect Answer Explanation

Choice E "effort," even choice A and B, in another circumstances, could also be the synonyms for the word "property."
Thus, only when the clue word "belongs to" is identified can the answer be determined.

Q25. Question Pattern: Which choice correctly describes the **sentence below**?
AP 5: Understanding the True Purpose   Find the explicitly stated true purpose of the sentence

■ **Question Keyword/Key phrase:** "In other societies, people think that art belongs to no one."
■ **Incorrect Pattern:** A) True artists do not exist—IW   B) Society concerns less on art—IW
  C) Society concerns less on artist—IW   **D) Society made the art**   E) Art actually made society—DC
■ **We Already Found the answer:** It's D. The answer was found before reading the passage.
■ **Relevancy Check:** The phrase "art belongs to no one" paradoxically emphasizes art belongs to everyone in society.
  However, it doesn't mean (A) artists do not exist. Nor does it mean choice B and C. The adverb "less" has a negative
  tone, contrasting to the positive tone of the phrase. Also, "concerned less" is not the author's main point.
  Choice E contradicts the passage description. It is the other way around.

D is the best answer. "Some society thinks that it has made the art, through the artist."
The author emphasizes that it is only through society that art can be created.

Q26. Question Pattern: According to the last sentence (lines 5-7), **an artwork is valued** by
AP 2: Summary Question   Summarize the sentence or the entire paragraph

■ **Question Keyword/Key phrase:** "an artwork is valued"
■ **Incorrect Pattern:** A) the market price—NI   **B) art that have impacted on people**   C) artist's skill—IS
  D) governmental support—NI   E) the age and reputation of artists—NI
■ **Relevancy Check:** Choices A, D, and E rely on general statements not stated in the passage.

B is the best answer. "An artwork is normally judged and valued by how much impact it has on..."
As stated above, artwork is valued by how much impact it has on people.
Choice C is plausible but insufficient explanation from the author's point of view.

Q27. Question Pattern: The main purpose of the passage is to
AP 1: Main Idea (Focus Shifts) Question Find the main idea of the entire passage or the paragraph

■ **Question Keyword/Key phrase:** "main purpose of"
■ **Incorrect Pattern:** A) praise great artists—NI **B) discuss the value of art** C) explain the importance of art education—NI D) compare art and science—NI E) celebrate Indigenous Aboriginal art—IS
■ **What Does The Question Really Ask?** *Find t*he keywords in each alternative. If the keywords from the passage—especially in SSAT Elementary level—do not appear in your choice, then, that choice has little chance to be the primary purpose of the passage, hence the incorrect answer.
■ **Reading Tip:** For the primary purpose question, pay special attention to the conclusion.

B is the best answer.   The passage starts out by questioning who owns the art, It then discusses the ownership of arts between artists and societies. Finally, in the last sentence, the author presents what factors value arts.

Incorrect Answer Explanation

Choice A) "great artists," C) "art education," D) "science" are not stated in the passage. Therefore, they should not even be considered as the possible answer for the primary purpose question. Choice E is mentioned only as the example, not as the primary purpose. Thus, it is Insufficient Information

Q28. Question Pattern: Based on the passage, **which person belongs to the people** in the above statement?
AP 7: Inference Question   Find the indirect suggestion behind the sentence

■ **Question Keyword/Key phrase:** "how much **people** appreciate it."
■ **Incorrect Pattern:** A) artist—IS B) art historian—NI C) Aboriginal Australians—IW D) pianist—NI **E) audience**
■ **We Already Found the answer:** It's E. The answer was found before reading the passage.
■ **What Does The Question Really Ask?** People who appreciate (viewing) the art should be the audience.
■ **Relevancy Check:** All the rest incorrect answers are, by and large, Irrelevant to the "people" in the question. For instance, choice C is a generalization because the passage states "aboriginal Australian artists, not the aboriginal Australians.

E is the best answer. "An artwork is normally judged and valued by impact it has on people,"
Choices A and D are art creators. They, by themselves, may as well be the audience, but they primarily create before appreciate arts. Choice B is incorrect because the job of art historian is mainly to study art, not to appreciate.

Test 6 Absolute Patterns for the analogy Section

AP2. Synonym/Antonym Find the similar or opposite meaning between the words

16. Production is to make as

A) arrival is to come   B) factory is worker   C) cost is to price   D) shop is to retailer   E) discount is premium

A is the best answer. Production is a synonym to make (verb) as (A) arrival is a synonym to come (verb).
Choice B is a part-whole relation in the Category Pattern. Choice C is incorrect. For "cost" is not a synonym to "price." It is the Category Pattern, not the Synonym Pattern as the Cost refers to the actual value of a product including the raw material while "price" is added value on top of the cost. Choice D is not in synonym relation either. For "retailer" is a human who runs the shop. Therefore, they are not the synonyms to each other. Choice E is in antonym relation.

AP4. Characteristic Pattern Find the Characteristic of Person, Place, Object, or Idea

17. Music is to Yoga as ear is to   A) exercise   **B) body**   C) gym   D) earphone   E) relax

B is the best answer. Music is heard through ears; yoga is practiced through body. Choices A, C, and E are associated with "Yoga, the secondary word in the question stem " but not with the entire question-stem. Choice D is associated with "music," the primary word in the question stem but not with the entire question-stem.

AP11. Subjective-Objective Pattern Find the Quality vs. Quantity, Tangible vs. Intangible Concept

18. Panda is to coyote as

A) video game is to online   B) bamboo is to tree   **C) cute is to ugly**   D) bear is to hibernation   E) eye is to black

C is the best answer. This question asks how we think or feel about certain animals.
Panda is known to be cute as coyote is known to be ugly. Choice A is Irrelevant words to the question-stem. Choices B, D, and E are associated with "Panda," the primary word in the question stem but not with the entire question-stem.

AP3. Purpose (Tool) Pattern Find the Purpose of Individual and the Goal, the Function of Tool

19. Gang is to teach as rob is to   A) bank   **B) teacher**   C) school   D) student   E) money

B is the best answer. Gang robs as teacher teaches. Choices A and E are associated with "gang," the primary word in the question stem but not with the entire question-stem. Choices C and D are associated with "teacher" but not with the entire question-stem.

AP11. Subjective-Objective Pattern Find the Quality vs. Quantity, Tangible vs. Intangible Concept

20. Speed limit is 50 miles as   A) success is to failure   B) knife is to gun

C) 20 Celsius is to 48 Fahrenheit   **D) boiling point is 100 degree**   E) grace is to ugly

D is the best answer. This question asks about quantifier. Both 50 miles and (D) 100 degree contain numeric quantifiers (numbers). Choices A and E are the antonym Pattern. Choice B is the Category Pattern.
Choice C is incorrect. "20 Celsius" is a numeric quantifier. Whereas "speed limit" and 'boiling point" are not.

ANSWER EXPLANATIONS FOR TEST 6

AP8. Production Pattern Find What Produces What and the Cause and Effect Relation

21. Food is to energy as

A) mountain is to vantage point   B) cup is to coffee   **C) sleep is to rest**   D) exam is to cheat   E) factory is to machine

C is the best answer. Food gives energy as (C) sleep gives rest.
Choices A and E show part-whole relations in the Category Pattern. Choice B shows a tool in the Purpose pattern. Choice D is irrelevant to the question-stem.

AP1. Category Pattern Find the Part and Whole Relation, the Same Type or Association

22. Swamp is to water as cola is to   A) pumpkin   B) bakery   C) bread   D) cake   **E) oil**

E is the best answer.
This question asks the similarity in all four words. Swamp, water, cola, and (E) oil are all liquid-base materials. Choice A is Irrelevant word. Choices B, C and D are associated with "cola or water" but not with the entire question-stem.

AP4. Characteristic Pattern Find the Characteristic of Person, Place, Object, or Idea

23. Mosquito is to bee as

A) cat is to butterfly   B) insect is to animal   C) pretty is to ugly   **D) disease is to pollination**   E) hot is to cold

D is the best answer. This question asks about the characteristics of certain animals.
Mosquito delivers disease as bee pollinates. Choices A, B, and E are, by and large, Irrelevant words to the question-stem. Choice C may be used to express as "mosquito is ugly as bee is pretty" with the Subjective-Objective Pattern. To do that, however, the words order should be flipped over.

AP1. Category Pattern Find the Part and Whole Relation, the Same Type or Association

24. White House is to president as

A) zoo is to zoologist   B) teacher is to school   C) house is to door   D) mother is to cook   **E) office is to father**

E is the best answer. President is in the White House as (E) father is in the office.
Choice A is incorrect because zoologist,—animal scientists, doesn't normally stay at the zoo. They study animals. "zoo" is more directly associated with "animals" not with zoologist. Choice B is incorrect because the words order is flipped over. Choice C is the part-whole in the Category Pattern. Choice D is irrelevant words to the question-stem.

AP1. Category Pattern Find the Part and Whole Relation, the Same Type or Association

25. Penguin is to camel as   A) cactus is to hot   B) tattoo is to skin   C) bird is to warm   D) flu is to cough   **E) cold is to hot**

E is the best answer. This question asks about the relations between animals and the regional temperature in which they live. Penguin normally lives in a cold region as (E) camel lives in a hot region.
Choice A is incorrect because "cactus" is a plant. It should, to follow the question-stem, use an animal. Choices B and D are irrelevant words to the question-stem. Choice C is incorrect because, unlike the distinctive features in the phrases "penguin in a cold region" and "camel in a hot region," "bird is to warm" has no such a logical association.

AP1. Category Pattern   Find the Part and Whole Relation, the Same Type or Association

26. Ant is to bird as eagle is to   A) sky   B) king   **C) insect**   D) beak   E) brave

C is the best answer. Ant is part of insect as eagle is part of birds. All the rest are associated with "eagle," but not with the entire question-stem.

AP1. Category Pattern   Find the Part and Whole Relation, the Same Type or Association

27. Surgery is to wilderness as

A) hunting is to hospital   B) medicine is to pill   C) nurse is to help   D) doctor is to kind   E) patient is to cure

A is the best answer. It asks for a place where a certain activity takes place.
Surgery is taken place at the hospital as hunting is taken place in the wilderness. Choice B is the Synonym Pattern. Choices C, D, and E are associated with "surgery," the primary word in the question stem, but not with the entire question-stem.

AP3. Purpose (Tool) Pattern   Find the Purpose of Individual and the Goal, the Function of Tool

28. Receipt is to shop as

A) ticket is to airplane   B) tip is to restaurant   C) sales tax is to expire   D) retail is to wholesale   E) good to goods

A is the best answer. Both the receipt and ticket are the proof of purchase. It indicates what we receive after purchasing something. Choice B is incorrect because "tip" is an expression of gratitude for the service rendered. "tip" is different from receipt or ticket in a sense that tip cannot be the used as a receipt for the sales. Choice C does not show any relation between the primary and secondary words. Choice D is the Category Pattern.
Choice E uses irrelevant words between the primary word and the secondary word in the question stem.

AP3. Purpose (Tool) Pattern   Find the Purpose of Individual and the Goal, the Function of Tool

29. Police is to badge as

A) kindergarten boy is to name tag   B) car is to plate   C) tire is to flat   D) dish is to restaurant   E) jail is to bar

A is the best answer. This question asks about the function of badge. Make sure to select the same human category as in the question-stem. Police badge identifies police as (A) the name tag worn by a kindergarten boy indicates his/her name. In identification purpose, both the badge and nametag are functional synonyms.
Choice B follows the question-stem in terms of identification purpose. "car," however, is nonhuman. Choices C, D, and E are all irrelevant to the question-stem.

AP3. Purpose (Tool) Pattern   Find the Purpose of Individual and the Goal, the Function of Tool

30. Rain is to cane as

A) grandma is to snow   **B) old is to umbrella**   C) young is to computer   D) father is to mother   E) sunglass is to dark

B is the best answer. This question is based on tools people use.
Umbrella is used in the rain. The old use cane. Choices A, C, and E use Irrelevant words between their primary and secondary words. Choice D is the antonym Pattern.

SSAT ELEMENTARY LEVEL

Reading & Verbal Section

Test 7

Test 7 Reading Section
Time: 30 Minutes, 29 Questions

Directions: Each reading passage is followed by questions about it. Answer the questions that follow a passage on the basis of what is stated or implied in that passage.

Questions 1-6 are based on the following passage.

Line   Music is an art that puts sounds together in a way that people like or find interesting. Most music includes people singing with their voices or playing musical instruments, such as the piano, guitar, or drums.
   There is no simple definition of music which covers all cases. Music is whatever people think
5 is music such as, sound which has rhythm, melody, pitch, timbre.
   The first musical instrument used by humans was probably the voice. The human voice can make many different kinds of sounds. Music is sound that has been organized by using rhythm, melody or harmony. If someone bangs **saucepans** while cooking, it makes noise. If a person bangs saucepans or pots in a rhythmic way, they are making a simple type of music.

1
Which of the followings can be rightfully called the music?
A) The biography of Mozart
B) Echoes from the mountain that sounds like singing
C) Rhythmic poetry written by Shakespeare
D) Drum beats for the full attack in a war
E) Whistle of grandpa

2
Which of the following is most similar situation to the statement in lines 8-9 (If someone...type of music)
A) A music teacher teaches students a music theory
B) A musician renders his first recital
C) An auto mechanic creates a wonderful sound using his tools
D) An opera singer sings a modern pop music
E) A boy practices song for Christmas

3

Read the sentence from line 4 in the box below.

> There is no simple definition of music which covers all cases.

The above statement describes which characteristic of music?

A) limited coverage

B) broad range

C) reaction by the audience

D) clarity

E) popularity

4

The qualities of music include all of the following EXCEPT

A) rhythm

B) melody

C) pitch

D) instrument

E) timbre

5

Which of the following was used as the first musical instrument by human?

A) drum

B) human voice

C) piano

D) guitar

E) violin

6

Which of the following can be used for the similar purpose to that of "saucepan" (line 8)?

A) Youtube music

B) piano

C) human voice

D) dog barking sound

E) chopsticks

Questions 7-12 are based on the following passage.

Line   Alice's Adventures in Wonderland is a novel written by Charles Dodgson, better known under the penname Lewis Carroll. It tells the story of a girl named Alice who falls down a rabbit-hole into a ———world populated by unique creatures acting as humans. The tale is filled with the lessons that schoolchildren were expected to memorize. The tale plays with
5   logic in ways that have made the story of lasting popularity with adults as well as children.

7

The primary purpose of the passage is to
A) criticize low-quality novels
B) describe the relationship between Charles Dodgson and Lewis Carroll
C) discuss the characteristics of adventure novels
D) point out readers' reaction to a novel
E) introduce briefly about a novel

8

Read the sentence from line 3 in the box below.

a _____ world populated by unique creatures acting as humans.

Which of the following can be used as the missing word in the underline?
A) fantastic
B) realistic
C) modern
D) pretty
E) democratic

9

Based on description in line 3, which of the following phrases would be included in the novel?
A) Her nose was so long that it reached to her toes
B) She is the frost in winter night.
C) The little cat laughed
D) David is Einstein at school.
E) Bark-Bark! Bark! The dog woke me up.

10

Which of the following statement is true?
A) The novel is written for children under 13
B) The novel is written by Charles Dodgson together with Lewis Carroll
C) Boys can expect the real world adventurers
D) The novel is being taught at school
E) The novel offers real lessons

11

According to the passage, what made the story popular?
A) Logic
B) Plays
C) Unique creatures
D) Wonderland
E) A rabbit

12

The last sentence of the passage primarily serves to
A) cite a well-known quote
B) raise a question
C) make a criticism
D) note a reason for its popularity
E) explain the origin of the story

Questions 13-17 are based on the following passage.

Line   A Fox once saw a Crow fly off with a piece of cheese in its beak and settle on a branch of a tree. 'That's for me, as I am a Fox,' and he walked up to the foot of the tree. 'Good-day, Mistress Crow,' he cried. 'How well you are looking to-day: how glossy your feathers; how bright your eye. I feel sure your voice must surpass that of other birds, just as your figure does; let me hear
5 but one song from you that I may greet you as the Queen of Birds.' The Crow lifted up her head and began to caw her best, but the moment she opened her mouth the piece of cheese fell to the ground, only to be snapped up by Master Fox. 'That will do,' said he. '**That** was all I wanted. In exchange for your cheese I will give you a piece of advice for the future .'Do not trust flatterers.'

13

"voice" in line 4 and "caw" in line 6 imply respectively as

A) lie *vs.* reality.
B) honesty *vs.* dishonesty
C) generosity *vs.* greed
D) wonder *vs.* plain
E) general *vs.* special

14

Which of the following statements would both the Crow and Fox eventually agree?

A) Flatterers should not be trusted
B) Fox cannot be trusted
C) Crow is the ugliest bird
D) Crow is the Queen of the Birds
E) True friends complement to each other

15

The Fox's praise in line 5, "I may greet you as the Queen of Birds" can be characterized as

A) honest
B) pride
C) flattery
D) respect
E) trust

16

The fox's character toward the crow can best be described as

A) respect
B) honest
C) not caring
D) deceptive
E) courageous

17

When the Fox said "That was all I wanted" in line 7, "That" refers to

A) the crow
B) voice
C) cheese
D) friendship with the Queen of Birds
E) flattery

Questions 18-23 are based on the following passage.

Line   Once upon a time there was an old cat, called Tabitha. Mrs. Tabitha was an anxious parent. She used to lose her kittens continually, and whenever they were lost, they always got into mischief! On baking day she determined to shut them up in a cupboard, but could not find Tom anywhere. Mrs. Tabitha went up and down all over the house, mewing for Tom. She looked in
5   the pantry under the staircase, and she searched the best spare bedroom that was all covered up with dust sheets. She went right upstairs and looked into the attics, but she could not find him anywhere. The old house was full of cupboards and passages. The walls were thick, and there used to be queer noises inside them, as if there might be a little secret staircase.
    Certainly there were odd little jagged doorways in the wainscot, and things disappeared at night,
10   especially cheese and bacon.

18

Read the statement from line 1 in the box below.

| Mrs. Tabitha was an **anxious** parent. |

Based on the above statement, what does "anxious" mean?

A) angry
B) concerned
C) cautious
D) diligent
E) lovely

19

The literary device mainly used in the story is

A) simile
B) metaphor
C) allusion
D) personification
E) climax

*Simile is a figure of speech involving the comparison of one thing with another
*Metaphor is an imaginative way of describing something.
*Allusion is an expression designed to call something to mind without mentioning it
*Climax is the most intense, exciting, or important point of something

20

Read the sentence from line 9 in the box below.

Which can most probably be replaced with **"things"**?

> Certainly there were odd little jagged doorways in the wainscot, and **things** disappeared at night

A) Tom

B) Oven

C) Cupboard

D) Foods

E) Ghost

21

Read the statement from line 4 in the box below.

> Mrs. Tabitha went up and down all over the house, **mewing** for Tom

The literary device used in the word "mewing" is

A) Hyperbole

B) Metaphor

C) Onomatopoeia

D) Personification

E) Alliteration

*Hyperbole refers to an exaggeration

*Metaphor is an imaginative way of describing something

*Onomatopoeia imitates the sound it is describing

*Personification gives human attributes to objects or animals

*Alliteration means two or more words in a row that all start with the same sound

22

Based on the story, who is most likely to have taken "things" in line 9?

A) Tom

B) Mrs. Tabitha

C) Mouse

D) The owner of the house

E) The children of the house

23

Mrs. Tabitha searched everywhere in the house EXCEPT

A) Baking oven

B) Pantry

C) Staircase

D) Bedroom

E) Attics

Questions 24-29 are based on the following passage.

Line   Astronomy is the study of the universe and everything in it. This includes stars, planets and galaxies as well as other things. The word astronomy comes from the Greek words astron which means star and nomos which means law. A person who studies astronomy is called an astronomer. Ancient people used the positions of the stars to navigate, and to find when was the
5   best time to plant crops. Since the 20th century there have been two main types of astronomy, observational and theoretical astronomy. Observational astronomy uses many observational equipment such as telescopes to observe or look at stars, galaxies and other astronomical objects. Theoretical astronomy uses math and computer models before observational astronomy.

24

Study subjects in astronomy include All but

A) Stars
B) Mars
C) Milky Way
D) Moon
E) Horoscope

*Horoscope: a forecast of a person's future

25

The author mentions "Greek" in line 2 mainly to

A) introduce astrophysics
B) introduce the origin of the word "astronomy"
C) tell astronomy is the oldest science
D) distinguish between observational and theoretical astronomy
E) compare the ancient and modern astronomy

26

Which of the following ancient Greek people would most likely use astronomy?

A) Farmers who developed an agricultural calendar based on stars location.
B) Teachers who taught Greek mythology
C) Armies prayed before Zeus status
D) People who used star sign to predict their future
E) A king who named his ship after Polaris

27

Which of the following statement is true of observational astronomy?

A) It is theoretical astronomy
B) It predicts our future
C) It uses telescopes
D) It was developed in ancient Greek period
E) It became known since the 16th century

28

Which statement is most strongly supported by the author?

A) Astronomy is important in our society
B) Astronomers should concern more with observation than with theory
C) Greeks still use astronomy to navigate sea
D) Observational astronomy is more important than theoretical astronomy
E) Observational astronomy uses many equipment

29

Theoretical astronomy is important in that it

A) helps searching for extraterrestrial life
B) does not have to use observational astronomy
C) requires no telescope
D) is used before the observational astronomy
E) can be used by regular folks

*extraterrestrial life = aliens

Verbal Test 7
20 MINUTES, 30 QUESTIONS

Directions: the synonym questions ask you to find the most appropriate synonym to the question.

The analogy questions ask you to find the most appropriate analogy to the question. Select the answer that best matches to the question.

Synonyms

Each of the following questions consists of one word followed by five words or phrases. You are to select the one word or phrase whose meaning is closest to the word in capital letters.

Sample Question:

ABILITY

A) mistake
B) **talent**
C) abandon
D) best student
E) late

1. DISSATISFIED
A) full
B) satiated
C) uncomfortable
D) happy
E) likable

2. TRADER
A) merchant
B) cheater
C) goods
D) market
E) international

3. ASSEMBLY
A) friendship
B) gathering
C) united
D) partial
E) loyalty

4. NAUSEA
A) approval
B) Austria
C) rejection
D) ocean
E) watery

5. PILGRIM
A) request
B) pray
C) religious
D) Mayflower
E) pioneer

6. SANE
A) rational
B) same
C) unequal
D) partial
E) holy

7. REPLICA
A) repeat
B) cane
C) clone
D) alone
E) together

8. MAGNIFICENT
A) rich
B) sticky
C) stone
D) small
E) medium

9. COUP
A) sedan
B) car
C) locomotion
D) revolution
E) development

10. VESTIGE
A) large
B) ocean
C) footprint
D) fingerprint
E) small

11. VOYAGE
A) excursion
B) ship
C) study
D) value
E) yacht

12. INFESTATION
A) festival
B) party
C) outdoor
D) fungus
E) disease

13. SCRUTINIZE

A) cheap

B) thrifty

C) inspect

D) saying

E) scant

14. MUTTER

A) easy

B) lively

C) like

D) complain

E) Center

15. EXTEND

A) small

B) short

C) prolong

D) large

E) Understand

Analogies

The following questions ask you to find relationships between words. For each question, select the answer choice that best completes the meaning of the sentence.

SAMPLE QUESTION

Q: River is to Ocean as:

A) better is to good

B) rain is to cloud

C) father is to mother

D) city is to country

E) fork is to spoon

This question is Degree Analogy question (small to big movement).

Ⓓ is the correct answer. Just as river is smaller than Ocean, so is city to the country.

Ⓐ is incorrect because the order is flipped over.

Ⓑ is incorrect because this is 'Production Analogy—what-produce-what.'

Ⓒ and Ⓔ are incorrect because there are no big and small relations between mother and father, so does fork to spoon.

16. Finger is to toe as

A) singer is to sing

B) tail is to fur

C) nose is to mouth

D) write is to walk

E) dance is to study

17. Earphone is to music as eyeglass is

A) lens

B) eye

C) round

D) a pair

E) book

18. Rabbit is to timid as
A) grass is to green
B) courageous is to eagle
C) zebra is to strip
D) fish is to swim
E) lion is to brave

19. Ash is to powder as water is to
A) cold
B) ice
C) transparent
D) white
E) liquid

20. Coach is to firefighter as train is to
A) extinguish fire
B) set fire
C) engine
D) siren
E) emergency

21. Opportunity is to father as
A) baby is to cute
B) chance is to daddy
C) U.F.O. is to Unidentified Flying Object
D) kiss is to love
E) live or die

22. Boring is to happiness as
A) cake is to bread
B) exciting is to unhappiness
C) enemy is to war
D) study is to hard
E) restaurant is to market

23. Computer is to Internet as
A) Wi-Fi modem is to network connection
B) music is to piano
C) swimming pool is to swimsuit
D) farm is to animal
E) electricity is to danger

24. Peanut butter is to peanut as
A) margarine is to melt
B) coffee is to bean
C) taste is to sweet
D) strawberry is to jam
E) expiry date is to instruction

25. Sun is to earth as
A) ocean is to stream
B) fire is to volcano
C) astronaut is to psychic
D) horse is to cow
E) male is to female

26. Comics is to rest as homework is to
A) wisdom
B) grade point
C) friend
D) fun
E) punishment

27. Threat is to fear as
A) bank is to banker
B) father is to grandfather
C) sister is to brother
D) yoga is to relaxation
E) dance is to popularity

28. Consumer is to spend as
A) factory is to manufacture
B) shopper is to Christmas
C) satisfaction is to guarantee
D) bank is to robbery
E) buyer is to seller

29. Royal is to excellent as
A) life is to death
B) king is to queen
C) kingdom is to heaven
D) luxury is to princess
E) beggar is to humble

30. Biologist is to whistle as
A) chef is to kitchen
B) police is to arrest
C) coach is to microscope
D) judge is to courtroom
E) car is to driver

SSAT ELEMENTARY LEVEL

Reading & Verbal Section

Test 7

Answer Explanations

TEST 7
READING SECTION

Please refer to the Reading Section AP Analyses

SYNONYM QUESTIONS
1 ~ 15

1	C
2	A
3	B
4	C
5	E
6	A
7	C
8	A
9	D
10	C
11	A
12	D
13	C
14	D
15	C

ANALOGY QUESTIONS NO. NO.16-30.

Please refer to the analogy Section AP Analyses

Test 7 Absolute Patterns for the Reading Section

Questions 1-6 are based on the following passage.

Music is an art that puts sounds together in a way that people like or find interesting. Most music includes (Q1) **people singing with their voices or playing musical instruments**, such as the piano, guitar, or drums. There is no simple definition of music which (Q3) **covers all cases**. It is an art form, and opinions come into play. Music is whatever people think is music. A different approach is to list the qualities music must have, such as, sound which has (Q4) **rhythm, melody, pitch, timbre**. The first musical instrument used (Q5) **by humans was probably the voice.** The human voice can make many different kinds of sounds. Music is sound that has been organized by using rhythm, melody or harmony.

If someone bangs saucepans while cooking, it makes noise. If a person (Q6) **bangs saucepans or pots in a rhythmic way,** they are making a simple type of music. (Q2) **If someone bangs saucepans while cooking, it makes noise.** If a person bangs saucepans or pots in a rhythmic way, they are making a simple type of Music

---

Q1. Question Pattern: Which of the followings can be rightfully **called the music**?
AP 7: Inference Question   Find the indirect suggestion behind the sentence

■ **Question Keyword/Key phrase:** "called music"
■ **Incorrect Pattern:** A) The biography of Mozart—NI   B) Echoes from the mountain that sounds like singing—NI
   C) Rhythmic poetry written by Shakespeare-IS   D) Drum beats for the full attack in a war-IS   **E) Whistle of grandpa**

E is the best answer.   The passage defines music as "people singing with their voices or playing musical instruments" "Whistle" is rhythmic melody created by human voice.

Incorrect Answer Explanation

A) "biography," B) "echoes," and C) "poetry" cannot be defined as music. D) "drum beats sound in a battlefield" is for the signal, therefore, rhythmic may it be, cannot still be called the music.

Q2. Question Pattern: Which of the following is most **similar situation** to lines 9-10 (If someone...type of)
AP 6: Analogy Question   Find the logically-supported similar situation

■ **Question Keyword/Key phrase:** "similar situation "
■ **Incorrect Pattern:** A) A music teacher teaches students a music theory—IW
   B) A musician renders his first recital—DC   **C) An auto mechanic creates a wonderful sound using his tools**
   D) An opera singer sings a modern pop music—DC   E) A boy practices song for Christmas—DC

C is the best answer.   The passage describes a simple melody played by non-musical instruments.
Choice C is the similar situation to the sentence in line 9.
Choice A "a music theory" is a theory, not a music. Choices B, D, and E are referring to normal music.

Q3. Question Pattern: The statement below describes which characteristic of **music**?
AP 5: Understanding the True Purpose   Find the explicitly stated true purpose of the sentence

- ■ **Question Keyword/Key phrase:** "There is no simple definition of music which covers all cases."
- ■ **Incorrect Pattern:** A) limited coverage—DC   **B) broad range**   C) reaction by the audience—NI
  D) clarity—DC   E) popularity—NI
- ■ **We Already Found the answer:** It's B. The answer was found before reading the passage.
- ■ **What Does The Question Really Ask?** "covering all cases" implies broad range.
- ■ **Relevancy Check:** Choices A and D contradict the passage statement. Choices C and E are irrelevant information.

B is the best answer. "Music is whatever people think is music."
As stated above, the author believes that there is no simple definition of music because its range is so broad.

Q4. Question Pattern: The **qualities of music** include all of the following EXCEPT
AP 2: Summary Question   Summarize the sentence or the entire paragraph

- ■ **Question Keyword/Key phrase:** "qualities of music"
- ■ **Incorrect Pattern:** A) rhythm—DC   B) melody—DC   C) pitch—DC   **D) instrument**   E) timbre—DC

D is the best answer. "the qualities music must have sound which has rhythm, melody, pitch, timbre"
As stated above, the passage does not include "instrument" as part of qualities of music.

Q5. Question Pattern: Which of the following was used as the first musical instrument by human?
AP 2: Summary Question   Summarize the sentence or the entire paragraph

- ■ **Question Keyword/Key phrase:** "the first musical instrument"
- ■ **Incorrect Pattern:** A) drum—NI   **B) human voice**   C) piano—Ni   D) guitar—Ni   E) violin—Ni
- ■ **We Already Found the answer:** It's B. The answer was found before reading the passage.
- ■ **What Does The Question Really Ask?** The answer for this question can be solved through a common sense. Before human invented any musical instrument, human's own voice must have been the first musical instrument.

B is the best answer. "The first musical instrument used by humans was probably the voice"
As stated above, it was humans voice that acted as the first musical instrument.

Q6. Which of the following can be used for the **similar purpose like that of saucepan** in line 9?
AP 7: Inference Question   Find the indirect suggestion behind the sentence

- ■ **Question Keyword/Key phrase:** "similar purpose to saucepan"
- ■ **Incorrect Pattern:** A) Youtube music—DC   B) piano—DC   C) human voice—DC   D) dog barking sound—NI
  E) chopsticks

E is the best answer. The passage describes "a person bangs saucepans or pots in a rhythmic way."
With chopsticks in choice E, rhythm for a simple music can be created. Both saucepan and chopsticks are non traditional musical instruments, yet create rhythm. Choices A, B, and C can create much more complex music than simple banging sounds of saucepan. Choice D "dog barking" can't create musical rhythm therefore irrelevant information.

ANSWER EXPLANATIONS FOR TEST 7

Questions 7-12 are based on the following passage.

(Q7) **Alice's Adventures in Wonderland is a novel written by** Charles Dodgson, better known under the penname Lewis Carroll. It tells the story of a girl named Alice who falls down a rabbit-hole into a ———**world populated by unique creatures (Q8 & Q9) acting as humans.** The (Q.10 & Q12) **tale is filled with the lessons** that schoolchildren were expected to memorize. The tale plays (Q11) **with logic in ways that have made the story of lasting popularity** with adults as well as children.

Q7. Question Pattern: The **primary purpose** of the passage is to
AP 1: Main Idea (Focus Shifts) Question Find the main idea of the entire passage or the paragraph

- ■ **Question Keyword/Key phrase:** "primary purpose"
- ■ **Incorrect Pattern:** A) criticize low-quality novels—DC
  B) describe the relationship between Charles Dodgson and Lewis Carroll—DC
  C) discuss the characteristics of adventure novels—NI   D) point out readers reaction to a novel—IS
  E) introduce briefly about a novel
- ■ **What Does The Question Really Ask?** The primary purpose question—in SSAT elementary level—is not extremely complicated. Choose the one that contains the broad and positive words. And don't choose anything that contains specific words or negative words.
- ■ **Relevancy Check:** Choice A "criticize" is a negative word seldom used in this sort of passage. Choice B uses people's names; therefore, it is specific details that are unlikely to be the answer for the primary purpose question. Choice D "readers" is a general statement that does not directly answer the question.

E is the best answer. "that have made the story of lasting popularity with adults as well as children."
As stated above, the correct answer E contains broad and positive tone to be fit in the primary purpose of this passage. Yes. It is to introduce briefly about a novel.

Incorrect Answer Explanation

Choice A is negative. The main tonality of the passage is held in a positive tone. Choice B is incorrect because, according to the passage—"penname," they are same person. Choice C is incorrect because it is not stated in the passage.

Q8. Question Pattern: Which of the following can be used in the underline?
AP 4: Word-In-Context Question   Find the clue words and keywords from the sentence

- ■ **Question Keyword/Key phrase:** "———-world populated by unique creatures **acting as humans.** "
- ■ **Incorrect Pattern: A) fantastic**   B) realistic—DC   C) modern—NI   D) pretty—NI   E) democratic—NI
- ■ **We Already Found the answer:** It's A. The answer was found before reading the passage.
- ■ **Relevancy Check:** Choice B contradicts the sentence description. The remaining choices do not reflect the sentence description, therefore, irrelevant words.

A is the best answer. Only in fantasy can animals act as a human.

Q9. Based on description in line 3, which of the following phrases would be included in the novel?
AP 6: Analogy Question   Find the logically-supported similar situation

SSAT ABSOLUTE PATTERNS

- **Question Keyword/Key phrase:** "line 3 (world...populated as humans),"
- **Incorrect Pattern:** A) Her nose was so long that it reached to her toes—NI B) She is the frost in winter night—NI.
  C) The big cat laughed D) David is Einstein at school—NI   E) Bark-Bark! Bark! The dog woke me up—NI.
- **We Already Found the answer:** It's C. The answer was found before reading the passage.
- **What Does The Question Really Ask?** This question asks for the literary device used in the novel, especially in line 3, wherein the animal characters are described in personification.
- **Relevancy Check:** Choice A is hyperbole that refers to an exaggerated statement. Choice B is metaphor that uses a figure of speech to compare two things. Choice D is allusion that calls something in mind without mentioning it. Choice E is onomatopoeia that is a word that describes sound.

C is the best answer. "fantastic world populated by unique creatures **acting as humans**"
Animal acting as human should basically use personification.
Choice C is Personification that gives human attributes to animals.

Q10. Question Pattern: Which of the following statement is **true**?
AP 2: Summary Question   Summarize the sentence or the entire paragraph

---

- **Question Keyword/Key phrase:** "true statement"
- **Incorrect Pattern:** A) The novel is written for children under 13—NI   B) The novel is written by Charles Dodgson together with Lewis Carroll—DC   C) Boys can expect the real world adventurers—DC
  D) the novel is being taught at school—NI   **E) The novel offers real lessons**
- **Relevancy Check:** Choice B is incorrect. As seen from the previous question, they are the same person.

E is the best answer. The *tale is filled with the lessons* that schoolchildren were expected to memorize.
As stated above, the novel offers real lessons.
                              Incorrect Answer Explanation
Choices A and D are not stated in the passage. Choice C contradicts the passage. It is not about the real word; it's a fantasy novel. For choice D, it is a fantasy and is not being taught at school.

Q11. Question Pattern: According to the passage, what made the **story popular?**
AP 2: Summary Question   Summarize the sentence or the entire paragraph

---

- **Question Keyword/Key phrase:** "story popular"
- **Incorrect Pattern: A) Logic**   B) Plays—NI   C) Unique creatures—IW   D) Wonderland—IW   E) A rabbit—IW
- **Reading Tips:** When in doubt, read the conclusion

A is the best answer. The concluding sentence states that the tale is filled with logic in ways that have made the story lasting popularity. Thus, the author attributes the logic as the main cause for its popularity.
All the rest are is irrelevant information that used only the meaningful words from the passage.

Q12. Question Pattern: The last sentence of the passage primarily serves to
AP 5: Understanding the True Purpose   Find the explicitly stated true purpose of the sentence

ANSWER EXPLANATIONS FOR TEST 7

- ■ **Question Keyword/Key phrase:** "last sentence"
- ■ **Incorrect Pattern:** A) cite a well-known quote—NI   B) raise a question—DC   C) make a criticism—DC
  D) note a reason for its popularity   E) explain the origin of the story—NI
- ■ **What Does The Question Really Ask?** As explained in the previous question, the last sentence focuses on the reason for its popularity.
- ■ **Relevancy Check:** Negative tones such as choice B and C cannot be the answer. For the novel maintains positive and informative tone.

D is the best answer. "The tale plays have made the story of lasting popularity"
Choice A is incorrect because there's no quote in the last sentence. Choice E is incorrect because the passage does not discuss the origin of the story.

Questions 13-17 are based on the following passage.

　　A Fox once saw a Crow fly off with a piece of cheese in its beak and settle on a branch of a tree. (Q16) **'That's for me, as I am a Fox,'** and he walked up to the foot of the tree. 'Good-day, Mistress Crow,' he cried. '(Q13 &15) **How well you are looking to-day: how glossy your feathers; how bright your eye. I feel sure your voice must surp Ass that of other birds**, just as your figure does; let me hear but one song from you that I may greet you as the Queen of Birds.' (Q14) **The Crow lifted up her head and began to caw her best,** but the moment she opened her mouth the piece of cheese fell to the ground, only to be snapped up by Master Fox. 'That will do,' said he. (Q17) **'That was all I wanted. In exchange for your cheese** I will give you a piece of advice for the future .'Do not trust flatterers.'

Q13. **Question Pattern:** "voice" in line 4 and "caw" in line 6 suggests that

AP **9: Relationships Question** Find the relationship between the cause and effect, characters, ideas

- ■ **Question Keyword/Key phrase:** "voice" compared to that of "caw""
- ■ **Incorrect Pattern: A) the first is a lie; the second is a reality**   B) the first is a honesty; the second is dishonesty—DC
  C) the first is generosity; the second is greed—NI   D) the first is wonder; the second is plain—NI
  E) the first is general; the second is special—NI

A is the best answer.   The first "voice" is the Fox's lie and the "Caw" is the real ugly voice of the Crow.
Incorrect Answer Explanation
Choice B contradict the statement. The 'voice" represents "dishonesty" of the Fox, and "caw" represents the truth of the crow.   Choices C and E are irrelevant words to both "voice" and "caw." Choice D is incorrect for the same reason as choice B.

Q14. **Question Pattern:** Which of the following statements would **both the Crow and Fox eventually agree**?
AP **9: Relationships Question** Find the relationship between the cause and effect, characters, ideas

- ■ **Question Keyword/Key phrase:** "both the Crow and Fox agree"
- ■ **Incorrect Pattern: A) Flatterers should not be trusted**   B) Fox cannot be trusted—IS   C) Crow is the ugliest bird—IS
  D) Crow is the queen of the birds—IS   E) True friends complement to each other—DC(TI)
- ■ **What Does The Question Really Ask?** The last sentence clearly states how both the fox and the crow may agree to each other. This question is difficult in that you are asked to find the mutual agreement between the fox and the crow—the two opposite characters in the story. It is easy to find the difference from the opposite characters. However, it is difficult to find the similarity from the opposite characters.

A is the best answer. The crow would agree with the statement "do not trust flatterers," which is the advice from the fox.

Incorrect Answer Explanation

Choice B and D are incorrect because the fox would not agree with them. Choice C is incorrect because the Crow would not agree. Choice E is incorrect because the tone between the fox and the crow should be negative, not positive.

Q15. Question Pattern: The **Fox's praise** (line 5) "I may greet you as the Queen of Birds" can be characterized as
AP 8: Understanding Attitude (Tone) Find the tonality: positive vs. negative, mental vs. physical

- ■ **Question Keyword/Key phrase:** "Queen of Birds" can be characterized "
- ■ **Incorrect Pattern:** A) honest—DC   B) pride—DC   **C) flattery**   D) respect—DC   E) trust—DC
- ■ **We Already Found the answer:** It's C. The answer was found before reading the passage.

C is the best answer. The comment by the Fox, whose only aim is to take the cheese from the crow, is nothing but flattery.

Incorrect Answer Explanation

Choices A and D contradict the fox's true intention for it only wants to steal cheese from the crow. The question focuses on the fox's flattery. In that sense, choices B and E become contradiction.

Q16. Question Pattern: The fox's character toward the crow can best be described as
AP 8: Understanding Attitude (Tone) Find the tonality: positive vs. negative, mental vs. physical

- ■ **Question Keyword/Key phrase:** "Fox's attitude toward the Crow"
- ■ **Incorrect Pattern:** A) respect—DC   B) honest—DC   C) not caring—NI   **D) deceptive**   E) courageous—NI

D is the best answer. *'That's for me, as I am a Fox,'* and he walked up to the foot of the tree. 'Good-day," As stated above, the fox's character is deceptive (lying).

Incorrect Answer Explanation

Choices A and B contradict the fox's attitude. Choices C and E are irrelevant words to the fox's attitude seen on the story.

Q17. Question Pattern: When the Fox said **"That** was all I wanted" in line 7, "That" refers to
Absolute Pattern 7: Inference Question   Find the indirect suggestion behind the sentence

- ■ **Question Keyword/Key phrase:** "**That** was all I wanted"
- ■ **Incorrect Pattern:** A) the crow—IW   B) the situation—NI   **C) cheese**   D) friendship with the Queen of Birds—DC   E) flattery—IW

C is the best answer. 'That was all I wanted. In exchange for your cheese I will give you a piece of advice"
The immediately following phrase "in exchange for your cheese" implies that the word "That" refers to cheese.
All the rest incorrect answers are irrelevant to the phrase and the word "cheese."

ANSWER EXPLANATIONS FOR TEST 7

Questions 18-23 are based on the following passage.

Once upon a time there was an (Q19) **old cat, called Tabitha. Mrs. Tabitha** was an **anxious** parent. (Q18) **She used to lose her kittens continually**, and whenever they were lost, they always got into mischief! On baking day she determined to shut them up in a cupboard, but could not find Tom anywhere. Mrs. Tabitha went up and down all over the house, (Q21) **mewing** for Tom. She (Q23) **looked in the pantry under the staircase**, and she searched the best spare bedroom that was all covered up with dust sheets. She went right upstairs and looked into the attics, but she could not find him anywhere. The old house was full of cupboards and passages. (Q22) **The walls were thick, and there used to be queer noises inside them,** as if there might be a little secret staircase. Certainly there were odd little jagged doorways in the wainscot, and **things** disappeared at night, especially (Q20) **cheese and bacon**.

Q18. Question Pattern: "Mrs. Tabitha was an **anxious** parent (line1)." what does "**anxious**" mean?
AP 4: Word-In-Context Question   Find the clue words and keywords from the sentence

- ■ **Question Keyword/Key phrase:** "anxious parent"
- ■ **Incorrect Pattern:** A) angry—EX   **B) concerned**   C) cautious—NI   D) diligent—NI   E) lovely—NI
- ■ **What Does The Question Really Ask?** For the easy word in the Word-in-Context question, always find the clue words from the passage.
- ■ **Relevancy Check:** The word 'anxious" is a fundamentally negative word. Thus, positive words like choice D and E can be safely removed.

B is the best answer. The immediately following phrase, "loosing her kids continuously" explains why Mrs. Tabitha was an 'anxious parent." Only choice B "concerned" can be used to represent the parent who habitually loses her child.

Incorrect Answer Explanation

Choices A and C are, although synonyms to "anxious," cannot be used to replace the word "concerned" in this sentence.

Q19. Question Pattern: The **literary device** mainly used in the story is
AP 4: Word-In-Context Question   Find the clue words and keywords from the sentence

- ■ **Question Keyword/Key phrase:** "literary device"
- ■ **Incorrect Pattern:** A) simile—NI   B) metaphor—NI   C) allusion—NI   **D) personification**   E) climax—NI

D is the best answer. "an old cat, called Tabitha. Mrs. Tabitha was an **anxious** parent"
As stated above, the passage uses personification—giving human characteristics to nonhuman—to describe cat as a human.

Incorrect Answer Explanation

*Simile is a figure of speech involving the comparison of one thing with another
*Metaphor is an imaginative way of describing something. *Allusion is an expression designed to call something to mind without mentioning it. *Climax is the most intense, exciting, or important point of something.

Q20. **Question Pattern:** Based on the story, which choice can most probably be replaced with **"things"**?
AP 7: Inference Question Find the indirect suggestion behind the sentence

■**Question Keyword/Key phrase:** "and **things** disappeared at night" .
■**Incorrect Pattern:** A) Tom—IW   B) Oven—NI   C) Cupboard—IW   **D) Foods**   E) Ghost—NI
■**Reading Tip:** Always read the following sentence next to the sentence in question.

D is the best answer. "and things disappeared at night, especially cheese and bacon."
As stated above, it is easy to identify what, along with cheese and bacon, disappeared at night.
Incorrect Answer Explanation
Other alternatives are incorrect because they are irrelevant to the following phrase "cheese and bacon."

Q21. **Question Pattern:** The **literary device** used in the word **"mewing"** (line 4) is
AP 4: Word-In-Context Question Find the clue words and keywords from the sentence

■**Question Keyword/Key phrase:** "Mrs. Tabitha went up and down all over the house, **mewing** for Tom."
■**Incorrect Pattern:**
A) Hyperbole—NI   B) Metaphor—NI   **C) Onomatopoeia**   D) Personification—NI   E) Alliteration—NI

C is the best answer. "mewing" refers to the sounds of cat. Onomatopoeia imitates the sound it is describing
Incorrect Answer Explanation
A) Hyperbole refers to an exaggeration   B) Metaphor is an imaginative way of describing something
D) Personification gives human attributes to objects or animals
E) Alliteration means two or more words in a row that all start with the same sound.

Q22. **Question Pattern: Who** would most likely have taken **"things"** in line 9?
AP 7: Inference Question Find the indirect suggestion behind the sentence

■**Question Keyword/Key phrase:** "Who"
■**Incorrect Pattern:** A) Tom—IW   B) Mrs. Tabitha—IW   **C) Mouse**   D) The owner of the house—NI
E) The children of the house—NI
■**What Does The Question Really Ask?** This inference question requires a bit of imagination based on the passage.

C is the best answer. The walls were thick, and there used to be queer noises inside them,
The phrases "queer noises inside," "odd little jagged doorways in the wainscot," "cheese and bacon" give us enough
clues that it must be a mouse that steals the foods.
Incorrect Answer Explanation
Choices A and B are cats in the story. The narrator speaks through Mrs. Tabitha's eyes, a cat. Mrs. Tabitha and her
children—also cats— live in the same house, not behind the walls. Therefore, the cats, by themselves, cannot be the
ones that steal cheese and bacon. Choices D and E are the people who cannot live behind the walls.

ANSWER EXPLANATIONS FOR TEST 7

Q23. **Question Pattern:** Mrs. Tabitha **searched everywhere** in the house **EXCEPT**
AP 2: Summary Question   Summarize the sentence or the entire paragraph

- ■ **Question Keyword/Key phrase:** "searched everywhere "
- ■ **Incorrect Pattern: A) Baking oven**   B) Pantry—DC   C) Staircase—DC   D) Bedroom—DC   E) Attics—DC
- ■ **What Does The Question Really Ask?** The question that contains the word "EXCEPT" is called the negative type of question. The negative type of question is especially difficult because it contains four true statements, all of which must be proven from the passage. The negative type of question takes more time, while it provides less probability, to find the correct answer. So, it is important to manage time. Also, remember that "EXCEPT" does not actually mean that the correct answer is unrelated to the passage. The word "EXCEPT" means "least" related words to the question.

A is the best answer. "She looked in the pantry...staircase...bedroom...attics,"
She looked everywhere EXCEPT Baking oven.

Questions 24-29 are based on the following passage.
   (Q24) **Astronomy is the study of the universe and everything in it. This includes stars, planets and galaxies** as well as other things. (Q25) **The word astronomy comes from the Greek words astron which means star and nomos which means law.** A person who studies astronomy is called an astronomer.
Ancient people used the positions of the stars to navigate, and (Q26) **to find when was the best time to plant crops.** Since the 20th century there have been two main types of astronomy, observational and theoretical astronomy. **Observational astronomy** (Q27 &Q28) **uses** many observational equipment such as **telescopes** to observe or look at stars, galaxies and other astronomical objects. **Theoretical astronomy** uses math and computer to predict models (Q29) **before the observational astronomy.**

Q24. **Question Pattern:** Study subjects in astronomy include All but
AP 2: Summary Question   Summarize the sentence or the entire paragraph

- ■ **Question Keyword/Key phrase:** "study subjects in astronomy "
- ■ **Incorrect Pattern:** A) Stars—DC   B) Mars—DC   C) Milky Way—DC   D) Moon—DC   **E) Horoscope**
- ■ **We Already Found the answer:** It's E. The answer was found before reading the passage.
- ■ **What Does The Question Really Ask?** This question—with the word "All but"—is another negative type of question. Read the previous question 23 for more detail.
- ■ **Relevancy Check:** Horoscope is a forecast of a person's future by reading stars in the sky, therefore is not a science.

E is the best answer.   Astronomy is the study of the universe and everything in it. This includes choice (A) stars, (B), (D) planets, and (C) galaxies with other things.

Q25. **Question Pattern:** The author mentions "**Greek**" in line 2 mainly to
AP 10: Structural Pattern of the Passage   Find the structural pattern of the paragraph or the passage

SSAT 8 Reading & Verbal Elementary Level

■ **Question Keyword/Key phrase:** "Greek"
■ **Incorrect Pattern:** A) introduce astrophysics—NI   **B) introduce the origin of a word "astronomy"**
   C) tell astronomy is the oldest science—NI   D) distinguish between observational and theoretical Astronomy—IW
   E) compare the ancient and modern astronomy—NI

B is the best answer. "The word astronomy comes from the **Greek** words astron **which means** star"
As stated above, the author uses Greek to introduce the origin of the word.

Incorrect Answer Explanation

Choices A, C, and E are incorrect because none of the information is stated in the passage. Choice D is mentioned in the passage but unrelated with this question.

Q26. Question Pattern: Which of the following ancient **Greek people would use astronomy**?
AP 6: Analogy Question   Find the logically-supported similar situation

■ **Question Keyword/Key phrase:** "Greek people would use astronomy"
■ **Incorrect Pattern: A) Farmers who developed an agricultural calendar based on stars location.**
   B) Teachers who taught Greek mythology—NI   C) armies who prayed before Zeus status—NI
   D) People who used star sign to predict their future—NI   E) A king who named his ship after Polaris—NI

A is the best answer.   The passage introduces some ancient Greek farmers used astronomy to find out when is the best time to plant crops.   Choice A corresponds to the statement.

Incorrect Answer Explanation

None of the rest incorrect answers are referring to scientific activities. They are unrelated to the study of astronomy.

Q27. Question Pattern: Which of the following statement is true of **observational astronomy**?
AP 2: Summary Question   Summarize the sentence or the entire paragraph

■ **Question Keyword/Key phrase:** "observational astronomy"
■ **Incorrect Pattern:** A) It is theoretical astronomy—DC   B) It predicts our future—NI   **C) It uses telescopes**
   D) It was developed In ancient Greek period—IW   E) It became known since the 16th century—NI
■ **Relevancy Check:** Choice B is incorrect. Known from the previous questions, astronomy is science and does not
   Predict the future, but astrology does.

C is the best answer. "Observational astronomy uses ...equipment such as telescopes"

Incorrect Answer Explanation

Choice A is incorrect because the passage divides astronomy into two types: observational and theoretical. They are different, and the former does not belong to the latter.
Choices D and E are incorrect because the passage states that it was developed in the 20th century.

ANSWER EXPLANATIONS FOR TEST 7

Q28. Question Pattern: Which statement is most strongly supported by the author?
AP 2: Summary Question   Summarize the sentence or the entire paragraph

---

■ **Question Keyword/Key phrase:** "supported by the author"
■ **Incorrect Pattern:** A) Astronomy is important in our society—NI(GE)
  B) Astronomers should concern more with observation than with theory—NI(GE)
  C) Greeks still use astronomy to navigate sea—NI
  D) Observational astronomy is more important than theoretical astronomy—NI
  E) Observational astronomy uses many equipment
■ **What Does The Question Really Ask?** This question can be solved simultaneously with the previous question and therefore requires no further passage reading.
■ **Relevancy Check:** Choices A and B rely on a general statements that do not directly answer the question. Choice C is—irrespective of true or not—irrelevant information to <u>scientific passage</u>.

E is the best answer. The passage states that observational astronomy uses many observational equipment such as telescopes.

Incorrect Answer Explanation

Choice D is not stated in the passage, and it is safe to believe both are equally important, just as both driving a car and learning traffic regulations are equally important for safe driving.

Q29. Question Pattern: Theoretical astronomy is important in that it
AP 2: Summary Question   Summarize the sentence or the entire paragraph

---

■ **Question Keyword/Key phrase:** "Theoretical astronomy "
■ **Incorrect Pattern:** A) helps searching for extraterrestrial life—NI
  B) does not have to use observational astronomy—DC   C) requires no telescope—IS
  D) is used before the observational astronomy   E) can be used by regular folks—NI
■ **Relevancy Check:** Choices A and E are irrelevant information and can be eliminated through common sense.

D is the best answer. The passage describes theoretical astronomy uses computer models before the observational astronomy. Theoretical astronomy is important in the sense that it is used before the observational astronomy.

Incorrect Answer Explanation

Choice B contradicts the passage. Choice C is incorrect. Of course, it does not use telescopes, but observational astronomy does. For not using telescopes, however, is only a characteristic and it does not mean it makes theoretical astronomy Important.

Test 7 Absolute Patterns for the analogy Section

AP1. Category Pattern Find the Part and Whole Relation, the Same Type or Association

16. Finger is to toe as

A) singer is to sing   B) tail is to fur   **C) nose is to mouth**   D) write is to walk   E) dance is to study

C is the best answer. Both fingers and toes have ten units each. (C) both nose and mouth have one unit each. Choice A is the purpose pattern. Choice B is the characteristic pattern. Choice D is distraction. With finger one cannot write; with toe, one cannot walk. It requires hands to write and feet to walk. Choice E are irrelevant words to each other.

AP3. Purpose (Tool) Pattern Find the Purpose of Individual and the Goal, the Function of Tool

17. Earphone is to music as eyeglass is   A) lens   B) eye   C) round   D) a pair   **E) book**

E is the best answer. Earphone is used to listen to the music as eyeglass is used to (E) read the book. Choices A and D, indicating part and whole relation with eyeglass, show no relation to the question-stem. Choice B is basically irrelevant word to the question-stem. Choice C describes the shape of eyeglass using the Degree Pattern.

AP7. Mental (Emotion) Pattern Find the Human Emotion or the Word related to Mentality

18. Rabbit is to timid as

A) grass is to green   B) courageous is to eagle   C) zebra is to strip   D) fish is to swim   **E) lion is to brave**

E is the best answer. This question is based on how we feel about a certain animal. We think rabbit is timid and (E) lion is brave. Choice A is the Characteristic pattern and is not related to the question-stem. Choice B follows the question-stem but the words order is flipped over. Choice C shows physical, not the mental characteristic of zebra. Choice D is the Characteristic Pattern describing fish's capability.

AP4. Characteristic Pattern Find the Characteristic of Person, Place, Object, or Idea

19. Ash is to powder as water is to   A) cold   B) ice   C) transparent   D) white   **E) liquid**

E is the best answer. This question asks about the characteristic of substances.
Ash is powder as water is (E) liquid.   All the rest are unrelated to the question-stem.

AP3. Purpose (Tool) Pattern Find the Purpose of Individual and the Goal, the Function of Tool

20. Coach is to firefighter as train is to   **A) extinguish fire**   B) set fire   C) engine   D) siren   E) emergency

A is the best answer. Coach trains athletes as firefighter (A) extinguishes fire.
The rest are associated with firefighter but not with the entire question-stem.

ANSWER EXPLANATIONS FOR TEST 7

AP2. Synonym/Antonym Find the similar or opposite meaning between the words

21. Opportunity is to father as

A) baby is to cute   **B) chance is to daddy**   C) U.F.O. is to Unidentified Flying Object   D) kiss is to love   E) live or die

B is the best answer. Opportunity is synonym to chance as father is synonym to (B) daddy.
Choices A and D are the Mental (Emotion) Pattern. Choice C is an acronym—abbreviation of certain word, not a synonym. Choice E is the antonym Pattern

AP2. Synonym/Antonym Find the similar or opposite meaning between the words

22. Boring is to happiness as

A) cake is to bread   **B) exciting is to unhappiness**   C) enemy is to war   D) study is to hard   E) restaurant is to market

B is the best answer. Boring is antonym to exciting as happiness is antonym to unhappiness. Note how the question-stem and the answer are paired to each other.
Choices A and C are the Category Pattern. Choice D is the Mental (Emotion) Pattern. Choice E has no pattern.

AP3. Purpose (Tool) Pattern Find the Purpose of Individual and the Goal, the Function of Tool

23. Computer is to Internet as   **A) Wi-Fi modem is to network connection**   B) music is to piano

C) swimming pool is to swimsuit   D) farm is to animal   E) electricity is to danger

A is the best answer. Computer is used to connect internet as (A) wifi modem is used to connect network.
All four words in the question-stem and the correct answer belong to the same internet category.
Choice B is the Purpose (Tool) Pattern but the words order is flipped over. And also, it is not the same category with the question-stem. Choices C and D are the Category Pattern. Choice E is the Mental (Emotion) Pattern

AP8. Production Pattern Find What Produces What and the Cause and Effect Relation

24. Peanut butter is to peanut as   A) margarine is to melt   **B) coffee is to bean**

C) taste is to sweet   D) strawberry is to jam   E) expiry date is to instruction

B is the best answer. Peanut butter is made of peanut as (B) coffee is made of bean.
Choice A is the Characteristic Pattern. Choice C is the Mental (Emotion) Pattern. Choice D follows the question-stem, except for the words order that is flipped over. Choice E is the association Pattern

AP5. Degree Pattern Find the Degree (Increase or Decrease), Find the Shape of place or thing

25. Sun is to earth as

A) ocean is to stream   B) fire is to volcano   C) astronaut is to psychic   D) horse is to cow   E) male is to female

A is the best answer. The Sun is bigger than the earth as ocean is bigger than stream.
Choice B is the Production Pattern. Choices C and D are the Category Pattern. Choice E is the antonym Pattern

AP3. Purpose (Tool) Pattern Find the Purpose of Individual and the Goal, the Function of Tool

26. Comics is to rest as homework is to   A) wisdom   **B) grade point**   C) friend   D) fun   E) punishment

B is the best answer. Comics is read for rest as homework is done to get (B) a grade point.

Choice A is not related to the question-stem. For the purpose of doing the homework is not gain wisdom. Choices C and D are not related to the question-stem. Choice E uses irrelevant words to the question-stem.

Absolute Pattern 7. Mental (Emotion) Pattern   Find the Human Emotion or the Word related to Mentality

27. Threat is to fear as

A) bank is to banker B) father is to grandfather C) sister is to brother **D) yoga is to relaxation**   E) dance is to popularity

D is the best answer. Threat causes fear as (D) yoga produces relaxation.
Choice A is the Purpose (JOB) Pattern. Choice B is the Degree Pattern. Choice C is the antonym Pattern.
Choice E has no relation between the primary and secondary word in respect to the question-stem.

Absolute Pattern 6. Definition Pattern   Find the Definition (Literal or Conceptual) of person, thing, and emotion

28. Consumer is to spend as   **A) factory is to manufacture**   B) shopper is to Christmas
      C) satisfaction is to guarantee   D) bank is to robbery   E) buyer is to seller

A is the best answer. Consumer spends money to buy goods as (A) factory manufactures goods.
Both the question-stem and the answer A belong to the same category in terms of relationships between producers and the consumer. Another coherence between the question-stem and choice A is that they both use the verb-forms "spend" and "manufacture." That is the major difference with other alternatives.
Choice B is incorrect because the word "Christmas" cannot be linked to the question-stem. Choices C and D are irrelevant words to the question-stem. Choice E is the antonym Pattern that does not match with the question-stem.

AP7. Mental (Emotion) Pattern Find the Human Emotion or the Word related to Mentality

29. Royal is to excellent as

A) life is to death   B) king is to queen   C) kingdom is to heaven   D) luxury is to princess   **E) beggar is to humble**

E is the best answer. This question is based on how we feel about a certain figure. Royal (family) is excellent as (E) beggar is humble. Choices A and B are the antonym Pattern. Choice C has little or no relation between the primary and secondary word. Choice D follows the question-stem but the words order is flipped over.

AP3. Purpose (Tool) Pattern Find the Purpose of Individual and the Goal, the Function of Tool

30. Biologist is to whistle as

A) chef is to kitchen   B) police is to arrest   **C) coach is to microscope**   D) judge is to courtroom   E) car is to driver

C is the best answer. Biologist uses a microscope as (C) coach uses a whistle.
Choices A and D show in their secondary words the places where people use for their work. Therefore, they are not the purpose pattern like the question-stem. Choice B shows people's job, not a tool.
Choice E follows the question-stem but the words order is flipped over.

SSAT

Reading & Verbal Section

Test 8

Test 8 Reading Section
Time: 30 Minutes, 29 Questions

Directions: Each reading passage is followed by questions about it. Answer the questions that follow a passage on the basis of what is stated or implied in that passage.

Questions 1-6 are based on the following passage.

> Science is what we do to find out about the natural world.
> It is the total of physics, chemistry, biology, geology and astronomy. Science makes use of mathematics, and it makes observations and experiments. Science produces accurate facts, scientific laws and theories. 'Science' also refers to the large amount of knowledge that has been found using this process.

1

Who would most likely work as a scientist?

A) A person fond of the natural world
B) A science fiction writer
C) A mathematicians
D) A school teacher
E) A man observes stars and predicts the future

2

The author states "It is the total of physics...and astronomy" (line 2) in order to

A) explain why science is difficult to learn
B) point out some popular science subjects
C) show science is in our everyday life
D) explain prerequisite to become a scientist
E) present the vast area of scientific study

3

Which of following subjects is NOT included in science?

A) Math
B) Biology
C) Geology
D) Astronomy
E) Alchemy

4

To be a scientist, one should be qualified to all of the following EXCEPT

A) be familiar with scientific laws
B) be good at mathematics
C) be ready to observe and experiment
D) be a nature lover
E) be knowledgeable in science

5

The passage is mainly concerned with scientist's

A) creativity
B) accuracy
C) modesty
D) wealth
E) courage

6

The primary purpose of the passage is to

A) think about the future science
B) explain the principle of science
C) discuss the early natural science
D) explain some limitations in science
E) describe the difference between science and other subjects

Questions 7-12 are based on the following passage.

Line
    Dipa loved to jump. She loved to climb trees. And most of all, she loved to run and play with her Puja Didi. Dipa lived in Agartala, the capital of Tripura. Agartala is green and beautiful with agarwood trees and pineapple, orange and litchi orchards. Her Baba was a national weightlifting champion. On most days, she went with him to the gymnasium, where he was a coach. Ma and
5 Baba wanted both their daughters to take up sports. So, at the age of five, Dipa started training.
    Gymnastics is a lot like acrobatics and aerobics. Quick movements. Tumbling and soaring. Fluid twists and turns. Breathtaking turns on narrow beams, Palette bars, vaults and uneven bars! Gymnastics needs balance, lots of mental effort, and control over muscles. One false step can mean a bad fall. Or a broken leg or an injured back!

7

Which choice best summarizes the main idea of the passage?

A) A Love story between Puja Didi and Dipa
B) Agartala, a beautiful place to live
C) A coach Baba
D) Dipa's love of gymnastics
E) How to become a great athlete

8

Dipa and Puja Didi share the general tone of

A) personal regret
B) open hostility
C) righteous anger
D) mild concern
E) cheerful eagerness

9

It can be inferred from the story that Agartala, where Dipa lived, is located in

A) a small village near the North Pole
B) an industrial complex
C) a small town in a war zone
D) a big city with a sport complex
E) a tropical island

10

Read the statement in the box below

> Gymnastics is a lot like acrobatics and aerobics. Quick movements. Tumbling and soaring. Fluid twists and turns.

Which of the following games best resembles Gymnastics?

A) Soccer
B) surfing
C) Baseball
D) Hockey
E) Basketball

11

Which equipment is NOT included in gymnastics?

A) Narrow beams
B) Palette bars
C) Uneven bars
D) Helmet
E) Vaults

12

Dipa feels that gymnastics requires all of the following qualities EXCEPT

A) Balance
B) Mental concentration
C) Muscle control
D) Creative idea
E) Accurate steps

Questions 13-18 are based on the following passage.

Line

This story is about my uncle named Sandy, who likes his camera so much, he always keeps it handy. Let's rewind to when Uncle Sandy was a little boy, Unlike his friends, he never dreamt of a fancy toy. Lost in books that spoke of magical creatures, Even in class, he never listened to his teachers. As time passed by, Uncle Sandy became a wildlife photographer,

5   While his friends became doctors, engineers and dance choreographers. Uncle Sandy didn't want to work in big offices, He wanted to take pictures of snakes, crocodiles and tortoises. So he decided to leave his family and friends behind, And took off to the jungles with freedom in mind. On his first expedition to the Western Ghats, He had his first encounter with a mysterious cat. Uncle Sandy has been on its trail ever since, Hoping to click a picture of it, for evidence. So

10 he decided to revisit the Western Ghats, Through its spiraling path in search of the cat.

13

Read this statement from lines 2

> Let's **rewind** to when Uncle Sandy was a little boy,

In which sentence below does the word "rewind" mean the same as the one in the sentence above?

A) Tom rewound the sad movie
B) Let's rewind the video game
C) Jim rewound the moment he fought with Gill
D) The motor rewinds the blades automatically
E) The repair shop rewound the fan blades

14

Why did Uncle Sandy not listen to his teachers in class?

A) He was always interested in taking pictures
B) He was always interested in wildlife
C) He wanted to have a fancy toy
D) He was slow at learning
E) He didn't want to study

15

The reference to Uncle Sandy's friends (line 5) serves to suggest

A) friendly nature of Uncle Sandy
B) maturity Uncle Sandy displayed even at his youth
C) some jobs that require big offices
D) interest Uncle Sandy had other than camera
E) Uncle Sandy's true desire

16

The passage states the purpose of Uncle Sandy's revisit to Western Ghats was to

A) leave from civilization
B) solve a mystery
C) live on the trail
D) hunt for the cat
E) get a picture of the cat

17

Based on the information in the passage, this story is written by

A) Uncle Sandy
B) Young Uncle Sandy when he was a boy
C) a nephew
D) aunt
E) a friend of Uncle Sandy

18

According to the story, which of the following statements is true?

A) The Western Ghats path was not straight
B) Uncle Sandy couldn't afford school education
C) Uncle Sandy caught the mysterious cat
D) Uncle Sandy took a photo of the cat
E) Uncle Sandy brought his family to the expedition

Questions 19-23 are based on the following passage.

Line

  Many years ago, there was an emperor, who was so excessively fond of new clothes, that he spent all his money on the finest suits.

  He had a different suit for each hour of the day. Just as you might say of any other king or emperor, "He is sitting in his council," people used to say of him, "He is sitting in his wardrobe."

5 One day, two rogues, calling themselves weavers said that they knew how to weave clothes of the most beautiful colors and elaborate patterns. The clothes made from their cloths were like no others, for they were invisible to everyone who was either unfit for their job, or extremely simple in the head.

  "These must, indeed, be splendid clothes!" Thought the emperor.

19

Read the statement from line 4 in the box below.

> "He is sitting in council," people used to say of him, "He is sitting in his wardrobe."

Which of the following statements most correctly interprets the above sentence?

A) The emperor concerned only about his clothes
B) The emperor served his kingdom well
C) The council and the emperor shared the same wardrobes
D) The emperor was well respected among people
E) The council was regularly held in the emperor's wardrobe.

20

According to the passage, the weave stuffs of the most beautiful colors can be visible only to those who

A) are simple in character
B) are fit for the office
C) are unfit for the office
D) are splendent
E) wear splendid clothes

21

Those unfit for the office may think that the Emperor wearing the splendid clothes is in fact

A) greedy
B) attractive
C) splendid
D) naked
E) courageous

22

Which of the followings would the Emperor most likely want to have?

A) new army
B) friends
C) invisible clothes to everyone
D) wisdom
E) splendid clothes

23

The splendid clothes (line 9) is in fact

A) not real
B) made of colorful fabric
C) extraordinarily simple design
D) unfit for the Emperor
E) visible

Questions 24-28 are based on the following passage.

Line   Now then, let us begin. When we are at the end of the story, we shall know more than we know now: but to begin. Once upon a time there was a wicked sprite, indeed he was the most mischievous of all sprites. One day he was in a very good humor, for he had made a mirror with the power of causing all that was good and beautiful when it was reflected therein, to look poor
5   and mean; but that which was good-for-nothing and looked ugly was shown magnified and increased in ugliness. In this mirror the most beautiful landscapes looked like boiled spinach, and the best persons were turned into frights, or appeared to stand on their heads.

24

Read the statement from lines 1-2 below.

> Now then, let us begin. When we are at the end of the story, we shall know more than we know now: but to begin.

What is the main reason that the author wrote as above?

A) The author show that he truly wants to communicate with the reader
B) The author warns that the story is beyond understanding
C) This is usually how authors start stories
D) The author doesn't know how to begin
E) The author wants to end the story soon

25

Read this statement from line 7

> the best persons were turned into frights, or appeared to stand on their heads

In which sentence below does the words "best Persons" mean the same as the one in above?

A) Tom is the best student in English class
B) Let's look for the best person for our company
C) David has a perfect body that everyone calls him the best person in the universe.
D) My car died again; let's find the best person.
E) Mom is the best person for Thanksgiving meals.

26

The passage describes that "boiled spinach" in line 6 was in fact

A) a cooked vegetable
B) a healthy food
C) the reflection of the beautiful landscapes
D) the ill-spirit
E) a wicked person

27

Which sensory device does the narrator primarily use throughout the passage?

A) Hearing
B) Smell
C) Sight
D) Taste
E) Touch

28

The story can best be found in

A) a realistic T.V. documentary
B) a historical biography
C) a whimsical novel
D) political cartoons
E) an encyclopedia

Verbal Test 8
20 MINUTES, 30 QUESTIONS

Directions: the synonym questions ask you to find the most appropriate synonym to the question.

The analogy questions ask you to find the most appropriate analogy to the question. Select the answer that best matches to the question.

Synonyms

Each of the following questions consists of one word followed by five words or phrases. You are to select the one word or phrase whose meaning is closest to the word in capital letters.

1. HACKNEYED
A) Boring
B) Interesting
C) Hockey rules
D) Surprise
E) Requirement

2. IMPERATIVE
A) unnecessary
B) required
C) king
D) relations
E) sadly

3. MUNDANE
A) exciting
B) boring
C) Monday work
D) weekly work
E) tiredness

4. PLACID
A) respect
B) warlike
C) peaceful
D) placement
E) organized

5. SPURIOUS
A) real
B) superior
C) arrogant
D) super
E) fake

6. STEALTHY
A) disclose
B) gaiety
C) excited
D) concealment
E) stealing

TEST 8

7. URBANE
A) polite
B) rude
C) country like
D) modern
E) wasteful

8. PERFIDY
A) friendship
B) loyal
C) treachery
D) fidelity
E) professional

9. ADVENT
A) departure
B) arrival
C) venture
D) explore
E) advertisement

10. ITINERANT
A) staying
B) ticketing
C) international
D) understand
E) traveling

11. CACHE
A) open
B) place
C) lazy
D) hiding place
E) spur

12. INCITE
A) instigate
B) ridiculous
C) recital
D) citation
E) ratio

13. APPEASE
A) peacemaker
B) excessive
C) shallow
D) anger
E) peace

14. DUPE
A) truth
B) bless
C) peace
D) deceive
E) cheer

15. ACME
A) malign
B) mail
C) bottom
D) pinnacle
E) foundation

16. Ear is to eye as toe is to
A) blood
B) finger
C) body
D) girl
E) boy

17. Engine is to car as
A) heart is to human
B) city is to building
C) chair is to leg
D) hat is to head
E) ocean is to fish

Test 8 Analogy questions 16-30

SAMPLE QUESTION
Q: River is to Ocean as:
This question is Degree Analogy question (small to big movement).

A) better is to good
B) rain is to cloud
C) father is to mother
D) <u>city is to country</u>
E) fork is to spoon

Ⓓ is the correct answer. Just as river is smaller than Ocean, so is city to the country.
Ⓐ is incorrect because the order is flipped over.
Ⓑ is incorrect because this is 'Production Analogy—what-produce-what.'
Ⓒ and Ⓔ are incorrect because there are no big and small relations between mother and father, so does fork to spoon.

18. Car plate is to name as
A) study is to insurance
B) fight is to win
C) number is to name tag
D) envelope is to stamp
E) metal is to clothe

19. Music is to earphone as star is to
A) microphone
B) telescope
C) book
D) cosmology
E) moon

20. Butter is to noodle as
A) bread is to soy source
B) coffee is to bean
C) soccer is to uniform
D) movie is to actor
E) girl is to boy

21. Hawaii is to desert as Sahara is to
A) country
B) wet
C) camel
D) islands
E) sand

22. Insect is to flower as
A) movie is to ticket
B) art is to artist
C) status is to exhibition
D) music is to concert
E) bee is to rose

23. Soccer is to rink as
A) child is to mom
B) student is to practice
C) boxer is to fight
D) hockey is to field
E) library is to book

24. Blood is to human as moisture is to
A) wet
B) gloomy
C) sky
D) cloud
E) dry

25. Rain is to monsoon as wind is to
A) breeze
B) hurricane
C) earthquake
D) volcano
E) camping

26. Mirror is to reflection as
A) coffee is to sleep
B) old is to young
C) bicycle is ride
D) hospital is to doctor
E) banana is to long

27. Chicken is to mammal as tiger is to
A) endangered animal
B) fast
C) cage
D) bird
E) furious

28. Stare is to glimpse as dime is to

A) dome

B) money

C) cent

D) dollar

E) quarter

29. God is to dying as

A) win is to luck

B) poor is money

C) thief is to jail

D) cure is to medicine

E) human is to immortal

30. Sky is to the blue as

A) ocean is to blue

B) star to pink

C) coffee is to red

D) chicken is to purple

E) fire is to white

SSAT ELEMENTARY LEVEL

Reading & Verbal Section

Test 8

Answer Explanations

The Pattern Analyses

ALL THE LOGIC AND RULES BEHIND
EVERY SINGLE SSAT QUESTION

TEST 8
READING SECTION

Please refer to the Reading Section AP Analyses

SYNONYM QUESTIONS
NO.1 ~ 15

1 A
2 B
3 B
4 C
5 E
6 D
7 A
8 C
9 B
10 E
11 D
12 A
13 E
14 D
15 D

THE ANALOGY QUESTIONS
NO.16-30.

Please refer to the analogy Section AP Analyses

ANSWER EXPLANATIONS FOR TEST 8

Test 8 Absolute Patterns for the Reading Section

Questions 1-6 are based on the following passage.

(Q4. & Q6.) **Science is what we do to find out about the natural world**. It is the total of (Q3.) **physics, chemistry, biology, geology and astronomy.** Science makes use of (Q1.) **mathematics,** and it makes observations and experiments. (Q5.) **Science produces accurate facts**, scientific laws and theories. 'Science' also refers to the large amount of knowledge that has been found using this process.

Q1. Question Pattern: Who would most likely **work as a scientist**?
AP 7: Inference Question   Find the indirect suggestion behind the sentence

---

■ **Question Keyword/Key phrase:** "work with science"
■ **Incorrect Pattern:** A) A person fond of the natural world—IW   B) A science fiction writer—NI
  C) A mathematicians   D) A school teacher—IS   E) A man observes stars and predicts the future—NI
■ **Relevancy Check:** B is incorrect because "writing science fiction" has nothing to do with working with science. Choice D is incorrect because it doesn't specify the subject the teacher specializes in. Choice E is fortune teller's job.

C is the best answer. "Science makes use of mathematics"
As stated above, mathematicians would most likely work with science.
Incorrect Answer Explanation
Choice A uses a trick by using the word "natural world" from the passage. "fond of," meaning "to have an affection for" is more appropriate to nature lovers or environmentalists, not to a scientist.

Q2. The author states "It is the total of physics...and astronomy" (line 2) in order to
AP 5: Understanding the True Purpose   Find the explicitly stated true purpose of the sentence

---

■ **Question Keyword/Key phrase:** "It is the total of physics...and astronomy"
  A) explain why science is difficult to learn—NI   B) point out some popular science subjects—NI
  C) show science is in our everyday life—NI   D) explain prerequisite to become a scientist—NI
  E) **present the vast area of scientific study**

D is the best answer. "It is the total of physics, chemistry, biology, geology and astronomy."
The clue words "total of" suggests vast area of scientific study.
All the other alternatives are irrelevant information not specified in the passage.

Q3. Question Pattern: Which of following subjects is **NOT included in science**?
AP 2: Summary Question   Summarize the sentence or the entire paragraph

---

■ **Question Keyword/Key phrase:** "subjects is **NOT included**"
■ **Incorrect Pattern:** A) Math—DC   B) Biology—DC   C) Geology—DC   D) Astronomy—DC   **E) Alchemy**
■ **We Already Found the answer:** It's E. The answer was found before reading the passage.
■ **Relevancy Check:** Alchemy is not a science. It is the medieval forerunner of chemistry.

E is the best answer. It is the total of physics, chemistry, biology, geology and astronomy.

SSAT ABSOLUTE PATTERNS

Q4. Question Pattern: To be a scientist, one should be qualified to all of the following **EXCEPT**
AP 7: Inference Question   Find the indirect suggestion behind the sentence

- ■ **Question Keyword/Key phrase:** "To be a scientist"
- ■ **Incorrect Pattern:** A) be familiar with scientific laws—DC   B) be good at mathematics—DC
  C) be ready to observe and experiment—DC   **D) be a nature lover**   E) be knowledgeable in science—DC

D is the best answer. As described in question 1, "nature" in the passage refers to the world observed and controlled by science. Choice D is irrelevant issue to science. All the rest are related to science, therefore true but incorrect.

Q5. Question Pattern: The passage is mainly **concerned with scientist's**
AP 2: Summary Question   Summarize the sentence or the entire paragraph

- ■ **Question Keyword/Key phrase:** "concerned with scientist's"
- ■ **Incorrect Pattern:** A) creativity—NI **B) accuracy** C) modesty—NI D) wealth—NI   E) courage—NI
- ■ **We Already Found the answer:** It's B. The answer was found before reading the passage.
- ■ **What Does The Question Really Ask?** Some questions can be solved with common sense.
- ■ **Relevancy Check:** Choice A, thinking from common sense, refers to the characteristic of artists. Choices C, D, and E are almost unrelated words to the academic characteristics of scientists in the passage.

B is the best answer. "Because Science produces accurate facts, scientists who conduct science should "
As stated above, science is based on accurate data and mathematics.

Q6. Question Pattern: The **primary purpose** of the passage is to
AP 1: Main Idea (Focus Shifts) Question Find the main idea of the entire passage or the paragraph

- ■ **Question Keyword/Key phrase:** "primary purpose "
- ■ **Incorrect Pattern:** A) think about the future science—NI   **B) explain the principle of science**
  C) discuss the early natural science— NI   D) explain some limitations in science—DC
  E) describe the difference between science and other subjects—NI

B is the best answer. "Science is what we do to find out about the natural world"
As stated above and defined in the first sentence, the primary purpose of the passage is to explain the principle of science.

Incorrect Answer Explanation
Choices A, C, and E are irrelevant information not stated in the passage. Choice D contradicts the passage wherein the author explains the vast area of scientific researches.

ANSWER EXPLANATIONS FOR TEST 8

Questions 7-12 are based on the following passage.

(Q7 & Q8) **Dipa loved to jump. She loved to climb trees.** And most of all, she loved to run and play with her Puja Didi. Dipa lived in Agartala, the capital of Tripura. Agartala is green and beautiful with agarwood trees and (Q9) **pineapple, orange and litchi orchards. Her Baba was a** national weightlifting champion. On most days, she went with him to the gymnasium, where he was a coach. Ma and Baba wanted Puja and Dipa to take up sports. So, at the age of five, Dipa started training. (Q10) **Gymnastics is a lot like acrobatics and aerobics. Quick movements. Tumbling and soaring. Fluid twists and turns.**
Breathtaking turns on (Q11) **narrow beams, Palette bars, vaults and uneven bars! Gymnastics needs** (Q12) **balance, lots of mental effort, and control over muscles. One false step can mean a bad fall. Or a broken leg or an injured back.**

Q7. Question Pattern: Which choice best **summarizes** the passage?
AP 1: Main Idea (Focus Shifts) Question Find the main idea of the entire passage or the paragraph

- **Question Keyword/Key phrase:** "summarizes"
- **Incorrect Pattern:** A) A Love story between Puja Didi and Dipa—NI   B) Agartala, a beautiful place to live—NI
   C) A coach Baba—IW   **D) Dipa's love of gymnastics**   E) How to become an Olympic athlete—EX
- **What Does The Question Really Ask?** The passage that contains several characters are in every sense quite confusing. Among many characters, focus on the main character, whose name appears most frequently. The main tone of the main character can be identified from the keywords. In this story, Dipa, the main character, loves to jump.
- **Relevancy Check:** Choices A, B, and C are incorrect because they—whether true statement—do not focus on the main character (Dipa) of the passage.

D is the best answer. "Dipa loved to jump. She loved to climb trees. And most of all, she loved"
The main character is "Dipa" and it is about her love of gymnastics.

Incorrect Answer Explanation

Choice A is incorrect because the passage states "Ma and Baba wanted Puja and Dipa to take up sports," from which we can tell that they are siblings. Choice E is extreme and not specified in the passage.

Q8. Question Pattern: Dipa and Puja Didi share the **general tone** of
AP 8: Understanding Attitude (Tone) Find the tonality: positive vs. negative, mental vs. physical

- **Question Keyword/Key phrase:** "general tone"
- **Incorrect Pattern:** A) personal regret—DC   B) open hostility—DC   C) righteous anger—DC   D) mild concern—DC
   E) cheerful eagerness
- **What Does The Question Really Ask?** The passage, seen from the previous question, starts with the positive tone. Therefore, the correct answer must also be positive that reflects the general tone of this story.
- **Relevancy Check:** All the rest incorrect answers are held in negative tonality.

E is the best answer.   "Dipa loved to jump...most of all, she loved to run and play with her Puja Didi"
As stated above, the general tone is positive; only choice E is positive.

SSAT ABSOLUTE PATTERNS

Q9. Question Pattern: It can be inferred from the story that **Agartala**, where Dipa lived, is located in
AP 7: Inference Question   Find the indirect suggestion behind the sentence

■ **Question Keyword/Key phrase:**   "Agartala"
■ **Incorrect Pattern:** A) a small village near the North Pole—DC   B) an industrial complex—DC
C) a small town in a war zone—DC   D) a big city with a sport complex—DC   **E) a tropical island**

E is the best answer. "Agartala is green and beautiful with agarwood trees and pineapple, orange"
As stated above, Agartala should probably be located in **a tropical island.**
A) "North Pole," B) "industrial," C) "war zone," and D) "a sport complex" do not agree with the passage description.

Q10. Question Pattern: Which of the following **games best resembles Gymnastics?**
AP 7: Inference Question   Find the indirect suggestion behind the sentence

■ **Question Keyword/Key phrase:**   "games resembles Gymnastics"
■ **Incorrect Pattern:** A) Soccer—NI   **B) Surfing**   C) Baseball—NI   D) Hockey—NI   E) Basketball—NI
■ **We Already Found the answer:** It's B. The answer was found before reading the passage.
■ **What Does The Question Really Ask?** Some questions can be solved with a common sense.
■ **Relevancy Check:** Choice B can be distinguished with A, C, D, and E in the sense that B is the individual sport while the rest are team sports.

B is the best answer.   The passage describes the movements required in gymnastics, which is very similar to surfing in the sense that it requires practiced body posture and balance. Also, they both are individual sports.

Q11. Question Pattern: According to the story, which of the following **equipment is not included** in Gymnastics?
AP 7: Inference Question   Find the indirect suggestion behind the sentence

■ **Question Keyword/Key phrase:**   "equipment is not included"
■ **Incorrect Pattern:** A) Narrow beams-DC   B) Palette bars-DC   C) Uneven bars-DC   **D) Helmet**   E) Vaults-DC
■ **We Already Found the answer:** It's D. The answer was found before reading the passage.
■ **What Does The Question Really Ask?** Some questions can be solved with a common sense.

D is the best answer.   It will be nonsense to wear a helmet while performing gymnastics.

Q12. Question Pattern: Dipa feels **gymnastics** requires all of following qualities EXCEPT
AP 2: Summary Question   Summarize the sentence or the entire paragraph

■ **Question Keyword/Key phrase:**   "gymnastics"
■ **Incorrect Pattern:** A) Balance—DC   B) Mental concentration—DC   C) Muscle control—DC   **D) Creative idea**
E) Accurate steps—DC
■ **Reading Tip:** When in doubt, read the conclusion.

D is the best answer. "Balance, lots of mental effort, and control over muscles. …requires accurate steps"
As stated above, Choice D "creative idea" is not mentioned.

ANSWER EXPLANATIONS FOR TEST 8

Questions 13-18 are based on the following passage.
This story is about (Q17) my uncle named Sandy, (Q14) **Who likes his camera so much,** he always keeps it handy. (Q13) **Let's rewind to when Uncle Sandy was a little boy,** Unlike his friends, he never dreamt of a fancy toy. Lost in books that spoke of magical creatures, Even in class, he never listened to his teachers. As time passed by, Uncle Sandy became a wildlife photographer.

While his friends became doctors, engineers and dance choreographers. (Q15) **Uncle Sandy didn't want to work in big offices,** He wanted to take pictures of snakes, crocodiles and tortoises. He had his first encounter with a mysterious cat. Uncle Sandy has been on its trail ever since, (Q16) **Hoping to click a picture of it, for evidence. So he decided to revisit the Western Ghats,** (Q18.) **Through its spiraling path** in search of the cat.

Q13. In which sentence below does the word **"rewind" mean the same** as the one in the sentence above?
AP 4: Word-In-Context Question   Find the clue words and keywords from the sentence

■ **Question Keyword/Key phrase:** "Let's **rewind** to when Uncle Sandy was a little boy,"
■ **Incorrect Pattern: A)** Tom rewound the sad movie—NI   B) Let's rewound the video game—NI
   C) Jim rewinds the moment he fought with Gill   D) The motor rewinds the blades automatically—NI
   E) The repair shop rewound the fan blades—NI
■ **We Already Found the answer:** It's C. The answer was found before reading the passage.
■ **What Does The Question Really Ask?** The question asks to distinguish figurative from literal meaning for the same word. The phase in question uses the word "rewind" in a figurative sense, saying "Let's go back to the time when...." The correct answer C also uses the word "rewinds" in a figurative sense, saying 'Jim thinks back to the moment..."
■ **Relevancy Check:** All the other incorrect answers use the word "rewinds" as a literal, physical meaning.

C is the best answer.   The word "rewind" used figuratively in the passage means "to turn back time."

Q14. **Question Pattern: Why did Uncle Sandy not listen** to his teachers in class?
AP 2: Summary Question   Summarize the sentence or the entire paragraph

■ **Question Keyword/Key phrase:** "Why did Uncle Sandy not listen"
■ **Incorrect Pattern: A) He was always interested in taking pictures**   B) He was always interested in wildlife—NI
   C) He wanted to have a fancy toy—NI D) He was slow at learning—NI   E) He didn't want to study—NI

A is the best answer.   "Sandy, who likes his camera so much,...Even in class, he never listened to.."
The story begins with the phrase "...who likes his camera so much, he always keeps it handy." The phrase "Even in class, he never listened to...." emphasizes uncle Sandy's obsession with picture taking.

Incorrect Answer Explanation

Choice B is distraction. Line 3 describes uncle Sandy as a wildlife photographer. Without having the word "photographer" the word "wildlife" drastically changes the intended meaning. Choices C, D, and E are irrelevant information, especially D and E use negative words while the passage describes him with positive tone.

Q15. **Question Pattern** The reference to Uncle Sandy's friends (line 5) serves to suggest
AP 3: Example Question   Find the primary reason for using the example sentence

SSAT ABSOLUTE PATTERNS

- ■ **Question Keyword/Key phrase:** "Uncle Sandy's friends"
- ■ **Incorrect Pattern:** A) friendly nature of Uncle Sandy—NI   B) maturity Uncle Sandy displayed even at his youth—NI   C) some jobs that require big offices—IW   D) interest Uncle Sandy had other than camera—DC
  E) Uncle Sandy's true desire
- ■ **What Does The Question Really Ask?** It is important to understand that the key phrase in the question: "Uncle Sandy's friends" is a mere example. As explained several times already, the correct answer lies not in the example sentence, but in the main idea that supports the example sentence.
- ■ **Relevancy Check:** Incorrect answers frequently use the words or phrase from the example sentence, instead of using the main idea.

E is the best answer. The passage states that Uncle Sandy didn't want to work in big offices, He wanted to take pictures, and that was his only true desire.

Incorrect Answer Explanation

Choices A and B are irrelevant information not specified in the passage. Choice C focuses on the example sentence not on the main purpose. Choice D contradicts the passage. The author has brought up this example to show that Uncle Sandy had no other interest but camera.

Q16. Question Pattern: Why did Uncle Sandy **revisit to Western Ghats**?
AP 3: The Example Question   Find the primary reason for using the example sentence

- ■ **Question Keyword/Key phrase:** "revisit to Western Ghats"
- ■ **Incorrect Pattern:** A) to leave from civilization—NI   B) to solve a mystery about a cat—NI   C) to live on the trail—NI   D) to catch the cat—EX   **E) to get a picture of the cat**
- ■ **Relevancy Check:** The phrase "revisit to Western Ghats" reveals that this is the example type of question. Just like the previous question, the main idea "Uncle Sandy's obsession with picture taking" must be the answer.

E is the best answer. He revisited to Western Ghats in the hope of taking the picture of the cat.
Choices A, B, C ,or D are neither stated in the passage nor can be the main idea of the passage.

Q17. Question Pattern: Based on the information in the passage, this story is written by
AP 7: Inference Question   Find the indirect suggestion behind the sentence

- ■ **Question Keyword/Key phrase:** "this story is written by"
- ■ **Incorrect Pattern:** A) uncle Sandy—IW   B) young Uncle Sandy when he was a boy—IW   **C) a nephew**
  D) an aunt—NI   E) a friend of Uncle Sandy—IW
- ■ **We Already Found the answer:** It's C. The answer was found before reading the passage.
- ■ **What Does The Question Really Ask?** The passage must be written by Uncle Sandy's nephew because the narrator calls him "my Uncle."

C is the best answer. "This story is about my uncle named Sandy, who likes his camera"

ANSWER EXPLANATIONS FOR TEST 8

Q18. Question Pattern: Which of the following statements is true?
AP 7: Inference Question Find the indirect suggestion behind the sentence

---

- **Question Keyword/Key phrase:** "true"
- **Incorrect Pattern: A) The Western Ghats path was not straight**
  B) Uncle Sandy couldn't afford school education—NI   C) Uncle Sandy caught the mysterious cat—NI
  D) Uncle Sandy took a photo of the cat—NI   E) Uncle Sandy brought his family to the expedition—DC
- **Relevancy Check:** Choice C and E are, as seen from the previous questions, cannot be the correct answer. For uncle Sandy went alone to the expedition, wishing to take pictures of the mysterious cat.

A is the best answer.   The passage states the path through the Western Ghats was spiraling, not straight
Choices B and D are not stated in the passage.

Questions 19-23 are based on the following passage.
   Many years ago, there was an Emperor, (Q22) **who was so excessively fond of** new clothes, that **he spent all his money in dress**. He did not trouble himself in the least about his soldiers; nor did he care to go either to the theatre or the chase, except for the opportunities then afforded him for displaying his new clothes. He had a different suit for each hour of the day; and as of any other king or emperor, one is accustomed to say, (Q19) **"he is sitting in council,"** it was always said of him, **"The Emperor is sitting in his wardrobe."** They gave out that they knew how to weave stuffs of the most beautiful colors, from which should have the wonderful property of (Q20 & Q21 & Q23) **invisible to everyone who was unfit for the office he held, or who was extraordinarily simple in character.** "These must, indeed, be **splendid clothes**!" thought the Emperor.

Q19. Question pattern Which of the followings most correctly interprets the statement below?
AP 5: Understanding the True Purpose Find the explicitly stated true purpose of the sentence

---

"he is sitting in council," it was always said of him, "The Emperor is sitting in his wardrobe."
- **Incorrect Pattern: A) The emperor concerned only about his clothes**
  B) The emperor served his kingdom well—DC   C) The council and the emperor shared the same wardrobes—NI
  D) The emperor was well respected among people-DC   E) The council was regularly held in the emperor's wardrobe-NI
- **We Already Found the answer:** It's A. The answer was found before reading the passage
- **Relevancy Check:** The tone in the above sentence is cynical. The answer therefore has to be negative. In that respect, choices B and D cannot be the answer.

A is the best answer.   "The Emperor is sitting in his wardrobe." Implies the Emperor concerns only about his dress. Choices C and E use the word "wardrobe" too literally. The "wardrobe" in the sentence is mainly used to insinuate the emperor's obsession with clothing.

Q20. Question pattern: The weave stuffs of the most beautiful colors can be visible only to those who
AP 2: Summary Question Summarize the sentence or the entire paragraph

---

SSAT ABSOLUTE PATTERNS

- ■ **Question Keyword/Key phrase:** "visible only to those "
- ■ **Incorrect Pattern:** A) are simple in character—DC **B) are fit for the office** C) are unfit for the office—DC D) are splendent—IW E) wear splendid clothes—IW

B is the best answer. The passage states that the clothes are *invisible* to everyone who *was unfit for the office* he held, or who was *extraordinarily simple* in character. It, then, means clothes are visible to those who are fit for the office.

Incorrect Answer Explanation

Choices A and C contradict the passage. Choices D and E used the key word "splendid" in a wrong way.

Q21. Question pattern: Those unfit for the office may think that the Emperor wearing the splendid clothes is in fact
AP 7: Inference Question   Find the indirect suggestion behind the sentence

- ■ **Question Keyword/Key phrase:** "Those unfit for the office may think "
- ■ **Incorrect Pattern:** A) greedy—NI B) attractive—DC C) splendid—DC **D) naked** E) courageous—NI
- ■ **We Already Found the answer:** It's D. The answer was found before reading the passage
- ■ **What Does The Question Really Ask?** The question asks for the opposite situation to the passage.
- ■ **Relevancy Check:** Choices A and E are irrelevant words to the overall character descriptions. Choices B and C contradict the passage description.

D is the best answer. "wonderful property of remaining invisible to everyone unfit for the office...
As stated above, those who unfit for the office might think that the Emperor is naked because it's invisible to them.

Q22. Question pattern: Which of the followings would the Emperor most likely want to have?
AP 2: Summary Question   Summarize the sentence or the entire paragraph

- ■ **Question Keyword/Key phrase:** "Emperor most likely want"
- ■ **Incorrect Pattern:** A) new army—NI B) friends—NI C) invisible clothes—IS D) wisdom—NI **E) splendid clothes**
- ■ **We Already Found the answer:** It's E. The answer was found before reading the passage.
- ■ **Relevancy Check:** Choices A, B, and D are not stated in the passage.

E is the best answer. "These must, indeed, be splendid clothes!"
In the passage the emperor is excessively fond of new clothes. The climax in the last sentence "splendid clothes!" emphasizes the emperor's obsession with clothes.

The Relevancy Check

Choice C is incorrect. Line 7 clearly states "invisible to everyone who was either unfit for their job..." In other words, the emperor wished to have a splendid clothes that is so magical as to be invisible to some people.

Q23. Question pattern: The splendid clothes in line 9 was in fact
AP 7: Inference Question   Find the indirect suggestion behind the sentence

- ■ **Question Keyword/Key phrase:** "splendid clothes "
- ■ **Incorrect Pattern: A) not real** B) made of colorful fabric—DC C) extraordinarily simple design—DC D) unfit for the Emperor—IW E) visible—DC

ANSWER EXPLANATIONS FOR TEST 8

A is the best answer. The passage mocks the emperor obsessed with clothing. The splendid clothes must be not real. Choices B, C and E are what two rogues, to fool the emperor, claimed to be the actual clothes. Therefore, they contradict the truth. Choice D is incorrect. The emperor believes the clothes is unfit only for people unfit for office.

Questions 24-28 are based on the following passage.
   (Q24) Now then, let us begin. When we are at the end of the story, we shall know more than we know now: but to begin. Once upon a time there was a wicked sprite, indeed he was the most mischievous of all sprites. One day he was (Q27 & Q28) **in a very good humor, for he had made a mirror** with the power of causing all that was **(Q25) good and beautiful** when it was reflected therein, to look poor and mean; but that which was good-for-nothing and looked ugly was shown magnified and increased in ugliness.
In this mirror (Q26) **the most beautiful landscapes** looked like **boiled spinach**, and the **best persons** were turned into frights, or appeared to stand on their heads; their faces were so distorted that they were not to be recognized; and if anyone had a mole, you might be sure that it would be magnified and spread over both nose and mouth.

Q24. **Question Pattern:** What is the main reason that the author wrote as below?
AP 10: Structural Pattern of the Passage   Find the structural pattern of the paragraph or the passage

Now then, let us begin. When we are at the end of the story, we shall know more than we know now:
■ **Question Keyword/Key phrase:** "main reason that the author wrote "
■ **Incorrect Pattern: A)** The author wants to show that he truly communicates with the reader
   B) The author warns that the story is beyond understanding—NI   C) This is usually how authors start stories-NI(GE)
   D) The author doesn't know how to begin—DC   E) The author wants to end the story soon—DC
■ **We Already Found the answer:** It's A. The answer was found before reading the passage.
■ **Relevancy Check:** Choice C uses a general statement that does not directly answer the question.
   Choices B and D contradict the intention of the author, who knows, in order to attract attention, exactly how to begin. Choice E contradicts the author's intention. He wants to start the story.

A is the best answer. The beginning of the story usually attracts reader's attention. The author is grabbing the reader's attention as if he is truly communicating with his reader.

Q25.**Question Pattern**: In which sentence does the words best persons mean the same as in the sentence?
AP 4: Word-In-Context Question   Finding clue words and keywords from the sentence in question

■ **Question Keyword/Key phrase:** "best persons were turned into frights, appeared to stand on their heads"
■ **Incorrect Pattern:** A) Tom is the best student in English class—NI B) Let's look for the best person for our
   company—NI   **C) David has a perfect body that everyone calls him the best person in the universe**
   D) My car died again; let's find the best person—NI E) Mom is the best person for Thanksgiving meals—NI
■ **We Already Found the answer:** It's C. The answer was found before reading the passage.
■ **What Does The Question Really Ask?** The sentence shows that the best person is the person with the best appearance.
■ **Relevancy Check:** Choice A can be interpreted as the smartest person. Choice B can be interpreted as the best staff for the job. Choice D refers to the best mechanic. Choice E means the best cook.

SSAT ABSOLUTE PATTERNS

C is the best answer. "the best persons were turned into frights, or appeared to stand on their heads"

Q26. Question Pattern: The passage describes that "boiled spinach" in line 7 was in fact
AP 2: Summary Question   Summarize the sentence or the entire paragraph

- ■ **Question Keyword/Key phrase:** "boiled spinach"
- ■ **Incorrect Pattern:** A) a cooked vegetable—IW   B) a healthy food—NI
  C) the reflection of the beautiful landscapes   D) the ill-spirit—IW   E) a wicked person—NI

C is the best answer.   The passage states even the most beautiful landscapes looked like boiled spinach.
Incorrect Answer Explanation
Choices A, B, and D are irrelevant information that only used meaningful words from the passage. Choice E is not stated in the passage

Q27. Question Pattern: Which sensory device does the narrator primarily use throughout the passage?
AP 10: Structural Pattern of the Passage   Find the structural pattern of the paragraph or the passage

- ■ **Question Keyword/Key phrase:** "sensory device"
- ■ **Incorrect Pattern:** A) Hearing—NI   B) Smell—NI   **C) Sight**   D) Taste—NI   E) Touch—NI
- ■ **We Already Found the answer:** It's C. The answer was found before reading the passage.
- ■ **What Does The Question Really Ask?** The main theme is the mirror created by the wicked spirit. The passage mostly describes about this mirror. Therefore, the "sight" is the answer.
- ■ **Relevancy Check:** All the rest are irrelevant information to the passage.

C is the best answer. "he had made a mirror with the power of causing all that was good and beautiful"

Q28. Question Pattern: The story can best be found in
AP 7: Inference Question   Find the indirect suggestion behind the sentence

- ■ **Question Keyword/Key phrase:** "The story"
- ■ **Incorrect Pattern:** A) a realistic T.V. documentary—NI   B) a historical biography—NI   **C) a whimsical novel**
  D) political cartoons—NI   E) an encyclopedia—NI
- ■ **We Already Found the answer:** It's C. The answer was found before reading the passage.
- ■ **What Does The Question Really Ask?** The story is fairy tail and can only be found in a whimsical novel rather than other sources in the alternatives.
- ■ **Relevancy Check:** All the remaining choices are irrelevant to the passage.

C is the best answer. "he had made a mirror with the power of causing all that was good and beautiful".

Test 8 Absolute Patterns for the analogy Section

AP1. Category Pattern   Find the Part and Whole Relation, the Same Type or Association

16. Ear is to eye as toe is to   A) blood   **B) finger**   C) body   D) girl   E) boy

B is the best answer. Both ear and eye have two units each. Both toe and finger have ten units each. Choices A and C are the same body category but don't follow the question-stem. Choices D and E are Irrelevant to the question-stem.

AP3. Purpose (Tool) Pattern   Find the Purpose of Individual and the Goal, the Function of Tool

17. Engine is to car as

A) heart is to human   B) city is to building   C) chair is to leg   D) hat is to head   E) ocean is to fish

A is the best answer. The Engine drives car as heart drives—by circulating blood—human body.
Choices B, C, and E are the Category Pattern specified in the parts and whole relations. For the students who may think the question-stem as the part-whole pattern, choice B, C, and E are certainly the part-whole pattern. They, however, are all flipped over in the word-orders.
Choice D is the Purpose (Tool) Pattern but is not following the question-stem as the 'hat' is unable to drive 'head.'

AP3. Purpose (Tool) Pattern   Find the Purpose of Individual and the Goal, the Function of Tool

18. Car plate is to name as

A) study is to insurance   B) fight is to win   **C) number is to name tag**   D) envelope is to stamp   E) metal is to clothe

C is the best answer. Car plate has numbers on it as the name tag has a name on it. In terms of usage, both the car plate and the name tag share the same purpose. Choices A and E are Irrelevant words to each other. Choices B and D are the Purpose pattern but do not follow the question-stem.

AP3. Purpose (Tool) Pattern   Find the Purpose of Individual and the Goal, the Function of Tool

19. Music is to earphone as star is to   A) microphone   **B) telescope**   C) book   D) cosmology   E) moon

B is the best answer. Earphone is used to listen to music as telescope is used to observe stars. Choices A and C are Irrelevant words to "star" Choices D and E are related to the word "star" but not to music, the entire question-stem

AP3. Purpose (Tool) Pattern   Find the Purpose of Individual and the Goal, the Function of Tool

20. Butter is to noodle as

A) bread is to soy source   B) coffee is to bean   C) soccer is to uniform   D) movie is to actor   E) girl is to boy

A is the best answer. Butter is used to bread as soy source is used to noodle. They all belong to foods category. Choice B is the Production Pattern. Choice C and D are the category pattern, unrelated to the question-stem. Choice E is the antonym Pattern

AP4. Characteristic Pattern   Find the Characteristic of Person, Place, Object, or Idea

21. Hawaii is to desert as Sahara is to   A) country   B) wet   C) camel   **D) islands**   E) sand

D is the best answer. Hawaii is islands as Sahara is desert. They all refer to the unique topographic characteristics. Choices A and B are Irrelevant to the question-stem. Choices C and E are related to "Sahara" but not to the entire question-stem

AP1. Category Pattern Find the Part and Whole Relation, the Same Type or Association

22. Insect is to flower as

A) movie is to ticket   B) art is to artist   C) status is to exhibition   D) music is to concert   **E) bee is to rose**

E is the best answer. Rose is part of flower as bee is part of insect. All four words belong to the nature.
Choice A is the Purpose (Tool) Pattern. Choices B and D are the Production Pattern. Choice C uses a part-whole in the Category Pattern, but is not the nature category as of the question-stem.

AP3. Purpose (Tool) Pattern Find the Purpose of Individual and the Goal, the Function of Tool

23. Soccer is to rink as

A) child is to mom   B) student is to practice   C) boxer is to fight   **D) hockey is to field**   E) library is to book

D is the best answer. Soccer is played in the field as hockey is played in the rink.
Choice A is the Category Pattern. Choices B and C are the Purpose (Tool) Pattern but they use humans. Choice E is the Purpose (Tool) Pattern, but not the same sport category.

AP1. Category Pattern Find the Part and Whole Relation, the Same Type or Association

24. Blood is to human as moisture is to   A) wet   B) gloomy   C) sky   **D) cloud**   E) dry

D is the best answer. Blood is in human body as moisture is in the cloud. Choice A refers to "blood" and "moisture" but not to "human" therefore cannot be the complete answer. Choices B and C are Irrelevant words to the question-stem. Choice E is antonym to "moist" but not related to the entire question-stem.

AP5. Degree Pattern Find the Degree (Increase or Decrease), Find the Shape of place or thing

25. Rain is to monsoon as wind is to   A) breeze   **B) hurricane**   C) earthquake   D) volcano   E) camping

B is the best answer. Monsoon is a heavier rain and hurricane is a stronger wind.
Choice A is the Degree Pattern as used in the question-stem but its degree moves in reverse order.
The rest are Irrelevant words to the question-stem

AP3. Purpose (Tool) Pattern Find the Purpose of Individual and the Goal, the Function of Tool

26. Mirror is to reflection as

A) coffee is to sleep   B) old is to young   **C) bicycle is ride**   D) hospital is to doctor   E) banana is to long

C is the best answer. The purpose of mirror is for reflection as the purpose of bicycle is for a ride.
Choice A is incorrect because coffee wakes people up. Choice B is the antonym Pattern
Choice D is the purpose pattern but involves human. Choice E is Irrelevant to the question-stem.

AP2. Synonym/Antonym Find the similar or opposite meaning between the words

27. Chicken is to mammal as tiger is to   A) endangered animal   B) fast   C) cage   **D) bird**   E) furious

D is the best answer. Chicken is bird animal as tiger is mammal. All the rest are related to 'tiger' but not to the entire question-stem.

ANSWER EXPLANATIONS FOR TEST 8

AP5. Degree Pattern Find the Degree (Increase or Decrease), Find the Shape of place or thing

28. Stare is to glimpse as dime is to   A) dome   B) money   **C) cent**   D) dollar   E) quarter

C is the best answer. Stare is stronger looking than glimpse as dime is greater than cent.
Choice A is Irrelevant word   Choice B is the Category Pattern to "dime" yet does not to respond to the entire question-stem.   Choices D and E use the Degree Pattern but the words orders are flipped over.

AP4. Characteristic Pattern Find the Characteristic of Person, Place, Object, or Idea

29. God is to dying as

A) win is to luck   B) poor is money   C) thief is to jail   D) cure is to medicine   **E) human is to immortal**

E is the best answer. God is immortal as human is to dying. Keep an eye on how the question-stem and the answer are paired to each other. Choices A, B, and C are Irrelevant words to the question-stem Choice D is the Purpose Pattern

AP4. Characteristic Pattern Find the Characteristic of Person, Place, Object, or Idea

30. Sky is to the blue as **A) ocean is to blue**   B) star to pink   C) coffee is to red   D) chicken is to purple   E) fire is to white

A is the best answer.   Both sky and ocean are blue color.
The rest are incorrect because each color does not properly represent the primary words.

SSAT ABSOLUTE PATTERNS

ABSOLUTE PATTERN SERIES

The College Board Official Test Reading Section

Tests 1 to 8 Analysis
SAT Absolute Pattern for the Reading Section is perfect for students who want to gain insights from the official college board test analyses.
This book is the only companion guide to the official publications that understands the algorithm in each question.

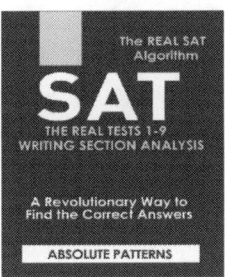

The College Board Official Test Writing Section

Tests 1 to 9 Analysis
SAT Absolute Pattern for the Writing Section is perfect for students who want to gain insights from the official college board test analyses.
This book is the only companion guide to the official publications that understands the algorithm in each question.

The Official Writing Section Tests Logic Chains from 1980 to Present.

This book offers the entire Logic Chains for the Writing Section from the college board old tests to the present tests.
The entire Logic Chains are regenerated through 8 practice tests.
Not a single question can escape from the Logic Chains presented in this book.

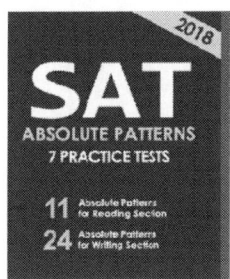

The Official Reading Section Tests Logic Chains from 1980 to Present.

This book offers the entire Logic Chains for the Reading Section from the college board old tests to the present one.
Not a single question can escape from this revealed Logic Chains. The entire Logic Chains are regenerated through 7 practice tests.

SSAT Absolute Patterns UPPER LEVEL 7 Practice Tests

12 **Hidden Patterns in the Analogy Section & 10 Absolute patterns in Reading Section**
SSAT Absolute Pattern is perfect for students who want to gain insights from the official test Logic Chains in Reading and Verbal Section.
This book is the only companion guide that understands the algorithm in each question.

ANSWER EXPLANATIONS FOR TEST 8

SSAT Absolute Patterns MIDDLE LEVEL 8 Practice Tests

***SSAT 12** Hidden Patterns in the analogy Section & 10 Absolute patterns in Reading Section*

SSAT Absolute Pattern is perfect for students who want to gain insights from the official test Logic Chains in Reading and Verbal Section.
This book is the only companion guide that understands the algorithm in each question.

SSAT Absolute Patterns ELEMENTARY LEVEL 8 Practice Tests

Students entering the SSAT for the first time rely on their own problem-solving methods. The mechanism in SSAT, however, is a bit more complex and therefore requires systematic understanding embedded on each question.
To thoroughly understand the patterns, please solve one question at a time and check the answer through the step-by-step pattern explanations.

ISEE Absolute Patterns UPPER LEVEL 7 Practice Tests

***ISEE 6** Hidden Patterns in the Sentence Completion & 10 Absolute patterns in Reading*

ISEE Absolute Pattern is perfect for students who want to gain insights from the official test Logic Chains in Reading and Verbal Section.
This book is the only companion guide that understands the algorithm in each question.

ISEE Absolute Patterns MIDDLE LEVEL 8 Practice Tests
***ISEE 6** Hidden Patterns in the Sentence Completion & 10 Absolute patterns in Reading*

ISEE Absolute Pattern is perfect for students who want to gain insights from the official test Logic Chains in Reading and Verbal Section.
This book is the only companion guide that understands the algorithm in each question.

ISEE Absolute Patterns LOWER LEVEL 8 Practice Tests

Students entering the ISEE for the first time rely on their own problem-solving methods. The mechanism in ISEE, however, is a bit more complex and therefore requires systematic understanding embedded on each question.
To thoroughly understand the patterns, please solve one question at a time and check the answer through the step-by-step pattern explanations.

Made in United States
Troutdale, OR
11/11/2023